THAT'S NOT WHAT THEY MEANT!

THAT'S NOT WHAT THEY MEANT!

RECLAIMING THE FOUNDING FATHERS FROM AMERICA'S RIGHT WING

MICHAEL AUSTIN

 Prometheus Books

59 John Glenn Drive
Amherst, New York 14228–2119

Published 2012 by Prometheus Books

Cover design by Jacqueline Nasso Cooke

Inquiries should be addressed to
Prometheus Books
59 John Glenn Drive
Amherst, New York 14228–2119
VOICE: 716–691–0133
FAX: 716–691–0137
WWW.PROMETHEUSBOOKS.COM

16 15 14 13 12   5 4 3 2 1

Library of Congress Cataloging-in-Publication Data

Austin, Michael, 1966-
    That's not what they meant! : reclaiming the Founding Fathers from America's right
wing / by Michael Austin.
        p. cm.
    Includes bibliographical references and index.
    ISBN 978-1-61614-670-2 (pbk.)
    ISBN 978-1-61614-671-9 (ebook)
    1. Founding Fathers of the United States. 2. United States—History—1783-1815.
3. United States—Politics and government—Philosophy. I. Title.

E302.5.A87 2012
973.3—dc23

                                                                    2012018460

Printed in the United States of America

For Karen

CONTENTS

APPENDIXES

FOREWORD

Michael Austin has done us all a great service in this book because he writes from the perspective of a concerned American who is not a zealot of the Right or the Left. He wants our understanding of the Founding Fathers to be based on what they said in the context in which they said it. We should not make up American history to suit a political party or any political or religious cause. In a more perfect union, we should be able to at least agree on the same facts.

Yet, as Austin demonstrates, mythmaking about the Founders is not a new phenomenon. It began almost as soon as the ink dried on the Declaration of Independence and the US Constitution. Austin coins the new and very useful word "Founderstein" to describe the practice—on both the right and the left—of taking snippets of quotations from various Founders to create a mythical ideal Founder, as if the Founders could be made into one person with one set of ideas. This is the same process of "proof texting" that has been used to take quotations from the Bible to fit various political or religious purposes. What results is a political monstrosity very much like Dr. Frankenstein's monster. It is simply wrong to meld the thoughts of a group of independent individuals from the eighteenth and early nineteenth centuries, who were frequently at odds with one another over major constitutional issues, into a single all-purpose abstraction to fit a particular agenda of twenty-first-century zealots.

"Founders" is not a singular word; it is plural. Yet today's right-wing political discourse would have us believe that one Founder can be substituted for all. A decade ago, I had the pleasure of serving as historical adviser to the National Constitution Center in Philadelphia when this new museum was established as the first to be dedicated to telling the story of the US Constitution. My assignments were to do historical research on the physical appearances and personalities of the signers of the Constitution and to work with artists and sculptors to create life-size bronze statues of the forty-two men who were in the room at Independence Hall on September 17, 1787, the day the US Constitution was approved by the Federal Convention.

The power of this exhibit rests with the fact that these signers (and three dissenters in the room that day who refused to sign) are rendered as accurately as we could make them on a human scale. It is art inspired by the historical record. These Founders are not raised up on pedestals; they are not ten feet tall. Our goal was to make them to look like people, not demigods. James Madison, at five feet four, was so small that one of his contemporaries called him "a half a bar of soap." In Signers' Hall he stands close to George Washington, the tall, regal, athletic general, who was almost a foot taller than Madison. Alexander Hamilton, a very small man, about the size of Madison, stands alone in the center of the room. His diminutive physical appearance seems out of character for the large role he played in American history. They did not call Hamilton the Little Lion for nothing. Benjamin Franklin, the oldest delegate at eighty-three, is seated in this display because he was ill during the convention and had to be carried into the hall. When you see the statues of the individual Founders, as close to the way they looked physically as we could make them (even though in bronze), you cannot help but realize that they were not one entity with interchangeable parts or ideas that can be manipulated to suit a twenty-first-century political agenda.

Walking among these statues gives visitors a sense that these were ordinary people who had been called upon to do an extraordinary job. They represented various interests, usually of their own states and regions of the country. Some delegates left the convention altogether because they did not like the direction of the deliberations. One who left in a huff was Robert Yates of New York, who became a leading Anti-Federalist. Yates fought against ratification of the Constitution through essays signed with the name "Brutus." This prompted Madison, Hamilton, and John Jay to their remarkable response: essays of their own, signed "Publius," which are revered in our time as the Federalist essays, the most powerful statements ever written on the meaning and purpose of government.

Only a handful of the delegates to the Federal Convention did most of the talking and debating at the convention, but each delegate played a role in the process. They were men of various backgrounds, intellectual attainments, and dispositions who managed to come together and find ways to compromise and create a new nation. They were not perfect, and neither was their work. But what they did in 1787, and what the states did in ratifying the Constitution, represented a remarkable advance in the concept of a republic that would be governed by leaders elected democratically by the people. We are still engaged in the constitutional process they started and gave to their generation and to all generations to follow.

This book is a clarion call that it is time for Americans to find ways to renew and revive civil discourse in our nation's affairs. This discourse can only be improved if we learn to solve the pressing issues of our time in a civil manner based on a fair understanding of history. The problems of this nation and of the world are now ours to solve. We can still find great inspiration from the Founders, but it is our world now, not theirs.

Out of respect for the millions of men and women who have sacrificed blood and treasure to create and maintain this nation, those of us alive today must find ways to come together to build a vibrant and responsible political process.

Elbridge Gerry of Massachusetts, one of the delegates to the Federal Convention who refused to sign the Constitution, was fearful of the excesses of too much democracy. He thought it would be too easy for people to be whipped into frenzy with false information. According to James Madison's notes at the Federal Convention, Gerry said, "The evils we experience flow from the excess of democracy. The people do not want virtue, but are dupes of pretended patriots."

Today, we have the Tea Party Patriots representing a groundswell of disenchantment with various aspects of government and public policy. While the Tea Party poses as a grassroots effort, and certainly has elements of a grassroots movement, a good deal of this has been orchestrated by right-wing groups from inside the Beltway. The Far Right seeks to establish a monopoly on American patriotism. Its technique is to co-opt the words of the Founders and twist them to fit its agenda. If you are not with the Far Right, you are part of the problem and may not be a patriotic American. Newt Gingrich calls President Obama's energy policy "anti-American." Can't we discuss the complex issue of energy without questioning the patriotism of the president? Name-calling may help in a political campaign, but it does not help one bit in governing the nation. We could elect a demagogue as president of the United States. Demagogic tactics work in elections. But demagogues cannot govern.

This is the thing that Gerry warned us about. It is too easy to dupe the public with extreme rhetoric and charges against the patriotism of fellow Americans. The real heroes of America, from all walks of life, do not go around wearing their patriotism on their sleeves and accusing others of being less patriotic or unpatriotic. They find ways to get the job done, whether that job is upholding justice, putting out a fire, defending the nation, educating our children, feeding the poor, healing the sick, building a bridge, or governing through pragmatic means and compromise. Our civil discourse will improve when we can again see one another as honest Americans who may simply disagree on the issues of the day.

Partisanship is part of politics. It always has been, and it always will be. George Washington didn't like "factions," as he called them, but he recognized they were part of human nature. Washington also said in his Farewell Address: "Of all the dispositions and habits which lead to political prosperity, religion and morality are indispensable supports." This concept has been essential to the success of the nation. This does not translate, however, into the idea that any one religion should hold more sway than any other in the governance of the nation.

This is not the place to enter into the long debate over whether the United States is a Christian nation and should be governed as such. But it is the place to say that the separation of church and state is an essential concept, too. Once God tells you the answer, there is no debating it, and there is no room for compromise with those of differing views. However, it is compromise that makes governance possible. Citizens and those holding government office should be informed by their religious beliefs and use them to act humanely, something all religions teach. But religion in politics far too often leads to intolerance and the loss of liberty.

We can be partisans. We can bring our religious beliefs and our sense of morality to civil discourse if we do it without demonizing those who disagree with us and without questioning the patriotism or the godliness of fellow Americans who have different views. The nation has survived by avoiding the extremes of the Right or the Left, and it has survived by keeping any single religious belief from having a monopoly on national politics.

While both sides of the political spectrum have tried to cast the Founders in roles to suit today's political, social, and religious agendas, right now it is the Far Right fringe that is the worst offender. From talk radio to political screeds in print, from cable news to the Internet, our national dialogue strongly resembles a form of political insanity. This book is part of the cure.

—Raymond W. Smock, PhD
Historian, US House of Representatives (1983–1995)

PREFACE

From the deliberatively provocative title of this book, many will assume—some hopefully and some disparagingly—that it has been written by a liberal historian out to settle scores. And while I have nothing against liberals, historians, or score settlers, I must admit from the start that these are not the perspectives I come from.

I am not a liberal; I am a moderate. I stand squarely in the center of American political discourse, inching a little bit to the left on social issues and a little bit to the right on economic ones. I have voted for and enthusiastically supported men and women from both political parties, and I have frequently criticized the excesses of extremists on both the left and the right. This book primarily focuses on the conservative extreme that, in recent years, has constructed a simplistic and intellectually indefensible narrative of America's Founding history to support a very narrow (and, ultimately, very modern) political agenda.

I am fully aware that liberal extremists do and say plenty of silly things; however, in the current historical moment, liberals are much less likely than conservatives to do and say the particular silly things I am looking at in this book. Liberals are much more likely to deny the importance of the Founding Fathers altogether, or to criticize them for being racist, sexist, and insensitive, than to lump them together into the ideologically incoherent proof texts that are the primary focus of this book. Where I have seen liberal abuses of history, I have made sure to point them out. But liberal silliness in general will have to wait for another book.

In discussing what I perceive to be the historical blinders of some conservatives, I have taken pains to distinguish extreme positions from the more reasonable and historically defensible positions of the conservative mainstream. As a centrist, I hold many of these latter positions myself, and I know that many genuine conservatives are as concerned as I am about the excesses of the extreme Right. I do not want to paint all conservatives with the same brush, nor do I want to become (as a friend recently admonished me not to become) the "Ann Coulter of the Left."

In addition to not being a liberal, I am also not a historian. By academic training, I am a literary critic specializing in textual analysis of eighteenth-century political novels and poems. In my previous books, I have explored such topics as the use of biblical narrative in *Robinson Crusoe*, the typology of *Paradise Regained*, and the evolutionary foundations of storytelling. I do not claim that these studies give me any scholarly expertise on America's Founding Fathers beyond some familiarity with eighteenth-century usage and a pretty good idea of how to use a library. I do not even have a radio show. I have written *That's Not What They Meant!* as a concerned American—somebody who wants to contribute something meaningful to the debates that shape our nation—rather than as a trained expert in any of the fields that intersect with my study.

Finally, I have no interest in settling scores, exposing hypocrisy, or saving the world from Glenn Beck and Mark Levin. This is the rhetoric of extremism—the rhetoric, in fact, of Glenn Beck and Mark Levin. Any rational corrective to their overheated discourse must begin with the assumption that the world, the Constitution, and the American way of life will not be destroyed by anybody's book or radio show—or even by the results of a single election. Rome did not fall in a day.

What I will do is disagree, often vigorously, about the way those on the right have used America's Founding history to support their very narrow and often extreme political agendas. I don't believe they are evil, and I certainly don't believe they are destroying America. They are, in fact, doing exactly what they are supposed to do: forming opinions, expressing their beliefs, and trying to get other people to agree with them. If anybody is destroying America, it is the liberals, centrists, and moderate conservatives who dismiss their arguments, often with contempt, but rarely with insight or understanding. Ideas, even the very bad ones, deserve a serious response.

In responding seriously to the arguments of the American Right, I have focused almost exclusively on book-length arguments by both commentators and political figures. Partly, this is from laziness. I have neither the time nor the inclination to track down, obtain, transcribe, and analyze thousands of hours of radio and television transcripts. But I also see these books as the permanent records of the debate. Through public libraries and, eventually, discount racks, readers will have easy access to all the contemporary books I cite in *That's Not What They Meant!*, allowing them to compare my arguments with those I am presuming to refute.

I do realize that relying on books presents a different problem in that many political figures do not write their own books. Every presidential candidate these days publishes a campaign autobiography or a manifesto, almost all of which are written by staff members or paid ghostwriters. This is true of broadcast personalities as well. Glenn Beck's book *Being George Washington* lists six writers and thirteen "researchers and contributors" on the title page, suggesting that Beck himself has become little more than a brand supervisor in his own media empire. In criticizing such books as the work of "Rick Perry" or "Glenn Beck," I am well aware that I am using a partial attribution at best—but I also believe that we are all responsible for the words we allow to appear under our own names.

In quoting from the words of the Founding Fathers, I have tried to use editions that will be widely available to readers. Whenever possible, I have used the Library of America editions of the writings of Franklin, Washington, Madison, Hamilton, Jefferson, Marshall, Paine, and Tocqueville. I have also relied heavily on the same publisher's two-volume *Debate on the Constitution* collection, edited by Bernard Bailyn. This invaluable resource reprints most of the Federalist papers, many of the Anti-Federalist papers, and the extant notes from the state-ratifying conventions that turned the proposed Constitution into the supreme law of the land. These volumes, combined with James Madison's *Notes of Debates in the Federal Convention of 1787*, have been my primary tutors in America's Founding history. I could not have asked for a better education.

Several of the primary sources are so important to my arguments that I could not work all the necessary passages into my own text without severely disrupting its flow. I struggled to find a way to incorporate these works into the chapters themselves, but, in the end, I chose to include them as appendixes. I have included these texts in their entirety (or, in one case, in relevant excerpts from a much longer work) at the end of the book, and I would encourage readers to test what I say against what these authors wrote whenever possible. In both the appendixes and the in-chapter citations, I have maintained the original spellings, grammar, and terminology used in the Founding documents, clarifying only to avoid potential ambiguity or misunderstanding.

I know that some will disagree intensely with much of what I say in the following pages, and I have tried to make it as easy as possible for readers to check my sources. I can only hope that some will do so and write their own books, casting me, whenever necessary, as the villain. For better or worse, the system the Founding Fathers created runs on opposition. It requires that we argue with each other—which is a very different thing from shouting at each other. To argue, we must first listen, then consider, and finally offer our own perspective—not as a last word, perhaps, but as a contribution to the debate that will make the discussion richer. All of us, either by being right or by being wrong, have something to bring to the table.

CHAPTER 1

HOW I LEARNED TO STOP WORRYING ABOUT GLENN BECK AND WRITE THIS BOOK

> There is no room in the city
> for respectable skills . . . and no reward for one's
>   efforts.
> Today my means are less than yesterday; come
>   tomorrow,
> the little left will be further reduced. So I'm going to
>   make for
> the place where Daedalus laid aside his weary wings.
> —Juvenal, *Satire 3*, lines 21–26

S omething is profoundly wrong in our country. Once, we were the world's undisputed military and economic superpower, but our standing has been jeopardized by corrupt rulers, profligate spending habits, and a population that has lost its spiritual moorings. Unchecked immigration has flooded our nation with cheap labor and a large population that does not even speak our language. But, even more than all this, we have forgotten the vision of our Founding Fathers and strayed from the path they set us upon.

That, at any rate, was the opinion of the Roman satirist Juvenal at the beginning of the second century CE when he wrote his famous third Satire. The country he reviles, of course, is Rome. The immigrants are the mercantile Jews and the libertine Greeks. And the Founding Fathers he invokes— Romulus, the stepchild of wolves and first king of Rome; and Numa, his pious successor—are figures of myth and legend. Like the great satirists of every era, Juvenal attacked his contemporaries by appealing to an inspirational but completely fabricated version of the golden past.[1]

Golden-age myths have been around for a long time. Confucius, Lao Tzu, and their followers filled their works with references to the epoch of the "good kings" of the past—rulers whose virtues were all but forgotten by the fifth century BCE. Three hundred years later, when seven separate kingdoms were contending for control of China, Confucius and Lao Tzu became the golden-age philosophers to whom people looked for wisdom. Similarly, the Old Testament records how the Hebrew prophets of the sixth century BCE excoriated their people for abandoning the faith of Abraham, Isaac, and Moses—the great patriarchs who themselves looked back to the Garden of Eden as the only true paradise humankind has ever inhabited.

These kinds of origin myths are necessary to shape people into a culture. Both France and England developed national identities at the end of the Middle Ages partly by hearkening back to the glorious reigns of Charlemagne and King Arthur—narratives that, though historically suspect, helped to forge groups of very different people into coherent nations with a common past and, therefore, a common future. Nearly every nation on earth today can point to at least one golden age—one time in history when its people enjoyed wiser rulers, better laws, fewer challenges, and greater prosperity than today. Such conceptions resist historical evidence spectacularly well because their purpose is not to explain the past but to influence the present.

The United States has not been exempt from the human race's tendency to sanitize and mythologize its origins. It would actually be strange if Americans did not turn figures such as George Washington and Benjamin Franklin into semidivine exemplars of courage, wisdom, and virtue. They really were amazing men who accomplished remarkable things. We don't have the time or the inclination to devote our lives to untangling historical complexities. It doesn't really matter whether George Washington told his father the truth about cutting down the cherry tree. He was the sort of person who would have done so, and that is all we need to know.

But, unlike most countries, America was founded in the full light of history—creating, in the process, thousands of primary documents for future generations to study. This wealth of documentary evidence has always made a difference in America's public discourse, making rigorous history of the Founding era possible—and, with it, much more sophisticated golden-age arguments than citizens of other nations have had access to. No Briton, for example, would seriously suggest the United Kingdom return to the "original intent" of the Lady of the Lake and require its chief executive to pull a sword out of a stone before assuming office. A significant portion of Americans, however, do believe the United States should return to the values of its Founding Fathers and set ourselves back on the course they charted for us.

Are they right? Should twenty-first-century Americans give serious attention to the philosophies of a group of privileged white men who lived more than two hundred years ago? My very simple answer to this question is yes, we should. The Founders were not perfect people, and we do not owe them any special allegiance because they set up our current political structure. They would be the first ones to tell us that we should hold to that structure only as long as it serves our needs.

However, the Founding generation in American history had an unusually high concentration of wise and insightful people who cared deeply about the country they were creating. We should always try to learn as much as possible from wise, insightful people who care deeply about things, as they usually have much to teach us. As we try to learn from the wisdom of the Founders, however, we must be careful not to mistake golden-age myths for political battering rams. Given the sheer immensity of their writings and the complexity of their arguments, it will always be easier to use the Founders for ammunition than for inspiration. Too often those who seem to advocate most forcefully for the values of the Founding Fathers simply want to co-opt the rhetorical power of the Founding myth.

This book will focus on one very specific golden-age myth that lies beneath much of the nonsense we see in contemporary American politics: the myth that the Founding Fathers held collective opinions about the important issues of their own day. They emphatically did not. With only a very few exceptions (such as the belief that the colonies should not be ruled by the British), any statement that begins "The Founders believed . . ." is destined to end in a historically unsupportable assertion of collective belief.

As the chapters in this book will show, the Founding Fathers were not men who agreed with each other about much of anything. But the golden-age myth requires collective opinions. No talk-radio host or stumping politician can say, "Some Founders believed X, some believed Y, and modern America is committed to Y instead of X, thus ignoring the intentions of X and giving preference to Y." There is no horsewhip or bully pulpit in such a statement, nor can it be used to attack an opponent's intelligence, character, or patriotism. But say, "The other guys are destroying America by turning us away from the values of the Founding Fathers," and people will stop turning the radio dial and listen to what you have to say—even if what you have to say is complete piffle.

And if you say it often enough, loudly enough, and angrily enough, you will probably land a six-figure book advance and a slot on Fox News.

THE FOUNDERS AND THE FRINGE

American history has not always had a group of men known collectively as "the Founding Fathers." The term dates back to Warren G. Harding's address to the Republican National Convention in 1916. Harding, then a freshman US senator from Ohio, opened the convention with a typical partisan speech about the evils of Democrats and the glory of Republicans. "The country, wearied afresh by a disappointing and distressing Democratic administration, is calling for Republican relief," he began. He then went on to say that "the essentials of constructive government and attending progress are abiding and unchanging. . . . We ought to be as genuinely American today as when the founding fathers flung their immortal defiance in the face of old-world oppressions and dedicated a new republic to liberty and justice."[2]

Harding continued to use the term "Founding Fathers" in his political speeches, culminating in his inaugural address as president of the United States in 1920. "I must utter my belief in the divine inspiration of the founding fathers," he told the cheering crowd. "Surely there must have been God's intent in the making of this new-world Republic. . . . Let us express renewed and strengthened devotion, in grateful reverence for the immortal beginning, and utter our confidence in the supreme fulfillment."[3] Given the acknowledged disaster that was the Harding presidency—he routinely competes with James Buchanan and Andrew Johnson for the title of "worst president in history"—his invention of the term may stand, in R. B. Bernstein's words, as "his most enduring political and intellectual legacy."[4]

Harding's coinage caught on and, for the past hundred years, has been a standard feature of political rhetoric in America. For most of that time, discussions of the Founding Fathers have been largely confined to negative definitions: the Founding Fathers represent all the things contemporary politicians aren't, and the world they inhabited is the paradise we either have lost or are on the verge of losing if we don't get our acts together and vote for X. As the events of the Founding era have receded further into the past, and as

original political contexts have been lost, the Founders have gradually transformed from historical individuals into members of a mythical collective
mind.

Since Harding's day, the Founding Fathers—transformed into a single
ideological entity—have been trotted out to support all manner of causes,
Left, Right, and center. No one party has had a monopoly on the use and
abuse of America's Founding history. Currently, however, the right wing of
the Republican Party has invested more than any other ideology in the creation of a Founding myth. This is especially true of the extreme right-wing
voices that have moved from talk radio to news TV to books that have dominated bestseller lists since the election of Barack Obama in 2008. Figures
such as Mark Levin, Sean Hannity, and Glenn Beck have taken a conspicu-
ously modern mixture of economic libertarianism and religious authoritari-
anism, combined it with an aggressively simplistic view of America's
Founding history, and produced a cohort of mythical heroes whose opinions
did not deviate in any significant way from their own.

Of all the right-wing figures currently on talk radio, nobody has done
more than Glenn Beck to make the Founding Father mythos part of the Far
Right's political agenda. Beck has built the publishing arm of his franchise
by repackaging the Founding Fathers for easy mass consumption—often
with comically inept results. His modern updating of *Common Sense*, for
example, tries to call Americans back to God in the name of Thomas Paine,
the most notoriously antireligious deist of the Enlightenment. And Beck's
book about George Washington's leadership style skips over the entire eight
years of Washington's presidency.[5]

It is easy to make fun of books such as these, but millions of people take
them seriously and believe they contain core truths about American history
that have been intentionally concealed by liberal scholars and politicians.
One of the bestselling political books of 2011, in fact, was Beck's *Original
Argument*, a modern updating of thirty-three of the Federalist essays combined with a heavy-handed analysis confirming that Hamilton, Madison, and
Jay all had the same political agenda as the twenty-first-century Tea Party.

Beck, to be sure, did not create this "translation" itself. For this, he relies
on the efforts of his collaborator, Joshua Charles, a piano-performance major
at the University of Kansas who (as he informs us in the introduction) com-
pleted the translation project during his senior year of college and managed
to get the essays into the hands of Beck, whom he considered a political idol.

Charles tells us that he undertook the "translation" because, when he read the original work, he felt "frustration trying to grasp what Publius was saying."[6]

Amateurish in places, Charles's translation is competent but far inferior to Mary Webster's *The Federalist Papers in Modern Language* (and even farther inferior to the original essays). It is in Beck's own contribution to the book—the introduction to each Federalist essay—that we see Madison, Hamilton, and Jay blended together with dozens of other early patriots to become an ideologically consistent mishmash of modern conservative opinions. In his thirty-three essay introductions, Beck refers to either "the Founders" or "our Founders" a total of twenty-five times. In contrast, he refers to Alexander Hamilton, James Madison, or John Jay (the actual authors of the Federalist papers) a combined total of once. In these introductions, we learn such dubious "facts" about the Founders as these:

> *Federalist* no. 1: *"The Founders believed America to be exception [sic], but some students are now being taught 'multiculturalism.'*[7] (Hamilton's primary argument in *Federalist* no. 1 is that America is *not* the exception but the rule, which other nations are watching carefully to see whether to follow its lead.)

> *Federalist* no. 9: *"The Founders did not want to concentrate power at the federal level."*[8] (This was a huge point of contention at the convention. Some of the delegates, including Hamilton, wanted nearly all power concentrated in a national government.)

> *Federalist* no. 17: *"A power grab by politicians at the federal level was something that our Founders could not really comprehend."*[9] (Not only did they comprehend it, they obsessed about it. Anti-Federalists made this their number-one talking point, and the fear of a national power grab almost prevented the ratification of the Constitution.)

> *Federalist* no. 28: *"The Founders believed that the union of states would have more power than the central government."*[10] (This was actually a minority position at the convention and one not reflected in either the Constitution or the Federalist papers. Madison argued strongly for a national veto over all state legislation. Other delegates wanted to abolish the states altogether.)

Federalist no. 84: *"The Founders thought a professional political class would be disconnected from their home states and prone to giving in to the temptations of power."*[11] (It would be difficult to imagine two better examples of professional politicians than Alexander Hamilton, who spent his entire adult life as a politician and paid virtually no attention to his adopted home state of New York, or James Madison, who was first elected to the Virginia legislature in 1776 at the age of twenty-five and left the presidency at the age of sixty-six after more than forty years of public service.)

I do not suggest that Beck gets these points wrong because the Founders really said the opposite of what he says they said. Rather, he gets them wrong because he collectivizes opinions that were never collective. His simplistic formulations fail to account for the debates, the compromises, and the passionate interplay of ideas that produced the Constitution. Beck's Founders walk in lockstep with the modern American Right. Like the Tea Party, Beck's Founders believe in small government, state supremacy, limited taxation, and public displays of religious belief.

Some of the Founders, of course, did believe in all these things; others believed in none of them. But most members of the Founding generation (like most Americans today) had complicated and continuously evolving opinions on these matters that simply cannot be accommodated by any convenient assertion of collective belief. Before we can claim to understand anything about the Founding Fathers, we must separate them from the collective myth and see them as actual individuals who believed a lot of different things.

DEFINING FOUNDERHOOD

Just who were the Founding Fathers, anyway? Given the importance most Americans attach to their opinions, one might think there was an authoritative list somewhere. But there isn't. The most common definition of the term is probably "anybody whose name I remember from the first nine weeks of American History in high school." Most people familiar with the era, however, do have a mental list of people from the Founding generation whom they consider important. While everybody's list is different, most have at least six names of men who, by an informal consensus, have become something like a top tier of America's Founding Fathers. The "big six" are:

- George Washington
- John Adams
- Thomas Jefferson
- James Madison
- Benjamin Franklin
- Alexander Hamilton

Even among the big six, we find tremendous differences in ideology and life experience. Three of them (Adams, Franklin, Jefferson) signed the Declaration of Independence; two of them (Washington, Hamilton) fought in the Revolutionary War. After the war, four of them (Washington, Franklin, Madison, Hamilton) attended the Constitutional Convention, while two of them (Jefferson, Adams) served as American ministers in Europe. Three (Washington, Jefferson, Madison) were Virginia plantation owners who owned slaves, and three (Franklin, Hamilton, Adams) were Northerners who supported abolition. Three (Washington, Adams, Hamilton) became staunch Federalists and worked to expand the power of the national government, and two (Jefferson, Madison) became the leaders of the opposition Republican faction. One of them (Franklin) died during the first year of the new government. Four of them (Washington, Adams, Jefferson, Madison) went on to become president, and one of them (Hamilton) was shot and killed by the sitting vice president in a duel that began as a political argument.

After the big six, the lists begin to diverge, depending on the political inclinations of the list makers, but some of the more likely suspects include John Jay, Patrick Henry, Thomas Paine, John Hancock, Gouverneur Morris, George Mason, John Marshall, Samuel Adams, James Monroe, and Elbridge Gerry. In her bestselling book *Founding Mothers*, Cokie Roberts adds such other deserving names as Abigail Adams, Mercy Otis Warren, Deborah Reed Franklin, Eliza Pinckney, and Martha Washington. Others apply the term *Founder* to any of the fifty-six signers of the Declaration of Independence, the fifty-five delegates to the Constitutional Convention, the thirty-nine delegates who actually signed the Constitution, or pretty much anybody who was alive in America during the late eighteenth century and didn't side with the British.

No definition, however, is going to give contemporary conservatives—or liberals or centrists, for that matter—a list of Founding Fathers whose positions completely match their own. What most all of us actually have is a list of Founding Fathers who agree with us about some things, disagree with us about other things, and couldn't even imagine most of the things we think about on a daily basis. Questions like, "Would the Founders define the Internet as 'interstate commerce'?" are fundamentally silly, though they form the basis of several recent bestselling books.[12] Such questions assume, quite incorrectly, that we can separate a political position from the historical circumstances that produced it.

We will never know what Thomas Jefferson or Alexander Hamilton would have thought about the capital-gains tax rate or the war in Iraq. But we can guess that they would have disagreed with each other about these issues as fiercely as they disagreed about almost everything else. Agreement was not their style. And we can reasonably suppose that if Thomas Jefferson, James Madison, Alexander Hamilton, and John Adams were all somehow transported to the twenty-first century and given a crash course on contemporary politics, they would fight with each other about almost all our issues as passionately and as frequently as they fought with each other about their own.

The various debates and disagreements of the Founding generation will constitute the primary focus of this book. Each of the Founders—no matter how we construct the list—had a unique outlook and a one-of-a-kind set of political opinions. None of them walked in lockstep with any of the others. However, they did organize themselves into factions that focused their debates in much the same way that political parties do today. Between 1777 and 1800, the men we now call "the Founding Fathers" organized themselves into four different major factions: two that dominated the political scene before the ratification of the Constitution and two that emerged during George Washington's first term as president. These factions are as follows:

- **THE FEDERALISTS (pre-1789):** The name *Federalist* was taken by the Framers and supporters of the Constitution. The name derives from the famous Federalist essays in support of ratification written by Alexander Hamilton, James Madison, and John Jay—with Jay playing a much smaller role than the other two. George Washington, John Adams, and Benjamin Franklin were also Federalists in this sense, while Thomas Jefferson, then the ambassador to France, wavered in public and private statements between the Federalist and the Anti-Federalist positions. The core belief of the first group of Federalists was that the Articles of Confederation were too weak to bind the states into a union and that the stronger central government provided by the Constitution was necessary to accomplish the task.

- **THE ANTI-FEDERALISTS:** Those who most favored a limited central government opposed the ratification of the Constitution, believing that the Articles of Confederation already provided the correct balance of power between the state and the federal governments. Such Revolutionary luminaries as Patrick Henry, George Mason, Samuel Adams, and John Hancock were Anti-Federalists who wrote and spoke against the Constitution and came very close to preventing its ratification. The Anti-Federalists believed that a strong central government would incline toward monarchy and that the states, rather than the federal government, should have the bulk of policy-making power. They feared the Constitution's creation of an independent judiciary, which they saw as potentially antidemocratic. They also tended to be the strongest proponents of public religious displays. One of their principal arguments against the Constitution was that it did not mention God.

- **THE FEDERALISTS (post-1789):** By the end of Washington's first term in 1792, the strong outlines of a two-party system—something not accounted for in the Constitution—had already emerged. The first majority party, the Federalists took their identity from the earlier faction of the same name, though many pre-1789 Federalists did not become Federalists in the new government. Those who did included George Washington, John Adams, and the acknowledged leader of the party, Alexander Hamilton. Federalists were strong supporters of commercial interests and were therefore favored by the financial establishment, much as Republicans are today. However, the Federalists also believed the United States needed a strong central government with more powers than those strictly enumerated in the Constitution. Hamilton was an early champion of a national debt and of direct taxation, and he advocated (and Washington eventually supported) the doctrine of "implied powers," through which he justified such extraconstitutional measures as the creation of the national bank.

As we will see in chapter 5, the confusion between the pre- and post-1789 definitions of the term *Federalist* is compounded by the fact that, before the Constitutional Convention in 1787, a "federalist" was a supporter of the Articles of Confederation—somebody who believed the United States should be a league of sovereign states rather than a single nation with a powerful central government. Thus, most federalists in 1786 became Anti-Federalists in 1787 and went on to become Republicans (rather than Federalists) in 1790.

- **THE REPUBLICANS:** Alarmed by Federalist incursions on state prerogatives, Thomas Jefferson and James Madison began forming an opposition party they referred to as the "Republicans" (the name would eventually be changed to "Democratic-Republicans" and then simply to "Democrats," leaving the "Republican" brand name open for future use by the party of Lincoln). Jeffersonian Republicans believed in strong state governments, limited federal government, and a strict-constructionist reading of the Constitution. However, they were also an agriculturalist party and were deeply suspicious of commerce and finance. In addition, of all the Founding Fathers, Jefferson and Madison held the strongest positions against the public support of religion.

These were the large ideological groupings in which the Founders carried out their debates with each other. Anyone today who wanted to hold the same political positions as any single Founding Father did would have to cross twenty-first-century party lines quite radically. Tea Party conservatives, for example, often cite Jefferson's and Madison's belief in a limited government and a strict interpretation of the Constitution. But these same Tea Party activists almost never talk about the same two men's rabid distrust of business, finance, and financial markets. And they simply have to close their eyes and pretend not to notice Jefferson's well-known hostility to the religions of his day.

Liberals, of course, fare no better. Though the modern Democratic Party traces its roots back to Thomas Jefferson, this genealogy is more myth than history. Modern Democrats share only part of Jefferson's agenda. Like Jefferson, they tend to be suspicious of moneyed interests and pride themselves on their commitment to recent immigrants, cultural minorities, and the poor.

However, they have usually tried to accomplish these Jeffersonian ends with the most Hamiltonian of means: a powerful federal government, a reliance on implied constitutional powers, and a lot of taxes.

As we fight with each other about many of the same issues the Founders did, we often imagine that things were different back then—that, somehow, men like Hamilton and Jefferson managed to disagree with each other without all the acrimony and partisanship we see every time we turn on the television. We instinctively believe politics doesn't have to be a blood sport. At some distant point in our nation's past, we want to believe, it was a more honorable affair.

But this is just another golden-age myth. America's politics (like everybody else's) have always been contentious, boisterous, and narrowly partisan. In many ways, the present age is the golden one. It has been decades since a president has had to send in armed forces to implement a Supreme Court decision and more than 150 years since anybody was beaten with a cane on the Senate floor. Nobody has been spit on in the House of Representatives for nearly two hundred years. And it has been a very long time indeed since an elected official has been killed—as three of the Founders, including Alexander Hamilton, were killed—in a duel with a political opponent.[13]

The Founding era had its share of Glenn Becks, too—though they were not nearly as calm or reasonable. In the eighteenth century, nobody had any expectation that journalists would be fair or balanced. Newspapers were party organs, pure and simple, and editors relished their roles as attack dogs. One such journalist, John Fenno, was recruited and paid by Alexander Hamilton to publish the *Gazette of the United States*, the staunch Federalist paper that functioned as something like the mainstream media and regularly attacked Jefferson and the Republicans. Not to be outdone, Jefferson hired the famous poet Phillip Freneau as a State Department translator—despite the fact that he spoke no language for which translation was necessary. Freneau's real job was to publish the *National Gazette*, which was decidedly anti-Hamilton, anti-Washington, and antigovernment.

Between 1791 and 1793, the two gazettes carried out open warfare with the nation's two emerging factions. Fenno depicted the Republicans as Jacobins and anarchists who wanted nothing more than to set up guillotines in the streets of Philadelphia and start decapitating wealthy industrialists and Federalist politicians. Freneau, for his part, presented the Federalists as crypto-monarchists in open league with the British to undo the American Revolution. Adams and Hamilton, they insisted, secretly plotted to make the presidency a hereditary office and to change its title to "king." In the meantime, the Federalists' primary objective (so the story goes) was to lay as many taxes as possible on poor farmers so that their meager wealth could be redistributed to the wealthy industrialists of the North.[14]

But Fenno and Freneau were just the precursors to the most colorful pundit of the day: Benjamin Franklin Bache (pronounced "Beech"), the editor of the Philadelphia *Aurora* and the grandson of Benjamin Franklin. Republican through and through, Bache built his career on attacking the Federalists—especially George Washington, the most revered figure in the nation, whom the *Aurora* regularly presented as an inept general, a closet aristocrat, and a betrayer of the American Revolution. Consider the following, very typical, broadside from Benny Bache:

> If ever a nation was debauched by a man, the American nation has been debauched by WASHINGTON. If ever a nation was deceived by a man, the American nation has been deceived by WASHINGTON. Let his conduct then be an example to future ages. Let it serve to be a warning that no man may be an idol, and that a people may confide in themselves rather than in an individual. Let the history of the federal government instruct mankind, that the masque of patriotism may be worn to conceal the foulest designs against the liberties of the people.[15]

During the presidency of John Adams, the besieged Federalists responded to Bache and other Republican editors by doing one of the stupidest things a major political party has ever done: they passed the Sedition Act (part of the group of laws known as the Alien and Sedition Acts), which made it a crime, punishable by imprisonment, to write or publish "false scandalous and malicious writing . . . against the government of the United States, or either house of Congress of the United States, or the President of the United States."[16] Bache was promptly arrested under this law and died of yellow fever while waiting for his trial, and the national backlash against the Alien and Sedition Acts helped propel Jefferson to the presidency in 1800. Federalists never regained power, and the memory of these patently unconstitutional laws has tarnished the reputation of the Federalist Party ever since.

In the pages of the *Aurora*, the *National Gazette*, and the *Gazette of the United States*—and dozens of other eighteenth-century American newspapers—we can find all the acrimony, overstatement, simplemindedness, and alarmism of modern talk radio and attack television. We even find the same themes: the evils of taxation, the perils of debt, federal power grabs, states' rights, tyrannical presidents, overreaching courts, an unjustifiable war (the quasi war with France), and an unwise peace. Then, as now, Americans were regularly assured that the country was on the brink of disaster.

But America survived. The Federalists did not turn the nation into a monarchy, and the Republicans did not soak the countryside in blood. For two hundred years, despite all the overheated political rhetoric to the contrary, America has continued to survive and prosper. We have not done so without challenges, to be sure. And we have not done so without Baches and Becks sprouting up in every generation to tell us our liberty and our national character depend on the result of the next election. It is a great tribute to the genius of the American people that the extremists have never been right.

THE REAL GOLDEN AGE

Those who see America's Founding era as a golden age are not entirely wrong. In many ways, it was. But it was not a golden age of good feelings and unfettered cooperation by wise and devoted patriots. The men we call Founders were as divided as a group of people with the same overall objectives could possibly be. Their ranks included monarchists, anarchists, and everything in between—a much greater diversity of views than we see in our political world today. They fought all the time, yet they managed to do remarkable things. They defeated the most powerful empire in the world without a trained army, they created the world's most enduring constitution, and they established a political tradition that has transferred power smoothly between different parties and factions for more than two hundred years.

The Founders accomplished these things not in spite of their disagreements but because of them, and because they put in place deliberative conventions capable of turning disagreements into powerful compromises. A system that required harmony, wisdom, or good intentions would have been doomed to fail, as people possessing these qualities will not always be in charge. But a system fueled by competition, disagreement, and a strong motivation to find solutions has human nature on its side and might just last forever.

The purpose of this book is to call out the incoherence of the right wing's historical narrative. To do this, I will examine some of the most significant debates that the Founders themselves participated in—debates that conservative extremists almost always ignore because they contradict the golden-age myth their rhetoric requires. By examining the debates and disagreements of the Founders, I do not wish to suggest that their opinions do not matter. I believe their opinions matter a great deal—not because they would expect us to adopt their beliefs (which, given the diversity of those beliefs, would be impossible) but because they showed us the way to turn differences of opinion into engines of democracy. If we are to find solutions to our present problems—and every generation of Americans has had its own problems—we must do so not by believing as the Founders believed but by arguing as they argued and, in the end, by compromising as they compromised, though we won't like it any better than they did.

In presenting themselves as the ideological heirs of a mythical group of ideologically coherent Founding Fathers, people like Glenn Beck, Mark Levin, and Sean Hannity have minimized the real conflicts among the Founders and presented individual opinions as collective truths. They have represented a narrow, blatantly partisan agenda as a divine mandate, and they have employed a dishonest historical narrative to demonize their opponents at every turn. They have, in other words, acted exactly as the Founding Fathers themselves acted more than two hundred years ago.

Most of the people we revere as Founders were as narrowly partisan and rhetorically manipulative as Glenn Beck and Mark Levin. However, they were not all narrowly partisan in the same ways, and the special genius of the political structure they created was the ability to harness disagreement for the public good. Most Americans today yearn for more civility in political discourse, or an end to gridlock and partisanship, but we should be careful what we wish for. Gridlock and partisanship make our government slow, but slowness is part of the overall design. The train to despotism usually runs on time; democracy requires patience, commitment, and a willingness to engage in an inherently oppositional political process.

America's Founding Fathers, for the most part, understood this well. These were men who argued with each other all the time about many of the things we argue about today. They rarely achieved consensus, but they built a great nation anyway. To replicate their success, we must first understand their process. We misunderstand the Founders when we try to turn their writings into a checklist of approved opinions for our own historical moment. Their real legacy to us is a political system—a system of disagreement, debate, and compromise—that has kept democracy vibrant in America for more than two hundred years.

CHAPTER 2

FOUNDERSTEIN: HOW TO TURN SIX DEAD WHITE GUYS INTO ONE POLITICAL MONSTER

The Founders believed that the union of states would have more power than the central government.
—Glenn Beck, *The Original Argument*

In establishing our system of separate powers, checks and balances, and federalism, **the Founders** limited Congress—and thus the will of the Positivists—to eighteen specific, enumerated, and delegated powers.
—Andrew Napolitano, *The Constitution in Exile*

Our Founding Fathers understood that every government becomes more susceptible to tyranny as it amasses more wealth and power. . . . **The Founders** also knew that, although local governments are capable of tyranny, the risk is less severe than it is at the national level.
—Senator Mike Lee, *The Freedom Agenda*

The [Supreme] Court has cleansed the schools of prayer, restricted how funds can be used in support of religious groups, prohibited some religious displays, and otherwise set out on a course to diminish or eliminate religious expression in the public square, ignoring **the Founders**' reservation of such decisions to the states.

—Rick Perry, *Fed Up!*

> **The Founders** understood the multiple benefits of reli-
> gion. They therefore aggressively promoted religion
> throughout American society.
> —David Barton, *Original Intent*

Anybody who spends enough time digging around in the graveyards of American political theory has met "Founderstein," an ideological monstrosity that, like Frankenstein's monster, borrows bits and pieces from those safely dead—from, that is, the speeches, published essays, letters, and journals of any number of different Founding Fathers, slapped together with absolutely no concern for context, rhetorical intent, or the tremendous differences between the individual Founders.

Each of the quotations opening this chapter is an example of a Founderstein, or an unjustifiable use of "the Founders" as an ideologically unified category. These quotations present, as settled collective opinions, assertions that were anything but. These issues—the balance of state and federal authority, the doctrine of enumerated powers, and the role of religion in the public square—were among the most important open questions of the Founding era. They are precisely the questions Hamilton, Jefferson, Madison, and Washington argued without ever coming to consensus.

The most common contemporary version of Founderstein might look something like this:

- Patrick Henry's fervent Christianity
- Benjamin Franklin's practical wisdom
- Thomas Jefferson's belief in limited government
- George Washington's view of America's providential role in history
- Alexander Hamilton's faith in markets
- James Madison's strict-constructionist view of the Constitution

Such a being would fit right in at a Tea Party rally and would certainly justify the common conception of "the Founding Fathers" among the conservative fringe. However, if we take these same men and combine another set of characteristics, we end up with a very different monster—one just as implausible as the first but designed for a different kind of political argument:

- Patrick Henry's implacable opposition to the Constitution
- Benjamin Franklin's sexual mores
- Thomas Jefferson's hostility toward organized religion
- George Washington's lifelong ownership of slaves
- Alexander Hamilton's dueling pistols
- James Madison's shifting political opinions

Here we have the Founderstein of the Left—the slave-owning, dueling crank who should not be revered but rather treated as an eccentric old uncle at a family picnic. But this creature never existed either. "The Founding Fathers" were not all devout Christians who sought to limit the power of government any more than they were all slave-owning atheists who wanted to expand the federal mandate. They were actual human beings with insights and moral lapses, virtues and vices, and, perhaps most important, little ability to agree with each other about much of anything.

At the heart of the Founderstein phenomenon lies a rhetorical need for unanimity. All the authors mentioned at the opening of this chapter would have been on solid ground if they had claimed "some of the Founders" held the positions being presented as collective, and, with a little work, they could have identified which ones. But identifying with just some of the Founders blunts the real assertion of these arguments: that people who disagree with them are bad Americans. Rather than give up this point—and the righteous indignation it inspires—these authors present open questions as settled ones and disputed assertions as universal principles, and, in the process, they assert a higher level of agreement among the Founders than the Founders themselves believed to be possible in this world.

Foundersteins are not creatures of this world. They come from the world of myth, where virtues are amplified and disagreements are suppressed. Only by invoking the world of myth can anybody say, "The Founding Fathers believed . . ." and end up with a historically coherent argument.

PROOF-TEXT PATRIOTISM

Founderstein monsters are created by proof-text citations. A proof text is an isolated quotation offered to support an argument. Unlike legitimate citations, proof texts rarely give sufficient information for readers to determine the context of a remark—or to answer questions such as "Who is the author of the quotation addressing?" "What specific questions is the author trying to answer?" or "What was the original purpose of the communication?" Proof texters ignore the differences between public speeches, private letters, and personal journals. They frequently change the original meaning of a text by removing words and phrases that get in the way of their interpretations, and they often build arguments by stringing together quotation after quotation with no sensitivity to the original context. Proof texting sometimes looks like scholarship, but it is a fundamentally different operation. Scholars draw conclusions from their research; proof texters draw research from their conclusions.

Proof-text argument has a long and distinguished history in the West, primarily because of its use in constructing arguments from the Bible. Many of the Founders came from Protestant sects that saw the Bible as something like thirty thousand separate one-paragraph pieces of evidence that could be combined in any order to support an assertion. In both England and America in the eighteenth century, it was completely acceptable to cobble together isolated verses from different parts of the Old and New Testaments in order to support almost any proposition, religious or political. It is no coincidence that some of the most egregious examples of proof-text patriotism in our own day come from those trying to prove the Founding Fathers were, with only a very few exceptions, Bible-believing evangelical Christians.

In the current political environment—in which strict-constructionist libertarians and evangelical conservatives have joined forces to create the Tea Party coalition—it is not at all surprising that the writings of the Founders have been made to support the same kinds of proof-text arguments that have traditionally rested on biblical citations. Disparate passages from Hamilton, Madison, and Franklin—like random verses from Isaiah, Job, and Mark— can be combined indiscriminately to produce a collective opinion that can then be presented as "what the Founders believed." And the collective opinion, once established, takes on the mantle of scriptural inerrancy. If "the Founders" believed it, it must be true.

One of the great advantages of proof texting, whether from the Bible or from the works of America's Founders, is that one seldom need bother with the original sources. Other people have already done the work and have collected the proof texts in Internet archives and in dictionaries of disembodied citations. One such publication is William Federer's massive *America's God and Country Encyclopedia of Quotations*, which goes out of its way to advertise itself to people who want to prove their point without actually reading primary texts. A plug for the book posted to a number of websites reads as follows:

> Have you ever heard an inspiring quote from one of our forefathers but had difficulty locating it when you really needed it? *America's God and Country Encyclopedia of Quotations* by William J. Federer is your solution. It is the most exciting, comprehensive book in print today highlighting America's Godly heritage. This 864-page reference book contains over 2,100 profound quotations from founding fathers, presidents, constitutions, court decisions and more. Entries are alphabetized and many are illustrated. With easy-to-use subject and source indexes, this book is nothing short of a gold mine for speeches, debates, articles, letters to elected officials, etc.[1]

Armed with Federer's massive tome, a web-enabled smartphone, and a Google app, no one need fear being caught without proof that the Founding Fathers were Christians, small-government enthusiasts, tax protesters, North American isolationists, or baked potatoes.

For examples of how this works in practice, look at the following two quotations from recent conservative bestsellers, both of which are trying to draw support for their agendas by citing Alexander Hamilton, and, by extension, all the Founding Fathers:

> Conservatives consider our founding document an expression of the framers' clear understanding of man's fallen nature. As Alexander Hamilton wrote in *Federalist* 51, "If men were angels, no government would be necessary. If angels were to govern men, neither external nor internal controls on government would be necessary. In framing a government which is to be administered by men over men, the great difficulty lies in this: you must first enable the government to control the governed; and in the next place oblige it to control itself."
> —Sean Hannity, *Conservative Victory*

> America is special because our rights come from God, but those rights must be protected by a central government that serves the people.
> —Glenn Beck, introducing the main point of Hamilton's *Federalist* no. 1 in *The Original Argument*

These two attempts to represent the opinions of a Founder illustrate the perils of trying to make serious arguments about the Founding Fathers with poorly researched, badly understood proof texts. Both Hannity and Beck imagine themselves to be proving something about how eighteenth-century politicians would view a modern political issue. Both appeal to the collective authority of the Founding Fathers on the strength of a single passage. And both get the original citation disastrously wrong.

Hannity's error is easy to see: Alexander Hamilton did not write *Federalist* no. 51; James Madison did, and this particular passage is one of the most famous things Madison ever wrote. This is not an innocent citation error. Attributing these words, and these sentiments, to Hamilton—whose Federalist essays argue for a considerably greater role for government than Madison's do—trivializes one of the most important conflicts of the Founding era. A serious student of the Founding era could no more confuse Madison and Hamilton than a serious Beatles fan could attribute "Yesterday" to John Lennon. Like the Beatles, the Founders did not come in interchangeable units.

The second passage is offered not as a quote from Alexander Hamilton but as a gloss of one of his most important essays: the introduction to the series of essays that we now call the Federalist papers. As discussed in chapter 1, radio personality Glenn Beck's 2011 book *The Original Argument* provides a "translation" of thirty-three of the essays, each introduced with a standard template that includes "The Message" (a capsule summary of the entire essay) and brief quotes from the original, each followed by a paragraph labeled "Relevance to Today." The second passage in this chapter's epigraph—"America is special because our rights come from God, but those rights must be protected by a central government that serves the people"— constitutes, for Beck, "the message" of *Federalist* no. 1.

But nothing in Beck's gloss has anything to do with the original *Federalist* no. 1. It just isn't there. In the first place, the essay does not say, allude to, or imply anything about God. In fact, not a single one of the fifty-one Federalist essays by Hamilton contains the words "God," "Christ," "Christian," "Providence," or "divinity." This is not to say that Hamilton did not believe in God; most of the available evidence suggests he was one of the more orthodox of the Founding Fathers. But his religious opinions cannot be derived from his Federalist essays.

Though it appears nowhere in *Federalist* no. 1, the claim that rights come from God would not have been controversial in the eighteenth century.

Hamilton did, in fact, make precisely this claim in the essay "The Farmer Refuted," which he wrote on the eve of the American Revolution. Beck quotes this essay (though not by name) in his general introduction to *The Original Argument*: "The sacred rights of mankind are not to be rummaged for among old parchments or musty records. They are written, as with a sunbeam . . . by the hand of divinity itself, and can never be erased or obscured by mortal power."[2] Had Beck simply posited "the rights of Americans come from God" as a claim of *Federalist* no. 1, he would have been guilty only of attributing something Hamilton said in one essay to another essay written eleven years later—careless, perhaps, but, in the grand scheme of things, forgivable.

But Beck takes his argument much further. For him, *Federalist* no. 1 is not about the derivation of natural rights; it is about American exceptionalism. "America is special," he pretends to summarize, "*because* our rights come from God." People in other countries—the nonspecial ones—cannot make the same claim. As Beck explains in the "Relevance to Today" portion of his introduction, "The Founders believed America to be exception [*sic*], but some students are now being taught 'multiculturalism,' the idea that no culture or country is superior to or better than another."[3]

There is nothing about American exceptionalism in *Federalist* no. 1. What Hamilton actually says (and what Beck quotes in his own argument) is that post-Revolutionary America is "an empire in many respects the most interesting in the world." And by "interesting," Hamilton does not mean "special," or "divinely favored," or even, in the modern sense of the word, "fascinating." He means, rather, that people around the world have a stake in, or an interest in, the success of the American experiment because it will show whether or not nonmonarchical self-government is possible—as he explains in the very next paragraph:

> It has been frequently remarked that it seems to have been reserved to the people of this country, by their conduct and example, to decide the important question, whether societies of men are really capable or not of establishing good government from reflection and choice, or whether they are forever destined to depend for their political constitutions on accident and force. If there be any truth in the remark, the crisis at which we are arrived may with propriety be regarded as the era in which that decision is to be made; and a wrong election of the part we shall act may, in this view, deserve to be considered as the general misfortune of mankind.[4]

Hamilton was absolutely correct. Much of the world, especially Europe, saw America as the most comprehensive experiment in republican government ever attempted. They watched the debate on the Constitution with great interest, knowing that if something other than a monarchy could succeed in America, it could succeed in other places as well. Hamilton presents America not as the exception but as the rule—a rule the rest of humankind could use to draw generalizations about human nature and republican government.

Hamilton does draw such a generalization about natural rights in "The Farmer Refuted," which he wrote to refute Loyalist arguments against revolution. Like most patriots in 1775, Hamilton believed Americans were justified in rebelling against the British Crown by the principle of natural rights. But, unlike Beck, he does not claim most-favored-nation status with God; rather, he insists all human beings have the exact same God-given rights that the American colonists do. "The nations of Turkey, Russia, France, Spain, and all other despotic kingdoms in the world, have an inherent right . . . to shake off the yoke of servitude," he writes, "and to model their government upon the principles of civil liberty."[5]

Nothing in *Federalist* no. 1—or in any of the citations Beck includes in his book—even begins to justify the gloss that "America is special because our rights come from God." The closest we can get is that America is interesting and the rights of everybody in the world come from God, and even this requires two separate quotations separated by nearly a dozen years. So how does Beck get away with calling "America is special because our rights come from God" *the* main point of *Federalist* no. 1?

The real question here is, how can someone who claims to revere the Founding Fathers justify such utter disregard for the integrity of their words?

LARRY SCHWEIKART AND THE
ART OF THE PROOF TEXT

The high-water mark of proof-text patriotism is Larry Schweikart's 2011 book *What Would the Founders Say?* Schweikart, a professor of history at the University of Dayton, became a conservative celebrity in 2010 when a book he coauthored six years earlier, *A Patriot's History of the United States*, earned Glenn Beck's on-air endorsement and soared to the top of the *New York Times* bestseller list. Schweikart began to appear regularly on Beck's television show and other Fox News programs—and several of his subsequent books also became bestsellers.

In *What Would the Founders Say?*, Schweikart sets out to prove—with a seemingly bottomless barrel of proof texts—that the Founding Fathers were conservative Christians, small-government advocates, and a collective personality whose views would not depart in any material way from the modern Tea Party platform. In the book, Schweikart assumes an astonishing level of uniformity in the beliefs of the Founders and claims a startling familiarity with how they would respond to the current political environment. We learn, among other things, that they would oppose labor unions and scoff at the food pyramid and that every one of them would likely "insist that the BLM [Bureau of Land Management] be burned down, and that the lands be unloaded as quickly as possible."[6]

Nobody can fault Schweikart for using quotations from the Founding Fathers to support conservative arguments. Some of the Founders, at various points in their lives, did indeed hold views that would fit well with modern conservative positions. But Schweikart does not build an argument from any historical context. Rather, like so many other proof-text patriots, he strings decontextualized quotations together to create historically incoherent assertions about the collective views of all the Founding Fathers at once.

Let's look at an example. In the eighth chapter of *What Would the Founders Say?*, Schweikart asks the question, "Should the United States tolerate high deficits and a large national debt?" No question could be more important to Tea Party conservatism in 2012, and if Schweikart wants to keep his string of bestselling conservative potboilers alive, he had better answer with a resounding no. But he has a problem. One of the first major debates between Hamiltonian Federalists and Jeffersonian Republicans was about this very issue, with Hamilton himself saying a number of positive things about a national debt. Not all the historical ducks are in Larry Schweikart's row.

While Schweikart could make a compelling argument that *some* Founders saw deficit spending as a bad thing—namely Jefferson and Madison—this would not serve his major purpose, which is to present contemporary conservatism as the only legitimate philosophical descendant of *all* the Founding Fathers. To achieve the unanimity his project requires,

Schweikart must deny the plain sense of some of Hamilton's most well-known writings. To do this, he resorts to one of the most intellectually dishonest passages I have ever read in a work purporting to be serious history. I will place the author's external citations in bold text:

> Hamilton's goal was to place in debt the wealthy to the government, not the other way around: **"The only plan that can preserve the currency is one that will make it in the immediate interest of the monied men to cooperate with the government in its support."** This was his mercantilist upbringing coming out. **"If all the public creditors receive their dues from one source,"** he wrote, **"distributed with an equal hand, their interests will be the same. And having the same interests, they will unite in support of the fiscal arrangements of the government."** Too many competing systems with their **"different provisions,"** he warned, would create **"distinct interests drawing different ways."** The federal government, he further reasoned, should neither be independent nor too much dependent. It should neither be **"raised above responsibility or control, nor should it want the means of maintaining its own weight, authority, dignity, and credit."**[7]

The most obvious problem with this paragraph, of course, is that it does not prove what it sets out to prove—that Hamilton wanted "to place in debt the wealthy to the government, not the other way around" (which, actually, doesn't even make sense). Some of the quotes in the paragraph talk about aligning the interest of wealthy Americans with the interests of the government. But the way Hamilton wanted to do this was by issuing government bonds, which the wealthy would purchase, thereby giving them a stake in America's success. And issuing bonds means going in debt to the bondholders.

However, the larger problem is with the quotations themselves. Schweikart presents them as if they were all part of the same unnamed source, but they are not. The four quotes come from three completely different texts, quoted out of three completely different collections of papers, addressing three completely different audiences:

- The first quotation comes from a private letter a very young Hamilton wrote to Robert Morris in 1780. Hamilton was a young assistant to General Washington during the Revolutionary War, and Morris was a wealthy financier who would soon become the Continental Congress's superintendent of finance. Hamilton, eager to test out his ideas, took the opportunity to write to Morris to outline the plan he was already forming for a national bank; one of the things he thought the bank should do was to issue bonds and, thereby, create internal stakeholders in America's success. Morris replied politely, and Hamilton continued serving in the army.[8]

- The second and third quotations come from the massive *Report on Public Credit* that Hamilton gave to Congress in 1790, ten years later, when he was secretary of the Treasury. The portions Schweikart quotes come from a long passage in which Hamilton argues that the federal government should assume all the war debts of the individual states because it would strengthen the credit of the United States to have a single method of paying these debts rather than thirteen different systems. This proposal was extremely controversial with those states that had already made progress in paying their war debts, and it was strongly opposed by both Madison and Jefferson. This quotation has nothing to do with placing wealthy Americans in debt to the United States; rather, it has to do with structuring existing debt, mainly to foreign countries, in a way that would enhance America's credit abroad.

- The fourth quotation comes from the sixth of six newspaper editorials Hamilton wrote in 1782, shortly after leaving Washington's general staff. The series was called "The Continentalist" and served as a precursor to Hamilton's *Federalist* contributions. In the passage Schweikart quotes, Hamilton is talking not about debt at all but about the need for a federal taxing power, and, specifically, a luxury tax. "The rich," he argues in the same paragraph, "must be made to pay for their luxuries."[9]

For a professional historian, this kind of indiscriminate citation is bad enough. In this particular passage, however, the proof texting becomes even more obvious when we look at the endnotes. The third quotation comes from the same source as the second and should be cited as such. Instead, however, Schweikart cites an additional source: Buckner Melton's *The Quotable Founding Fathers*—a mother lode of proof-text citations with 2,500 quotes arranged by subject and completely stripped of context. As it happens, this particular citation is a mistake. The cited quote cannot be found in Melton's volume. But fourteen of the thirty-four direct quotations in the chapter *can* be found there, exactly as Schweikart quotes them, almost all without any context whatsoever (though he officially cites the book only one other time).

Schweikart's recipe for a popular bestseller is simple: start with a few random quotations, strip them carefully of any historical context, combine them, throw in an overbearing ideological agenda, and stir. And make darn sure Glenn Beck likes the final product.

PROOF-TEXT PATRIOTISM AND THE MYTH OF COLLECTIVE OPINION

The best thing about a Founderstein monster is that you don't have to pull all your pieces from the same Founder. The Founderstein phenomenon relies on a collectivizing logic that legitimate historians reject. To prove that, say, Benjamin Franklin would have supported a capital-gains tax cut, you would have to work pretty hard to establish that Franklin could have understood the concept of a capital gain, demonstrate that he believed the sorts of people who realized capital gains were good for the economy, explain his general philosophy on taxation, and so on. A person would have to read a lot of primary texts to make such an argument convincingly.

All the difficulty evaporates, however, when we assume the Founders all believed alike. Then we can construct chains of reasoning that move from Hamilton to Adams to Franklin and back to Hamilton and not worry about getting any particular Founder's views wrong. Since we don't need context to make such arguments, we can get all the quotes we need right off the Internet or from other proof-text collections. A person could fill many pages with quote strings like these and never actually read a primary text. Many have.

Let's look at an example from one of Glenn Beck's most recent books, *Being George Washington*. The premise of the book is innocuous enough: George Washington was a great man because he adopted some very specific character traits that we can all adopt as well. Therefore, any of us can "be George Washington" by mastering such simple virtues as honesty, courage, punctuality, and attention to detail. Who wouldn't want to be George Washington?

But being George Washington apparently also requires certain civic virtues and certain views of the Constitution. In a chapter of the book devoted to Washington at the 1787 Constitutional Convention, Beck insists that we must (like George Washington) bind ourselves to the original purposes of the men who wrote the Constitution. To help us along, he creates four summary principles that constitute something of a "Mere Constitutionality" for those who want to be George Washington. I will quote the first and the fourth of these principles below:

(First Principle) The Constitution recognizes the existence of natural law. In the Declaration of Independence Thomas Jefferson referred to "the laws of Nature and Nature's God." Natural law recognizes the existence of God and acknowledges that God established a natural order of things for this earth and the people of this earth.

(Fourth Principle) The Constitution was created on the assumption that America would function under a free-market economy, recognizing and protecting property rights. John Adams wrote: "All men are born free and independent, and have certain natural, essential, and unalienable rights, among which may be reckoned the right of . . . protecting property."[10]

Both of these propositions give us a lot to argue about. It is not at all obvious, for example, that the Jeffersonian notion of "natural law" included a God that modern American Christians would recognize as such. Like many Enlightenment thinkers, Jefferson saw God as something like the sum total of the laws of nature rather than as a personal deity who interacted with the human race. Furthermore, neither Jefferson nor Adams would have even understood the term *free-market economy* as we understand it today. Jefferson, in particular, saw America as a primarily agrarian economy, and he viewed all kinds of financial markets with suspicion.

Two facts, however, are beyond dispute: (1) that Jefferson did not attend the Constitutional Convention in Philadelphia in 1787, and (2) that Adams wasn't there either. At the time, the two men were ministers to, respectively, France and England, and they knew only as much about the Constitution as they read in letters from home. Both the Declaration of Independence and the Constitution of Massachusetts (the source of the Adams quotation) are very different things from the US Constitution. No rational standard of proof allows Beck's claim (that "the Constitution recognizes the existence of natural law") to be supported with his evidence (that in "the Declaration of Independence Thomas Jefferson referred to 'the laws of Nature and Nature's God'"). The correct text to cite in demonstrating what the Constitution says would be the Constitution.

But there has never been a time in human history when rational arguments have persuaded more people than paranoid screeds. Proof texting works—and works well—because human beings are hardwired to gravitate toward evidence that confirms our existing beliefs. Researchers call this "confirmation bias" and have proved it time after time under rigorous experimental conditions. This is a cognitive predisposition that cuts across ideological boundaries. Human beings of all philosophical and ideological persuasions will give more credence to a piece of evidence that confirms their beliefs than they will to a similar piece of evidence that contradicts their beliefs. This is because we base most of our opinions on nonrational considerations and then search for evidence to justify and explain what we have chosen to believe.

As an example of how confirmation bias supports proof-text argument, consider the following two quotations from John Adams:

> Religion and virtue are the only foundations, not only of republicanism and of all free government, but of social felicity under all governments and in all the combinations of human society.

> The United States of America have exhibited, perhaps, the first example of governments erected on the simple principles of nature. . . . It will never be pretended that any persons employed in that service had interviews with the gods, or were in any degree under the influence of Heaven.

On their face, these quotations would seem to contradict each other, at least partially, on whether America was founded on religious principles. Both, however, are irresistible as proof texts because they are short, self-contained expressions of positions that many people today hold. In fact, I chose both of them, more or less at random, from websites that consist primarily of proof texts for their respective positions. The first comes from the Christian Apologetics & Research Ministry and the second from Positive Atheism's Big List of John Adams Quotations.[11]

The contradiction between these two statements seems strange only because we are accustomed to seeing major historical figures as completely consistent in their views—though we know most people aren't consistent about such things at all. I would fail the consistency test miserably if thousands of historians combed through every letter, e-mail, public address, blog post, and academic argument I have ever written. Why would we expect a Founding Father to be any different? If we just think about it for a minute, we will realize a number of factors could be responsible for such an inconsistency:

- **Genre:** The first quotation comes from a private letter, while the second comes from Adams's *A Defence of the Constitutions of Government of the United States of America*, which he wrote while in England in an attempt to influence the Constitutional Convention in the United States. Like most of us, Adams spoke very differently in private correspondence than in official documents.[12]
- **Audience and Purpose:** The audience in the first quotation is Dr. Benjamin Rush, one of the more devout Christians among the Founding Fathers. The audience for the second quotation is the world in general—and, specifically, the Americans who would soon be discussing and voting on a new Constitution. Adams's very different purposes for writing these texts could easily account for the difference in emphasis.
- **Time Frame:** Adams's letter to Benjamin Rush was written in 1811; his *Defence of the Constitutions* was written in 1786 and 1787. It is quite possible that Adams changed his mind about some things over the course of twenty-five years. Most of us change our minds about things—even very important things—over long periods of time.
- **Context:** In his letter to Rush, Adams is giving qualified agreement to his pious friend, who has advised him to leave "a posthumous address to the citizens of the United States" concerning, in part, "religious virtues." Adams replies that, while he agrees "in sentiment" with the importance of religion, he does not believe it would be wise to make a posthumous statement, lest his family be "charged with hypocrisy." In his political pamphlet, Adams is stressing that the American Revolution proved government authority "can be grounded on reason, morality, and the Christian religion, without the monkery of priests or the knavery of politicians."[13]

Subjected to this kind of analysis, both quotations lose their luster. Neither one quite means what its proof-texting proponents would like it to mean.

The first quotation comes from the "I agree with you in principle" statement that one often makes when disagreeing with a close friend. The second represents a clear attempt to separate religion, which the author supports, from established clergy, which he opposes.

But most people don't want to have to conduct a full-scale textual analysis every time they encounter a proof text. That's hard work—and it is unlikely to give us the clarity we need to pursue our own opinions without reservation. When presented with potentially contradictory evidence such as the two John Adams quotations above, most people will choose the one that supports their view and declare it "what Adams really meant" while similarly finding reasons to discount the other quotation: it is out of context, out of character, or a cynical manipulation by ideologically motivated evildoers. This is precisely how confirmation bias works.

Even a single quotation can mean radically different things when situated within different narratives. Proof-text arguments usually don't just take quotations out of the original context; they replace that context with a new one made of the story the proof texter is trying to tell. Consider the following fairly straightforward passage from a speech George Washington gave to a group of Delaware Indians in 1779, when, as commander of the Continental army, he was trying to secure their allegiance against the British:

> You do well to wish to learn our arts and ways of life, and above all, the religion of Jesus Christ. These will make you a greater and happier people than you are.[14]

Now look at how this quotation has been embedded into two very different narratives about George Washington's religious beliefs. The first example comes from a well-known evangelical who sponsors a ministry devoted to establishing the religious nature of America's Founding Fathers. The second comes from a left-leaning Unitarian minister who holds firmly to a belief in the separation of church and state:

> Perhaps George Washington . . . provided the most succinct description of America's educational philosophy when Chiefs from the Delaware Indian Tribe brought him three Indian youths to be trained in American schools. Washington first assured the Chiefs that "Congress . . . will look upon them as their own children," and then commended the Chiefs for their decision, telling them that

> You do well to wish to learn our arts and ways of life, and above all, the
> religion of Jesus Christ. These will make you a greater and happier people
> than you are. Congress will do everything they can to assist you in this
> wise intention.

By George Washington's own words, what youths learned in America's
schools "above all" was "the religion of Jesus Christ."[15]

It requires no great effort—and many have done so—to string together an
impressive series of pious-sounding phrases from Washington's writings
to certify that the first president was a true believer. He was culturally
Christian, to be sure, but throughout volumes of correspondence, public
and private, Washington mentions Christ by name only once, in a 1799
address to the chiefs of the Delaware Indians composed almost certainly
by an adjutant.[16]

What are we to make of such radically different narrative contexts for the
same quotation? Neither author gets any facts wrong. Washington did indeed
tell the chiefs that Congress would educate their children, and he did
admonish them to learn the "religion of Jesus Christ." But it is also true that
this is the only occurrence of the words "Jesus Christ" in some ninety volumes of the first president's papers and letters. The quotation in question can
legitimately be used to support either narrative. And this is my point. A collection of proof texts—whatever the ideology of its author—proves nothing
because proof-text citations can be used to support anything.

We are fortunate to live at a time when the writings of the remarkable
men and women of the Founding generation are widely available to anybody
who wants to read them. Just a few years ago, this was not the case. When I
was a college student in the 1990s, only those with access to major research
libraries could read the collected works of Alexander Hamilton or Thomas
Jefferson. Most of us had to make do with heavily edited selections or expen-
sive—and still not exhaustive—anthologies. All that has changed. Internet
sites such as Google Books and Project Gutenberg now make complete original texts available at no cost. These books can be read on computer screens,
tablet computers, electronic readers, smartphones, and other devices that can
display simple text. The actual words of the Founders have never been more
available to Americans.

The same is true for serious yet accessible scholarship of the Founding era. Historians and biographers have long been attracted to the early American republic, which has been well represented in academic books and articles for years. Trade book publishers have also gotten into the game. Distinguished academic historians who are also good writers—figures such as Pauline Mayer, Gordon Wood, Ron Chernow, Carol Berkin, Edward Larson, Mary Beth Norton, and James Simon, to name just a few who have been important to my own understanding—have been presenting the best insights of contemporary history to mainstream audiences for years.

But too much information can often have the same results as no information at all. As the Internet has made available entire libraries of once-limited information, it has also created a market for people who can read, digest, synthesize, and summarize that information for average readers. Given the difficulty of many of the original texts and the complexity of much of the scholarly work, the market for easy-to-read, ideologically comforting commentary on the works of the Founding Fathers has grown dramatically with the advent of the so-called constitutional conservative movement in American politics. Unfortunately, however, the voices that have risen to meet this demand often mistake shouting for scholarship and simplistic dogma for political principle. And they have interests that go well beyond historical accuracy, scholarly integrity, or simply getting it right.

CHAPTER 3

THE FALLACY OF "ORIGINAL INTENT"

It was—and typically still is—a fundamental maxim of law to determine the intent of the authors of a statute before attempting to apply it.

—David Barton, *Original Intent*

You will find it frequently said in judicial opinions of my court and others that the judge's objective in interpreting a statute is to give effect to "the intent of the legislature." This principle, in one form or another, goes back at least as far as Blackstone. Unfortunately, it does not square with some of the (few) generally accepted concrete rules of statutory construction. One is the rule that when the text of a statute is clear, that is the end of the matter. Why should that be so, if what the legislature *intended*, rather than what it *said*, is the object of our inquiry?"

—Justice Antonin Scalia, "A Matter of Interpretation"

Nearly every problem of the modern era stems from America's neglect of the Constitution and its Framers. On this point, at least, right-wing radio hosts agree. The Framers understood that universal healthcare was a federal overreach, that taxes should always be low, and that public schools (whatever they were) would always need prayers. They put all this in the Constitution, too, for those who know how to read it. We simply need to understand and allow ourselves to be governed by their worldview, as expressed in their letters, journals, speeches, and public papers—all of which should bear directly on our understanding of the Constitution. This, in a nutshell, is the interpretive strategy known as "original intent."

For most fringe conservatives, original intent is the only acceptable standard to use in interpreting the Constitution. We must, in other words, evaluate our own laws and policies by what the Framers meant rather than simply by what they said. In *Arguing with Idiots*, Glenn Beck goes as far as to translate parts of the Constitution himself, "from English to Idiot," so that there can be "no doubt as to what our Founding Fathers really intended."[1] Sean Hannity insists Republicans must "be known far and wide as the party that is committed to constitutional government," which, he adds, means "respecting the Constitution as written and according to its original intent."[2] And Mark Levin argues that the only judges who actually uphold their oath of office are those who "look to the intent of the Constitution and the intent of the Framers when deciding a Constitutional question."[3]

To discover the original intent, these same fringe conservatives tell us, we must look outside of the text of the Constitution for evidence of what its Framers really thought. We must examine, as Levin writes in *Liberty and Tyranny*, both the text itself and "a variety of original sources—records of public debates, diaries, correspondence, notes, etc." These sources will tell us what the Founders *really* thought about issues that may be ambiguous in the Constitution itself. Such an approach is "the only standard that gives fidelity to the Constitution."[4]

There is a certain naive logic to the original-intent approach; it corresponds with the way most of us read literature. If we want to understand what Nathaniel Hawthorne really meant in *The Scarlet Letter*, we might very plausibly read his letters, journal entries, other novels, and public statements in search for his real views on concepts, such as sin and redemption, that are crucial to *The Scarlet Letter*. As a literary critic, I have spent most of my professional life operating under precisely these assumptions, which (French deconstruction aside) can lead to excellent and productive readings of novels and poems.

But constitutional interpretation is nothing like literary history. For one thing, Nathaniel Hawthorne was a single individual, not hundreds of people working from different starting points to form a consensus based on compromise. Even more important, however, *The Scarlet Letter* is not a legal document. Nobody will ever go to jail for reading it incorrectly, nor will it ever determine the shape of the government or the protection of civil rights. One of my primary assertions in this book is that original intent, while a reasonable strategy for understanding the meaning of literature, is a spectacularly bad standard for interpreting the law of the land.

Most of the fallacies of the original-intent position can be seen in the works of one of the fringe conservatives most associated with the doctrine: David Barton, the founder of the WallBuilders ministry, a Texas-based organization dedicated to "presenting America's forgotten history and heroes, with an emphasis on the moral, religious, and constitutional foundation on which America was built."[5] Barton has written a dozen or so books on topics such as education, race relations, and the right to bear arms. His bestselling work, though, is the five-hundred-page *Original Intent: The Courts, the Constitution, and Religion*, currently in its fifth edition.

Barton's magnum opus (like several other books he has written on the subject) consists largely of proof-text quotations; as he brags in the preface, it contains "hundreds of the Founders' direct declarations on many of the constitutional issues which America continues to face today." He does not limit his citations to the thirty-nine men who actually signed the Constitution or to the fifty-five who participated in its construction. Rather, he supports his constitutional interpretation with "some two hundred fifty individuals" who "exerted significant influence in, provided leadership for, or had a substantial impact on the birth, development, and establishment of America as an independent, self-governing nation."[6]

This kind of analysis makes two deeply problematic assumptions: (1) that the text of the Constitution is insufficient to establish its meaning and must be supplemented by the writings of the Founders in other contexts, and (2) that the writings of any Founder—not just those who had something to do with the crafting of the Constitution or the Bill of Rights—can be used to shed light on the meaning of both documents. From his starting position, Barton quite predictably proof texts his way to a Constitution that "aggressively promoted religion throughout American society" until "the departure from that practice was facilitated by the laxness of the citizenry in understanding, and of the Court in upholding the Constitution's original intent."[7]

As evidence of the Constitution's original intent, Barton includes hundreds of quotations by such figures as Samuel Adams, Noah Webster, Patrick Henry, John Quincy Adams, William Findley, and John Hancock—none of whom were actually at the convention and most of whom ardently opposed the Constitution during the ratification debate. Only a small fraction of the quotations Barton includes to establish the original intent of the Framers actually come from Framers. To accept his conclusions, therefore, we would have to grant the premise that we can take anything ever written or said by any of 250 people and use it to establish the meaning of a document written in the summer of 1787 by fifty-five specific individuals, only thirty-nine of whom actually signed it.

There is simply no acceptable rationale for interpreting the Constitution according to the intentions and opinions of people who had nothing to do with its construction and who opposed its ratification once it was constructed. The overwhelming majority of Barton's proof-text citations do not even support his original-intent position. But what about those that do? Should we not give credence to quotations from James Madison, Alexander Hamilton, Roger Sherman, Charles Pinckney, and the other Founders who attended the Constitutional Convention in 1787?

Absolutely not! The private opinions of these men do not matter to the legal interpretation of the document they produced. I do not say this as an America-hating liberal who sees the Constitution as a "living, breathing document" that can mean anything we want it to mean. I believe we must interpret the Constitution according to the meaning of its words, with careful attention to how those words were used in their historical context. Words mean things, and those meanings matter.

Interpreting the Constitution according to the meaning of its words as they were understood at the time—the jurisprudential standard known as *originalism* or *textualism*—is very different from interpreting it according to the intentions of its authors. The Framers drafted the Constitution, but they did not ratify it, and, by their own design, their deliberations were not made available to the people who did. Any interpretation that cannot be derived from the text itself, placed in the linguistic context of the time, has no rational claim to authority. Supreme Court justice Antonin Scalia—a dedicated originalist often incorrectly cited by the Right as a believer in original intent—makes this case clearly in his lecture "A Matter of Interpretation":

> It is simply incompatible with democratic government, or indeed, even with fair government, to have the meaning of a law determined by what the lawgiver meant, rather than by what the lawgiver promulgated. That seems to me one step worse than the trick the emperor Nero was said to engage in: posting edicts high up on the pillars, so they could not be easily read. Government by unexpressed intent is similarly tyrannical.[8]

If we truly believe, as the Founders did, that sovereignty ultimately lies with the people, then we have no business basing our legal interpretations on the intentions of the political elite as derived from extratextual sources (letters, debates, journal entries, etc.) that were not available to the general population. As much as we revere the Framers, their constitutional opinions are no more authoritative than those of anybody else who read the document at the time. And on most of the things we argue about today, the Framers' opinions were no more consistent than our own.

Those who argue for original intent often promote the similar interpretive strategy of "legislative intent" or "legislative history" as a guide for interpreting the Constitution's several amendments. This practice involves searching through records of the congressional debates for speeches and statements about—and sometimes earlier versions of—the amendment. As Scalia points out, appeals to legislative history are even more problematic than appeals to original intent. "I reject the use of legislative history on principle, since I reject the intent of the legislature as the proper criterion of the law," Scalia explains. He also argues that examining legislative history "does not even make sense for those who *accept* legislative intent as the criterion. It is much more likely to produce a false or contrived legislative intent than a genuine one. The first and most obvious reason for this is that, with respect to 99.99 percent of the issues of construction reaching the courts, there *is* no legislative intent, so that any clues provided by the legislative history are bound to be false."[9]

For an example of a "false or contrived legislative intent," let's return to Barton, who inadvertently demonstrates just such an interpretive fallacy when discussing the passage of the First Amendment in 1789. To "prove" the Framers only intended to prohibit the federal government from choosing a national church from among several Christian denominations, Barton turns to the *Annals of Congress* to cite the debate that preceded the passage of the First Amendment's Establishment Clause:

It was—and typically still is—a fundamental maxim of law to determine the intent of the authors of a statute before attempting to apply it. Therefore, to discover the legitimate scope of protections and prohibitions intended in either the First Amendment or Article VI, investigate the records from that era rather than relying on an interpretation concocted by the Court two hundred years *ex post facto*.

   Begin, for instance, by investigating the various proposals for the First Amendment. Notice that of George Mason (a member of the Constitutional Convention and "The Father of the Bill of Rights"):

> All men have an equal, natural and unalienable right to the free exercise of religion, according to the dictates of conscience; and that no particular sect or society of Christians ought to be favored or established by law in preference to others.

James Madison proposed:

> The civil rights of none shall be abridged on account of religious belief or worship, nor shall any national religion be established. . . .

The records are succinct; they clearly document that the Founders' purpose for the First Amendment is *not* compatible with the interpretation given it by contemporary courts. The Founders intended only to prevent the establishment of a single national denomination, not to restrain public religious expressions.[10]

Barton draws exactly the wrong conclusion from his evidence. Early drafts of a piece of legislation do not tell us what the legislature *intended*; they tell us what the legislature *rejected*. Had the Congress actually wanted to limit the First Amendment's protection to different Christian sects, they would have voted for Mason's version of the text. Had they wanted to limit the antiestablishment language to the establishment of a national religion only, they would have voted for Madison's version. Their rejection of these early versions tells us precisely what they did not want to say. To use these early versions to try to fix a positive legislative intent—even if one does believe such a thing matters—subjects the text to interpretive violence bordering on hostility.

Such fallacies as original intent and legislative intent have no place in a democracy. They are, rather, a theological approach to interpreting the meaning of a text. When gods deign to speak, anything they have to say is relevant to deriving the divine intent, which is the whole point of theology. But the Founders were not gods, and the Constitution is not Holy Writ but a compact entered into by specific people at a specific time in history. The words of its Framers matter a great deal; their intentions—unless clearly stated in their words—do not matter at all. It staggers the mind that, under the name of preserving liberty, fringe conservatives such as Levin and Barton seriously suggest the three hundred million Americans alive today should be governed by the unpromulgated intentions of fifty-five men who have been dead for two hundred years.

THE FRAMERS ON THE FRAMERS' INTENT?

Many of the Founding Fathers would have been extremely surprised to learn that 230 years after they created it, their Constitution was still governing the country they loved. For some of them, this would have come as a pleasant surprise. For others, however, it would have been a nasty shock, as they believed every generation should renegotiate its own social contract instead of being bound by the will of its ancestors.

Of all the Founders, it was Thomas Jefferson, the figure most revered by small-government libertarians, who most forcefully rejected the idea that one generation's opinions could bind another generation's politics. In a 1789 letter to James Madison from his station in Paris, Jefferson wrote:

> The question Whether one generation of men has a right to bind another, seems never to have been started either on this or our side of the water. Yet it is a question of such consequences as not only to merit decision, but place also, among the fundamental principles of every government. The course of reflection in which we are immersed here on the elementary principles of society has presented this question to my mind; and that no such obligation can be transmitted I think very capable of proof. I set out on this ground which I suppose to be self evident, "that the earth belongs in usufruct to the living;" that the dead have neither powers nor rights over it.[11]

Jefferson further says, "Every constitution then, and every law, naturally expires at the end of 19 years. If it be enforced longer, it is an act of force, and not of right."[12] Had Jefferson prevailed in his opinion, the United States would now be working on its twelfth Constitution.

For very good reasons, we have rejected Jefferson's advice. A Constitutional Convention every other decade—during which the foundational rules of government and society could be rewritten at will—would hardly promote stability or long-term thinking. Fortunately, the Constitution has proved to be a remarkably enduring document because it provides needed political stability while, at the same time, creating a process that leaves most decisions in the hands of the people currently living under it. This would not have been possible if previous generations of Americans had felt themselves bound by the eighteenth-century worldview that produced the Constitution.

Perhaps the greatest irony of the original-intent position is that it baldly contradicts the actual original intent of the Framers, who very clearly did not intend for future generations to interpret the Constitution in light of their unexpressed opinions. To prevent such a thing from happening, they decided, at the end of the Philadelphia Convention, not to publish the records of their discussions and debates. As Professor H. Jefferson Powell writes in his well-known 1985 article "The Original Understanding of Original Intent," there is "no indication that they expected or intended future interpreters to refer to any extratextual intentions revealed in the convention's secretly conducted debates."[13]

As Powell documents in his superbly researched article, nearly every relevant statement by a Framer rejects the idea that the Constitution should be interpreted by extratextual considerations. Hamilton makes this case clearly in his 1791 brief to Washington about the constitutionality of the national bank—a brief that, Powell rightly concludes, amounts to an "absolute rejection of what modern intentionalists would regard as evidence of 'intent.'"[14]

> Whatever may have been the intention of the framers of a constitution, or of a law, that intention is to be sought for in the instrument itself, according to the usual and established rules of construction. Nothing is more common than for laws to express and effect more or less than was intended. If, then, a power to erect a corporation in any case be deducible, by fair inference, from the whole or any part of the numerous provisions of the Constitution of the United States, arguments drawn from extrinsic circumstances regarding the intention of the convention must be rejected.[15]

By 1796, there were very few things Hamilton and Madison agreed upon. The former had become the de facto leader of the Federalists, who supported a strong central union, while the latter had joined with Jefferson to lead the Republicans, who supported strong states and limited federal power. Nonetheless, Madison took precisely the same position that Hamilton did on the question of the Framers' intent. During a tense congressional debate on a resolution aimed at forcing Washington to hand over sensitive diplomatic files to the House of Representatives, a member of Congress quoted from the minutes of the Virginia ratification convention in an attempt to fix the meaning of the Constitution. Madison, however, rejected any extratextual method of ascertaining the intent of the document. According to the *Annals of Congress,*

Mr. M[adison] said, he did not believe a single instance could be cited in which the sense of the Convention had been required or admitted as material in any Constitutional question.

But, after all, whatever veneration might be entertained for the body of men who formed our Constitution, the sense of that body could never be regarded as the oracular guide in expounding the Constitution.[16]

Like most of the Framers, Madison believed the intention that really mattered was that of the citizens who ratified the Constitution—the people of the United States through their representatives in the ratifying conventions. In practice, this translates into what Scalia calls an "objectified intent," or the sense that a reasonable person would have understood when reading the law at the time it was written.[17] In determining this sense, of course, it can be useful to examine some extra-constitutional sources—not only the writings of Framers, but also the thoughts and opinions of generally educated men and women in the Founding era who read the Constitution and reflected on its meaning.

The most important thing we will learn from these sources, however, is that the most hotly contested portions of the Constitution did not flow from anybody's original intent. Intentions determined the starting positions of the delegates, but compromise shaped the final result—and a compromise is, by definition, a position nobody started out with. To understand this point, we now turn to two of the most important compromises the convention reached—both of which received only tepid support from any of the delegates and both of which resolved seemingly unresolvable conflicts and became enduring elements of the American Constitution.

ORIGINAL INTENT AND THE GREAT COMPROMISES

Most historians acknowledge that the Constitutional Convention was effective because the delegates managed to move from their deeply entrenched positions to the remarkable compromises that created the Constitution. These compromises, however, make it impossible to locate the collective intent of the Framers in the words or opinions of the delegates. The reason is simple: the compromises the convention reached often embodied positions that did not represent the actual opinion of any of the delegates.

The most famous and consequential compromise of the convention was the agreement to form a bicameral legislature with one house based on equal representation and one based on proportional representation. Without this compromise, no Constitution would have been possible. The large states (Massachusetts, Pennsylvania, and Madison's Virginia) felt anything other than proportional representation would be undemocratic. The small states, on the other hand, already had equal representation under the status quo, and they saw no reason to give it away.

Initially, Madison used his convention allies to push through a proposal for proportional representation in both houses of Congress. It soon became clear, however, that the smaller states simply weren't going to participate in a government that left them with less power than they had under the Articles of Confederation, which gave each state's delegation a single vote. Madison's coalition could win a bare majority of votes (six states to five), but he could do so only at the expense of the stronger union most of the delegates desired. Six states were enough to win the point, but not enough to form a government.

To resolve the impasse, some of the delegates began to gravitate toward a compromise proposed earlier in the convention by Connecticut delegates Roger Sherman and Oliver Ellsworth. This "Connecticut Plan" was built on the assumption of a bicameral legislature, but it stipulated proportional representation in the lower house and equal representation for each state in the upper house—the exact system we have today. Not a single delegate came to the convention with the intention to create the representative structure that ended up in the Constitution. Madison opposed the compromise to the very end. He felt that both reason and natural law were on the side of proportional representation. In the end, however, Madison accepted the compromise and went on to champion the legislative model it created.

With one exception only, Madison accepted all the modifications to his original plan with equanimity. He won some, he lost some, and he emerged from the convention to become one of the new Constitution's greatest defenders. But one of his failures at the convention continued to sting him throughout the ratification process: his failure to secure a veto for the federal legislature on state laws that it found unacceptable. Madison proposed such a veto in the Virginia Plan, and he brought it before the convention on June 8, just one week into the proceedings. Madison took the convention floor to argue that he could not but regard an indefinite power to negative [veto] legislative acts of the States as absolutely necessary to a perfect system. Experience had evinced a constant tendency in the States to encroach on the federal authority; to violate national Treaties; to infringe the rights & interests of each other; to oppress the weaker party within their respective jurisdictions. A negative was the mildest expedient that could be devised for preventing these mischiefs.[18]

The delegates rejected this proposal as an infringement on state rights. But Madison would not be deterred. He believed that, without a national check on state laws, state governments would become majoritarian tyrannies with the power to destroy the rights of the minority. He would later write to Jefferson that "a constitutional negative on the laws of the States" would be necessary "to secure individuals ag[ain]st encroachments on their rights."[19] Madison proposed the veto again on July 17, and it lost by an even larger margin than before.

After the second vote, however, something tremendously important happened, though at the time it seemed nothing but an afterthought to the intense debate over the federal veto. Luther Martin, perhaps the most openly anti-nationalist delegate at the convention, proposed a resolution that "the Legislative acts of the United States made by virtue and in pursuance of the Articles of Union, and all treaties made and ratified under the authority of the United States, shall be the supreme law of the respective states." This resolution—which Martin made largely to prevent any further talk of a veto—was accepted by the other delegates *nemine contradicente* (without objection) and became the basis for Article VI, Section 2 of the Constitution, sometimes known as the Supremacy Clause.[20]

Martin later admitted that his resolution had been a trick. As the most ardent supporter of state sovereignty at the convention, he had little use for the supremacy of a document that he had no intention of supporting. He tried, rather, to construct the resolution in such a way that it would apply to state laws and not to state constitutions, thus preserving the supremacy of states at the constitutional level. The drafters of the final document, however, eventually closed this loophole.[21]

Martin's trick poses a dilemma for those who advocate an "original intent" interpretation of the Constitution: Whose original intent do we take as authoritative? Madison's intent was to push the federal veto throughout the convention. Martin's was to trick the delegates into supporting state sovereignty without even knowing it. And the rest of the delegates simply accepted the resolution without comment or debate. We can never know what motivated their acceptance, though we can guess it had something to do with getting Madison off his hobbyhorse and back to the business of designing a Constitution.

When the convention was over, Madison continued to feel he had lost the most important battle of the summer. The letter he sent to Jefferson along with a copy of the new Constitution contains a 2,500-word digression lamenting the absence of the federal veto. He argues that the veto was necessary for three reasons: (1) to prevent insuperable conflicts between local and national governments, (2) to protect the rights of individuals from hostile majorities at the state level, and (3) to prevent a dominant religious sect from unjustly imposing its will within a state. Madison feared these issues would soon jeopardize the stability of the republic.

Nonetheless, Madison went on to coauthor the Federalist essays and to defend every aspect of the Constitution against the attacks of the Anti-Federalists. Luther Martin, on the other hand, left the convention early, refused to sign the Constitution, and became the leader of Maryland's Anti-Federalist opposition. Though neither man had really wanted the supremacy clause, it emerged as a logical outcome of their intense disagreement over the proper relationship of the states to the federal government.

Remarkably, however, the supremacy clause quickly became an almost-perfect compromise between the two original positions, giving each side almost everything it had wanted to begin with. In the hands of the courts, it became a powerful tool to strike down oppressive or overreaching state laws, beginning with the *Ware v. Hilton* decision in 1796—seven years before the *Marbury v. Madison* decision settled the question of judicial review. During the civil rights movement, the supremacy clause was a crucial tool for enforcing school desegregation, voting rights, and other principles of basic fairness that contradicted state laws in the South.

Both of these examples show the true genius of a constitutional process that allows for significant progress without general agreement. The Framers did not make compromises because they were the sort of people who liked to make compromises. They made compromises because it was the only alternative to failure. And the system they created works much the same way. The Framers created a government of diffuse, overlapping, and self-interested sovereignties—all of which have enough power to prevent forward movement on almost any initiative or proposal. No matter how deeply committed we are to our views, other people, committed to other views, can always frustrate the actions we support. Such a system creates tremendous incentives for compromises and temporary political alliances. It is a good system for governing a country that represents many different values and interests. It is a very bad system, however, for a single individual to use to translate his or her intent directly into settled law.

BIRTHRIGHT CITIZENSHIP: WHERE TEXTUALISM AND ORIGINAL INTENT PART WAYS

As we have seen, the interpretive standard of original intent (focusing on the extratextual opinions of the author) is often confused with the standard of textualism (focusing on the meaning of the words in their original context). Often, these two strategies produce similar interpretations, but just as often, they do not. No contemporary question demonstrates the difference better than the issue of birthright citizenship, the practice of granting automatic citizenship to children born in the United States regardless of the citizenship of their parents.

Nearly every judge, law professor, and legal scholar in the country believes the Fourteenth Amendment protects birthright citizenship through its first sentence: "All persons born or naturalized in the United States, and subject to the jurisdiction thereof, are citizens of the United States and of the State wherein they reside." Nearly every talk-radio host and right-wing politician, on the other hand, believes the Fourteenth Amendment does no such thing. It was, they argue, an amendment designed to grant citizenship to freed slaves, not immigrant children, and any other interpretation misrepresents the intent of the Framers.

Pulitzer Prize–winning columnist George Will—only an occasional visitor to Glennbeckistan—also believes there is no constitutional basis for granting citizenship to the children of illegal immigrants. In fact, in a March 2010 op-ed for the *Washington Post*, Will stakes out a position that has made him one of the intellectual architects of the anti-birthright-citizenship movement. He points out, accurately, that, at the time the Fourteenth Amendment was ratified, there was no such thing as an "illegal immigrant" because "no law had ever restricted immigration." To understand the meaning of the text, he argues, we need to ask ourselves what the Framers would have thought if they could have foreseen our generation's problems:

> If those who wrote and ratified the 14th Amendment *had* imagined laws restricting immigration—and had anticipated huge waves of illegal immigration—is it reasonable to presume they would have wanted to provide the reward of citizenship to the children of the violators of those laws? Surely not.[22]

This statement takes the original-intent fallacy to a new level. In the absence of source material, it directs us to try to consider what the writers of the Fourteenth Amendment would have thought about a problem they did not have. If judges actually took George Will seriously (of which there is little danger), they could justify just about anything on the grounds that the Framers were the sort of people who probably would have thought it was a good idea.

To his credit, Will does quote one of the authors of the Fourteenth Amendment, Senator Lyman Trumbull of Illinois—who said that the phrase "subject to the jurisdiction of the United States" meant "subject to its complete jurisdiction," which (Will assumes) would not include foreign nationals. Other fringe conservatives point to a speech by Senator Jacob M. Howard in the floor debate on the Fourteenth Amendment:

> This amendment which I have offered is simply declaratory of what I regard as the law of the land already, that every person born within the United States, and subject to their jurisdiction, is by virtue of natural law and national law a citizen of the United States. This will not, of course, include persons born in the United States who are foreigners, aliens, who belong to the families of ambassadors or foreign ministers accredited to the Government of the United States, but will include every other class of persons.[23]

There can be little doubt that Senator Jacob Howard believed, when casting his vote on the Fourteenth Amendment, that it would not grant citizenship to the children of foreigners. It is quite possible that everybody else in Congress at the time felt the same. I will even grant, for the sake of argument, Will's assumption that if the authors of the amendment had been able to look into the future and see our generation's illegal immigration problem, they would have clarified what they meant by "under the jurisdiction thereof."

But they didn't. The Framers of the Fourteenth Amendment wrote a straightforward law that listed only two requirements for citizenship: (1) that a person be born in the United States, and (2) that a person be under the jurisdiction of the United States. Neither of these conditions is particularly controversial. Anybody born within the recognized boundaries of the United States meets the first criterion, and anybody who is subject to the laws of the United States—and who can be punished by American courts for violating those laws—meets the second. No judge or serious legal scholar suggests that illegal aliens are not under the jurisdiction of the United States—that we should give them immunity from our laws and decline to prosecute them when they commit crimes. Any state that took this assertion seriously would have to reorganize its judicial system to deport, rather than prosecute, illegal aliens who commit crimes.

And yet, the current fringe-conservative position is based entirely on asserting that this clause does not mean what it clearly says. "Illegal aliens are subject to the jurisdiction of their home country," writes Mark Levin, "as are their children, whether they are born in their home country or the United States."[24] Legal analyst Garrett Epps points out the absurdity of positions like this:

> This argument doesn't pass the laugh test. Does anyone doubt that American police have the power to arrest "illegal" aliens for crimes committed on American soil? Does anyone seriously contend that people injured in auto accidents are barred from suing "illegal" alien drivers? And those are the parents. Remember the Clause is about the *child*, born and present in the United States. Any power the law has over children of American citizens at the moment of their birth on American soil, it also has over American-born children of aliens. Child welfare authorities can take them away from their parents as part of an abuse or neglect investigation. The civil-justice system can attach their property if it is a subject of a dispute. They have no immunity from American law, any more than do their parents.[25]

Levin also asserts that "there is no legislative history supporting the absurd proposition that the Fourteenth Amendment was intended to empower illegal aliens to confer American citizenship on their own babies merely as a result of their birth in the United States."[26] In this, he is at least partially correct. As so many fringe conservatives have pointed out, the authors of the Fourteenth Amendment could not have anticipated the question of illegal immigration; therefore, there is no reason they would have discussed it in their debates. Levin is absolutely correct to point to the lack of any legislative history supporting birthright citizenship. If legislative history mattered in constitutional interpretation, he would have a valid point. But, as we have already seen, legislative history is even less relevant than legislative intent.

The current debate on birthright citizenship is not, as it has been presented on the right, a debate between constitutional "strict constructionists" who care about the original meaning of the text and irresponsible "judicial activists" bent on passing law from the bench. It is, rather, a debate between textualists, who care about the original meaning, and intentionalists, who focus on the original intent. And this is where those of us who actually believe the text of the Constitution matters must part ways with the conservative fringe. Living under the rule of law means being accountable for what the Constitution says rather than for the ultimately unknowable intentions of its authors. The text of the Fourteenth Amendment is almost ridiculously clear: if a person was born in the United States, and if this person was, at birth, subject to the laws of the United States, then he or she is a citizen.

I am not suggesting that birthright citizenship is a good idea. In fact, I think it is a very bad idea. Conservatives are absolutely correct to point out that the birthright-citizenship clause creates a powerful incentive for illegal immigration and that illegal immigration is stretching the resources of many states to the breaking point. As a sovereign nation, the United States has both a right and an obligation to control its borders, and those who come here illegally flout our laws and our sovereignty. We need to do something about this problem.

But the something cannot include sidestepping the supreme law of the land because it has become inconvenient. Nor can it mean applying the deeply flawed and fundamentally undemocratic standard of original intent to try to wrest the Constitution away from the words on the page. The Constitution itself is very clear about the remedy for a problem the original Framers did not foresee: a constitutional amendment, in this case, one stipulating that citizenship is conveyed only to children born in the United States when at least one parent is already a citizen or a legal resident.

Republican senators David Vitter and Rand Paul proposed just such an amendment in early 2011, and I wish it well. To their credit, Vitter and Paul rejected the calls of many in their party to end birthright citizenship by legislative fiat—choosing, rather, to take the Constitution seriously. The constitutional amendment they propose has an uphill climb to ratification. It must first be approved by a two-thirds supermajority in both houses and by three-fourths of the individual state legislatures. But the Constitution is supposed to be hard to change. An amendment is supposed to require a broad consensus that something is wrong and needs to be fixed. If such a consensus exists, let's get busy and amend. If it does not exist, let's stop rummaging around the archives trying to determine the original intent of a statute whose literal meaning could not be clearer.

CONCLUSION

The constitutional system works largely because of its minimalism. It is a very different document from the Code of Hammurabi or the law of Moses. These legal codes were designed to govern people; the Constitution was designed to give people a mechanism for governing themselves. This means that the Constitution is sometimes ambiguous by design—that phrases such as "necessary and proper" or "cruel and unusual" require careful interpretation from the perspective of the generation doing the interpreting. When determining whether keelhauling constitutes "cruel and unusual punishment," for example, we should focus not on how common such a punishment was in the eighteenth century but on how uncommon it is in the twenty-first. That each generation do so for itself is the clear intent of the document.

Those who pore over the letters and diaries of the Framers looking to support narrow political agendas (whatever those agendas are) are a lot like the die-hard Beatles fans who used to play the albums backward looking for proof that Paul McCartney was really dead. Not only will they never find what they are looking for, they will end up missing out on a lot of the great stuff that comes with doing it right. The Framers of the Constitution were wise and committed men who designed one of the best mechanisms for self-government ever created. Rather than looking at this remarkable process, however, some conservatives have taken the stance that Americans should replace self-government with government by conjecture and clairvoyance.

I do not mean to suggest that we should not take the opinions of the Founders seriously when they talk about the Constitution. Madison, Hamilton, Jefferson, and the other Founding Fathers created a body of political theory that deserves to be studied for its own merits. And, though understanding how these men read and understood the Constitution does not give us an authoritative Framers' intent, it does help us define a range of acceptable interpretations by showing us how some of the people of the time construed its objective meaning. However, this is a very different thing from trying to construe the meaning of a law by guessing at the unstated intentions of the author.

The view of original intent propounded by many on the right is directly at odds with the democratic principles they espouse, the common sense they advocate, and even the Supreme Court justice they revere. This difference between "original meaning" and "original intent" may seem slight, but it separates Scalia's mainstream conservatism from that of the conservative fringe. Scalia himself alluded to this distinction in a 1997 lecture at the Manhattan Institute for Policy Research. When asked whether or not he would consider scaling back the application of the Bill of Rights to the states through an originalist reading of the Fourteenth Amendment, he replied, "I am an originalist. I am a textualist. I am not a nut."[27]

Unfortunately, many of those driving public opinion and government policy in the era of the Tea Party cannot say the same.

CHAPTER 4

THE FOUNDERS ON RELIGION AND LIBERTY

> George Washington's practice of Christianity was lim-
> ited and superficial, because he was not himself a
> Christian. In the enlightened tradition of his day, he
> was a devout Deist—just as many of the clergymen
> who knew him suspected.
> —Barry Schwartz, *George Washington: The Making of*
> *an American Symbol*

> Were George Washington living today, he would
> freely identify with the Bible-believing branch of evan-
> gelical Christianity that is having such a positive influ-
> ence on our nation.
> —Tim LaHaye, *Faith of Our Founding Fathers*

Here, in a nutshell, is what we know for sure about the religious beliefs of our first president: He was either a confirmed deist or an evangelical Christian—or maybe a typical Anglican vestryman who thought fondly, but not often, of God. He was either heavily influenced by Freemasonry, or he participated casually in Masonic rites to facilitate social connections. He was a passionate Christian, or he intentionally avoided mentioning Jesus Christ in public, or he saw Jesus as a great but not divine teacher. Religion might have been the most important thing in his life, or it might have been a convenient way for him to instill a sense of duty in others. He might have been deeply influenced by Enlightenment rationalism, or he might have rejected it as an affront to his faith. And the rest of the Founding Fathers thought pretty much the same way.

Washington's religious beliefs are hard to pin down because he was intensely private about them. Most historians now believe he was both a reasonably devout Anglican and a committed Freemason—not an unusual pairing in the eighteenth century. Many of his public statements about God used either deistic language ("Providence" and "God of Nature") or Masonic terms ("the Grand Architect of the Universe"). He avoided public prayers and religious ceremonies but, by most accounts, observed religious devotions in private. Though he appears to have been influenced by both Enlightenment deism and evangelical Christianity (such as it was in the eighteenth century), those who attempt to place him firmly in either camp do so only by ignoring real scholarly evidence and cherry-picking his words.

Cherry-picking Washington's words is not difficult. He wrote a lot. Editors at the University of Virginia have been working on his collected papers since 1968 and have produced sixty-three of a projected ninety volumes representing more than 135,000 separate manuscripts. Somewhere in these millions of words—many of which can be searched electronically for high-value catchphrases—we can find ample proof texts to establish that George Washington was whatever our current political arguments require him to be. That, after all, is how proof texting works.

As the most important symbol of America's Founding, Washington has become a highly contested battlefield for today's religious factions. But most of the other Founders have received similar treatment. Over the past century or so, a staggering amount of proof texting has gone into "proving" things about the religious nature of America's Founding. Both liberals and conservatives have learned to play the game like seasoned chess masters going through standard opening sequences by rote. A typical opening gambit from the Right might go something like this:

> I have examined all religions, as well as my narrow sphere, my straightened means, and my busy life, would allow; and the result is that the Bible is the best Book in the world. It contains more philosophy than all the libraries I have seen.
>
> —John Adams[1]

> It is the duty of every man to render to the Creator such homage. . . . Before any man can be considered as a member of Civil Society, he must be considered as a subject of the Governor of the Universe.
>
> —James Madison[2]

A more beautiful or precious morsel of ethics I have never seen; it is a document in proof that I am a real Christian; that is to say, a disciple of the doctrines of Jesus.

—Thomas Jefferson[3]

Whoever shall introduce into public affairs the principles of . . . Christianity will change the face of the world.

—Benjamin Franklin[4]

It cannot be emphasized too strongly or too often that this great nation was founded, not by religionists, but by Christians; not on religions, but on the Gospel of Jesus Christ.

—Patrick Henry[5]

As proof texts go, these are all darn good. Each speaks to significant religious feelings on the part of the Founding Fathers, and most of them single out Christianity as the religion the Founders felt significantly about. Collectively, they make it very difficult to argue that the Founders were atheists, or deists, or even that they were skeptical about Christianity. This is why social conservatives offer these quotations—and many like them—as proof that, whatever liberal academic historians say, America was founded by devout Christians much like themselves.

But the other side hasn't played their opening move yet. When they do, we find another treasure trove of quotations that just as persuasively—and just as inaccurately—demonstrate that the Founding Fathers were committed secularists and Bible haters. A typical opening from a left-wing proof texter might include such chestnuts as:

When we read the obscene stories, the voluptuous debaucheries, the cruel and torturous executions, the unrelenting vindictiveness, with which more than half of the Bible is filled, it would be more consistent that we call it the word of a demon than the word of God. It is a history of wickedness that has served to corrupt and brutalize mankind; and, for my own part, I sincerely detest it, as I detest everything that is cruel.

—Thomas Paine, 1794[6]

I am a Christian, in the only sense that he would have wished any one to be; sincerely attached to his doctrines, in preference to all others; ascribing to himself every *human* excellence; & believing that he never claimed any other.

—Thomas Jefferson[7]

Thirteen governments [of the original states] thus founded on the natural authority of the people alone, without a pretence of miracle or mystery, and which are destined to spread over the Northern part of that whole quarter of the globe, are a great point gained in favor of the rights of mankind.

—John Adams[8]

Some books against Deism fell into my hands; they were said to be the Substance of Sermons preached at Boyle's lectures. It happened that they wrought an effect on me quite contrary to what was intended by them; for the arguments of the Deists, which were quoted to be refuted, appeared to me much stronger than the refutations; in short, I soon became a thorough Deist.

—Benjamin Franklin[9]

As the Government of the United States of America is not, in any sense, founded on the Christian religion; as it has in itself no character of enmity against the laws, religion, or tranquility, of Mussulmen; and, as the said States never entered into any war, or act of hostility against any Mahometan nation, it is declared by the parties, that no pretext arising from religious opinions, shall ever produce an interruption of the harmony existing between the two countries.

—Article 9 of the Treaty of Tripoli, ratified unanimously by the US Senate in 1797 and signed by President John Adams[10]

These quotations show a very different group of Founding Fathers— many of whom have the same names as the ones in the first set of quotations. These Founders were secularists at best. They saw Christianity as a corrupt tradition perverted by centuries of power-hungry priests. And they believed America was founded by exceptional human beings with no help from the divine.

To the student of actual rather than proof-text history, the answer to the question "What did the Founding Fathers believe about religion and its role in society?" goes something like this: The Founding Fathers believed all sorts of things. Some of them were devout Christians who never questioned their faith, others were Christian deists or Unitarians who believed Jesus

Christ was an exceptional but not divine moral teacher, and others still were non-Christian deists who believed in a nonpersonal "watchmaker God" who created the laws of nature and then disappeared. Many of them held all three of these beliefs at some point in their lives, and some of them would waver between orthodox Christianity and deism in the space of a single day.

Furthermore, the personal religious beliefs of the Founders do not always explain how they felt about the role of religion in the public sphere. Some were personally devout but believed private devotion was best served by a strict separation between church and state. Others were not particularly religious in private but still saw religion as a good tool for promoting civic virtue. And others felt the states should be free to establish religions as they saw fit.

From all this religious diversity emerged a fairly coherent Founding compromise: America would be an officially secular nation that would vigorously protect everybody's freedom of worship and belief. Unlike most European nations, which officially preferred their state churches and occasionally tolerated others, America would offer its citizens actual religious liberty, which meant those of any religion, or no religion at all, would be free to participate fully in the political community.

RELIGIOUS LIBERTY IN VIRGINIA AND BEYOND

Right-wing mythology holds that liberals and other enemies of America have been intentionally misunderstanding the separation of church and state for the last two hundred years. Neither Thomas Jefferson nor anybody else (they insist) ever meant to suggest that the government should not actively promote Christianity. All the Founders meant to do was prevent the federal government from singling out any particular version of Christianity for tax support. "Very simply, the Founding Fathers did not want a single federal denomination to rule America," writes Christian activist David Barton, "but they did expect basic Biblical principles and values to be present throughout public life and society."[11]

This argument goes well beyond asserting that people have the right to practice their religion in a public setting (which nobody actually disagrees with). Barton and others flatly claim (1) that the Founders used the word *religion* as a synonym for *Christian denomination* and intended to exclude non-

Christians from the guarantee of religious freedom, (2) that they wanted both federal and state governments to support Christianity generally (but nondenominationally) through tax dollars and public policies, and (3) that any mention by the Founders of "separation of church and state" meant only that "the federal government could not interfere with public religious expression."[12] Evangelical celebrity author Tim LaHaye (coauthor of the Rapture-inspired Left Behind series) makes the ultimate purpose of the Right's position exceptionally clear: "If we as a nation do not soon return our official public policy to the Christian consensus of our Founding Fathers and the Biblical principles of law that have provided the freedoms we've enjoyed for over two hundred years, it is just a matter of time before we lose those freedoms."[13]

LaHaye's call to return to "Biblical principles of law" is difficult to square with the actual text of the Constitution, which mentions nothing about God or the Bible and almost nothing about religion at all. The only passage in the Constitution that applies even remotely to religion is the statement in Article VI that "no religious Test shall ever be required as a Qualification to any office of public Trust under the United States." With the ratification of the Bill of Rights in 1789 came the two clauses of the First Amendment that form the basis for most of the religious precedents in American constitutional law: (1) "Congress shall make no law respecting the establishment of religion," and (2) "or prohibiting the free exercise thereof."

In their books, both Barton and LaHaye insist on the most-restrictive possible understanding of the Establishment Clause (that it prohibits only the legal establishment of a single state religion at the federal level) and the least-restrictive possible understanding of the Free Exercise Clause (that it permits the government to support and subsidize the religious practices of the Christian majority as long as it does not single out a specific denomination). Armed with mountains of proof texts and virtually no understanding of historical context, Barton and LaHaye play to the Right's persistent fear that secular humanists are persecuting them and trying to take away their natural rights to say prayers in public schools, read the Ten Commandments in public buildings, and look at Nativity displays in front of City Hall.

In asserting that the Founding Fathers wanted to base American law on the Bible and publicly endorse the Christian religion, conservatives are not entirely wrong. But they are not entirely right either. Some of the Founding Fathers felt exactly this way and said so repeatedly. Some did not. The

Founders debated this issue as vigorously and contentiously in their own time as we do in ours. Consequently, there are a lot of different opinions that can reasonably be asserted as those of "the Founding Fathers." If we really want to understand what the Founders thought about the role of religion in society, we must look at the entire debate, which, most historians believe, began in Virginia.

Before the Constitution was even imagined, the principles of religious liberty that would eventually predominate in the Constitutional Convention were worked out in the long struggle for disestablishment in the Virginia legislature—a struggle that pitted Thomas Jefferson and James Madison against Patrick Henry and other Revolutionary luminaries. The controversy surrounded the Act for Establishing Religious Freedom (see appendix A), which Jefferson drafted in 1777 but was not passed until 1786.

The bulk of the law's text can be found in the long, polemical introduction, which makes such strong statements as "to compel a man to furnish contributions of money for the propagation of opinions which he disbelieves and abhors, is sinful and tyrannical" and "our civil rights have no dependence on our religious opinions, any more than our opinions in physics or geometry." The enforceable portion of the law stipulates:

> We the General Assembly of Virginia do enact that no man shall be compelled to frequent or support any religious worship, place, or ministry whatsoever, nor shall be enforced, restrained, molested, or burthened in his body or goods, nor shall otherwise suffer, on account of his religious opinions or belief; but that all men shall be free to profess, and by argument to maintain, their opinions in matters of religion, and that the same shall in no wise diminish, enlarge, or affect their civil capacities.[14]

Jefferson's proposal, to do away with any state support of religion whatsoever, was too radical for the Virginia legislature at the time. When he introduced the bill in 1779, it was roundly defeated; in its place the legislature offered a series of half measures designed to decrease the influence of the Anglican Church without disestablishing it entirely. But Jefferson's proposal refused to die. In 1786, after the Revolution was over and Jefferson was away in France, James Madison resurrected the proposal as part of a dispute with Patrick Henry and secured its passage.

The Virginia debate shows, among other things, how difficult it is to take seriously the Christian Right's generalization that Founders wanted to prevent establishing a single federal denomination but never intended to separate church and state. They did, and they did not—it all depends on which Founders we are talking about. There was never anything like an official Founder position on the relationship between church and state. In fact, in the ten years that religious establishment was debated in Virginia, legislators and their constituents moved through four distinct positions, each of which represented the opinions of a group of men who can reasonably be considered Founding Fathers.

Denominational Establishment

When the disestablishment debate began, the Anglican Church had been the established church of Virginia for 170 years. This meant that in Virginia, as in England, the church was an official part of the state. It had the power to levy taxes, punish heresy, compel church attendance, and confiscate the property of dissenters. By 1776, many of these provisions were no longer enforced, as Presbyterians, Baptists, and other dissenters outnumbered Anglicans throughout the state. But state support through religious levies remained in place and was defended vigorously by the now-minority Anglicans. At the dawn of the American Revolution, however, few Virginians wanted to continue supporting a church whose official head was the king of England.

Limited Religious Tolerance

In 1776, when the Virginia legislature met to create a new constitution, it adopted a series of reforms aimed at placating dissenters. The great beneficiaries of these measures were non-Anglican Protestants, who were exempted from the religion tax. The official establishment remained in effect, and, as Jefferson biographer Merrill Peterson explains, "Virginians could still be punished for heretical opinions . . . [and] Parish levies on members of the Church were suspended but not abolished."[15] While Trinitarian Protestants were accorded a nearly full measure of religious tolerance, "Unitarians [non-Trinitarian Christians] and freethinkers might be declared unfit parents and have their children taken from them," and "Roman Catholics were excluded from the mantle of toleration and burdened with legal disabilities." In November of 1776, Jefferson took to the floor of the legislature to ask, "Has the state a right to adopt an opinion in matters of religion?"[16] His own answer to this question was the now-famous Act for Establishing Religious Freedom.

Nondenominational Establishment

By 1784, very little was left of established religion in Virginia. Anglicans—now called "Episcopalians" to de-emphasize their ties to England—were a distinct minority. Across the state, church atten-dance was down and church buildings were falling into disrepair. Patrick Henry lamented the state of affairs, arguing that "the general diffusion of Christian knowledge hath a natural tendency to correct the morals of men, restrain their vices, and preserve the peace of society."[17] Rather than trying to undo the de facto disestablishment of Anglicanism, Henry proposed to establish Christianity generally as the official religion of Virginia and abolish "all distinctions of preeminence amongst the different societies or communities of Christians."[18] Henry proposed a general tax for the support of Chris-tian churches whose proceeds would be shared by all denominations "for a Minister or Teacher of the Gospel of their denomination, or the providing places of divine worship."[19]

Religious Liberty

By the time the Virginia House of Delegates took up Henry's bill, Jefferson had already left for France. His closest political ally, James Madison, remained in Virginia and led the opposition to the bill. Madison argued, as Jefferson had before him, that genuine religious liberty required that the government allow religious practices and doctrines to circulate freely, neither helping nor hindering any partic-ular idea or affiliation. In practice, this meant that the state should not do anything that amounted to supporting religion, which included (1) not allowing any religion or denomination to claim more authority from the state than any other, and (2) not allowing public money to support religious practices in any way.

The third and fourth positions in this progression correspond closely to today's "conservative" and "liberal" positions on religion in the public square. People like Tim LaHaye and David Barton—who argue the Founders always intended America to be a Christian nation and were only trying to prevent the establishment of a single denomination—echo Patrick Henry's position almost exactly. They hold that America is officially Christian and should unapologetically promote Christian values and Christian worship in the public square.

Among contemporary commentators, Mark Levin has become a leading spokesman for nondenominational establishment. In the "On Faith and the Founding" chapter of *Liberty and Tyranny*, Levin argues that

> a theocracy is not established if certain public schools allow their students to pray at the beginning of the day, or participate in Christmas or Easter assemblies; or if certain school districts transport parochial students to their religious schools as part of the district's bus route; or certain communities choose to construct a manger scene on the grounds of their town hall or display the Ten Commandments above their courthouse steps. . . . Some might be uncomfortable or offended by these events, but individuals are uncomfortable all the time over all kinds of government activities. Some might oppose the use of their tax dollars to support these events. So what? Individuals oppose the manner in which government uses their tax dollars all the time.[20]

Levin's arguments in 2009 are exactly the same as Patrick Henry's arguments in 1785: (1) that the state should be allowed to promote some religious ideas and not others, depending on the values of the community; and (2) that government bodies should be allowed to use tax dollars to support religions unequally, as long as "a theocracy is not established." It would be difficult to construct a pair of propositions that more closely represent what Thomas Jefferson and James Madison fought against for ten years.

And yet Levin, like right-wing commentators everywhere, continues to use *the Founders* as a collective term for a single ideology. "The Founders," he argues, "rejected the establishment of a national religion, leaving the states free to make their own decisions"[21] (not Madison, who proposed a constitutional amendment to extend the establishment ban to states). Moreover, for "the Founders, faith is not a threat to civil society but rather vital to its survival"[22] (not for Jefferson, who consistently advocated a philosophical system of pure reason and rejected faith in the supernatural). With this issue, as with so many others, one can appeal to a collective Founding ideology only at the expense of historical coherence.

In their rabid support of Henry's nondenominational establishment position, modern social conservatives do indeed invoke one of the positions held by some Founding Fathers—Patrick Henry, to be sure, but also George Washington, who saw great social value in public religious activities, and John Adams, who had no desire to remove state sponsorship of all religious activities. But they also reject—fundamentally and dishonestly—the stated views of both James Madison and Thomas Jefferson, who dissented vigorously from Henry's proposal—not because they were hostile to religion but because they believed true religious freedom required a laissez-faire approach by the state.

MADISON'S "MEMORIAL AND REMONSTRANCE"

We need not spend a lot of time wondering what James Madison really thought about the connection between church and state. Unlike Washington, who held his religious opinions close to his chest, or Jefferson, whose published views are often contradictory, Madison held systematic, transparent, and consistent views on church and state throughout his life. During the Virginia disestablishment debate, he published his "Memorial and Remonstrance against Religious Assessment" (see appendix B), a small pamphlet that lays out as clear a definition of *religious liberty* as any Founding Father ever constructed. Anybody who tries to take seriously the Right's argument that the Founding Fathers never intended to separate church and state must either pretend that James Madison never existed or argue that he was not a Founding Father.

The principal assertion of "Memorial and Remonstrance" is that the freedom of religious belief is a fundamental human right that is not affected by the social contract. When they enter a society, people do not surrender any portion of their right to believe as they choose. Therefore, the government can have no legitimate role in supporting, or in opposing, any religious opinion. "The religion then of every man," Madison writes, "must be left to the conviction and conscience of every man; and it is the right of every man to exercise it as these may dictate."[23] The state can simply have nothing to say about what people choose to believe about God because religious opinions do not fall within the scope of government's limited power.

The state's only legitimate role in religion lies in protecting all people's religious freedom equally—and this means the state can do nothing to give one set of religious beliefs more rights than another. Madison entirely rejects the argument that religious liberty applies only to different denominations of Christianity, as such a restriction would mock the fundamental laws of nature that make minds free. "Who does not see that the same authority which can establish Christianity, in exclusion of all other Religions," he asks, "may establish with the same ease any particular sect of Christians, in exclusion of all other sects?"[24]

Madison also insists that the same freedom that applies to religious belief must apply to nonbelief and that "whilst we assert for ourselves a freedom to embrace . . . the Religion which we believe to be of divine origin, we cannot deny an equal freedom to those whose minds have not yet yielded to the evidence that has convinced us."[25] This is simply a logical extension of how Madison understood liberty of conscience. Having liberty means being able to believe anything at all. While the state can proscribe and punish religious behavior that conflicts with the social order, it can neither legislate what people should believe nor fail to protect all belief—including nonbelief—equally.

As the purpose of "Memorial and Remonstrance" was to defeat a religious assessment, its primary objection is to taxation used to support religious activities. The amount of the support is irrelevant, as any amount of money compromises the principle of equal religious liberty and "the same authority which can force a citizen to contribute three pence only of his property for the support of any one establishment, may force him to conform to any other establishment in all cases whatsoever."[26] By burdening non-Christians and nonbelievers with the cost of Christian instruction, Madison argues, Henry's religious assessment

> violates the equality which ought to be the basis of every law, and which is more indispensible, in proportion as the validity or expediency of any law is more liable to be impeached. If "all men are by nature equally free and independent," all men are to be considered as entering into Society on equal conditions; as relinquishing no more, and therefore retaining no less, one than another, of their natural rights.[27]

For Madison, government can protect the religious freedom of all citizens equally only by requiring the state to be completely neutral on religious matters, neither promoting nor punishing any variety of belief or nonbelief. "In matters of religion," he insists, "no man's right is abridged by the Civil Society [and] religion is wholly exempt from its cognizance."[28] This concept of government noncognizance of religion underlies Madison's lifelong commitment to the liberty of conscience, as Vincent Phillip Muñoz explains in his first-rate scholarly work *God and the Founders*:

> Madison championed a "religion blind" constitution, a constitution that prohibits the state from taking cognizance of religion. In Madison's view, the state may not classify citizens on the basis of religious beliefs or religious affiliation, which means that government actors may neither privilege nor penalize institutions, religious citizens, or religiously motivated conduct as such. . . . The principle of religious noncognizance accounts for Madison's political actions, statements, and writings made as a state legislator, congressman, president, and elder statesman.[29]

Without the noncognizance principle, Madison realized, it would be too easy for a religious majority to turn the government into a mechanism for invading the rights of a minority. Anticipating his classic argument in *Federalist* no. 10, he writes, "True it is, that no other rule exists, by which any question which may divide a Society, can be ultimately determined, but the will of the majority; but it is also true that the majority may trespass on the rights of the minority."[30] To prevent the state from becoming an instrument of religious persecution—as it had become nearly everywhere in the world that Madison knew about—religion itself must be taken out of the government's sphere of influence.

After engineering a resounding defeat of Henry's assessment plan, Madison reintroduced Jefferson's Act for Establishing Religious Freedom, which passed in 1786 as resoundingly as it had failed seven years before. Jefferson was in France at the time and unable to participate in the debate. After the legislature passed the bill, though, Madison wrote immediately to Jefferson, telling him that "the steps taken throughout the Country to defeat the Gen[era]l Assessment, had produced all the effect that could have been wished. . . . The enacting clauses past without a single alteration, and I flatter myself have in this Country extinguished for ever the ambitious hope of making laws for the human mind."[31]

Madison held these views on church and state consistently throughout his political career. Historian Garry Wills writes that Madison, as a delegate to the Constitutional Convention, "promote[d] a document that goes beyond the Articles of Confederation, which did not require a religious oath for holding office, by *forbidding* such oaths (Article VI)."[32] As the author of the Bill of Rights, Madison created the First Amendment, which explicitly constitutionalizes his view that the government should neither promote nor punish any kind of religious belief: "Congress shall make no law respecting the establishment of religion, or prohibiting the free exercise thereof." During the congressional debates over the Bill of Rights, Madison also proposed an amendment that would have prevented any state from infringing on the religious freedom of its citizens.[33] The amendment failed, and it would not be until the middle of the twentieth century that states would be formally prohibited from establishing religion.

As a legislator and as president, Madison also worked to ensure that the federal government remained noncognizant of religion. He opposed many of the combinations of church and state we take for granted today, such as giving state support to religious organizations for purely charitable purposes and hiring state-supported chaplains in the military and in the Houses of Congress.[34] He also vetoed bills that placed the federal government in the position of supporting religion, such as an 1811 act to set aside a parcel of public land in Mississippi for use by a Baptist church. In his veto message to Congress, Madison makes it very clear that, in his opinion, any diversion of federal funds to religious organizations constituted "establishment" and violated the First Amendment:

> Because the bill in reserving a certain parcel of land of the United States for the use of said Baptist Church comprises a principle and precedent for the appropriation of funds of the United States for the use and support of religious societies, contrary to the article of the Constitution which declares that "Congress shall make no law respecting a religious establishment."[35]

The Madisonian noncognizance doctrine lies at the heart of many twentieth-century Supreme Court decisions that the Right sees, incorrectly, as attacks on religion. Under Madison's criteria, no state entity can divert any official attention or financial resource (including the labor of its employees) to an activity that promotes a specific religious perspective. School-sponsored prayers and public displays of religious symbols (unless presented in a non-religious context) simply do not meet the noncognizance test. Such activities require that the state give recognition to some religious practices and not others, and they divert public resources to the promotion of religious ideals that are not universal.

JEFFERSON AND THE WALL OF SEPARATION

As Wills explains, most of what we now know about Thomas Jefferson's religious belief "is drawn from sources denied to his contemporaries." His views were "sufficiently unorthodox for him to take care that they not become generally known. He refused to be drawn into a public defense of them, and he was chary about letting even the most trustworthy people see his private writings on Jesus, Christianity, and the Churches."[36] During the bitterly contested election of 1800, Jefferson had been routinely labeled an atheist by Hamilton and other Federalists—a smear that nearly cost him the presidency. In fact, Jefferson was not an atheist. He could best be described as something between a Unitarian and a Christian deist. He believed in a somewhat more personal God than most deists did, and, though he did not accept the divinity of Jesus Christ, he considered him the greatest moral teacher ever born.

While Jefferson kept his personal religious beliefs to himself, he loudly trumpeted his belief in religious liberty for all—the very principle he promulgated in the Virginia Statute for Religious Freedom. At the end of his life, Jefferson counted his authorship of the statute as one of his greatest achievements. At his direction, his gravestone reads, "Here was buried Thomas Jefferson, author of the Declaration of American Independence, of the Statute of Virginia for Religious Freedom, and father of the University of Virginia." Significantly, "third president of the United States" did not make the cut.

In contemporary American political discourse, however, Jefferson's well-documented and finely nuanced position on religious liberty is usually reduced to a single catchphrase, "a wall of separation between church and state," taken from an 1802 letter to a Baptist organization in Connecticut. Few phrases in American history have been explained and expounded upon as much as this one. Since the 1940s, when Supreme Court justices began to use this phrase to support controversial decisions about the Establishment Clause, both liberals and conservatives have developed their own mutually exclusive histories of what Jefferson meant to say when he penned these words to the Danbury Baptist Association (see appendix C).

For liberals, the "wall of separation" phrase is the smoking gun that proves the Founders wanted to separate religion and public life completely. Jefferson intended this to be an authoritative interpretation of the First Amendment, and many on the left accept him at his word, despite the fact that it was written thirteen years after the Bill of Rights was adopted and by someone who was not even in the country when the First Amendment was debated.

Conservatives, on the other hand, have developed a litany of explanations for Jefferson's most troublesome metaphor. Some acknowledge that Jefferson actually did favor the separation of church and state and simply dismiss him, as Tim LaHaye does, as a "closet Unitarian who had nothing to do with the founding of our nation" (apparently, writing the Declaration of Independence was not enough to get Jefferson into the club).[37] Others insist this is an isolated statement Jefferson dashed off without any real thought about the implications of his metaphor. Still others—most notably, Christian broadcaster Pat Robertson—argue that Jefferson is telling the Baptists that he would like to help them but cannot because he is unfairly constrained by the Establishment Clause in the First Amendment.[38]

The most common conservative argument, though, is that liberals have been intentionally taking Jefferson out of context for most of the last century. Barton, for example, insists that "in his letter, Jefferson made clear that the 'wall of separation' was erected not to limit public religious expressions but rather to provide security against governmental interference with those expressions, whether private or public."[39] In his book *The Myth of Separation*, Barton creates a context for the Danbury letter that has absolutely no basis in historical fact:

> Although the statesmen and patriots who framed the Constitution had made it clear that no one Christian denomination would become the official denomination, the Danbury Baptists expressed their concern over a rumor that a particular denomination was soon to be recognized as the national denomination. On January 1, 1802, President Jefferson responded to the Danbury Baptists in a letter. He calmed their fears by using the now infamous phrase to assure them that the federal government would not establish any single denomination of Christianity as the national denomination.[40]

This is pure fiction. Other than the date and the author, everything Barton says here flatly contradictions the historical record. The Danbury Baptists were not concerned about a rumor of national establishment; they were protesting the state-level establishment of the Congregational Church in Connecticut. Jefferson was not trying to reassure them of anything; rather, he was using their letter to him as a platform to make a political proclamation he could publish widely to refute the common Federalist charge that he was an atheist. And his "wall of separation" metaphor was specifically designed to establish the unconstitutionality of an activity that Barton himself consistently presents as proof of the religious nature of the Founding Fathers: the presidential proclamation of national days of fasting and prayer.

To get the heart of Jefferson's letter, we must first realize that established denominations were still common in the states. Though Madison had tried to apply the First Amendment prohibition of religious establishment to the states in the Bill of Rights, he had been unsuccessful. Consequently, many of the Southern states continued to support the Episcopal Church, while three of the New England states—Massachusetts, New Hampshire, and Connecticut—officially supported the Congregational (Puritan) Church. Throughout the United States, evangelical Christians, especially Baptists, were strong proponents of disestablishment in all the states—taking Virginia as a model—so that they would not be forced to pay taxes to support religions not their own.

In Connecticut, historian Derek Davis explains, the Danbury Baptist Association had become a leading force in the Baptist Petition Movement, "an organized effort by Connecticut Baptist leaders to arouse the conscience of the Congregational majority in Connecticut to end its status as the state's official religion."[41] They approached Jefferson, the author of the Virginia Statute for Religious Freedom, as an ally in their cause, somebody who could help them end religious discrimination at the state level:

> Our sentiments are uniformly on the side of religious liberty—that religion is at all times and places a matter between God and individuals—that no man ought to suffer in name, person, or effects on account of his religious opinions—that the legitimate power of civil government extends no further than to punish the man who works ill to his neighbors; But, sir, our constitution of government is not specific. . . . And therefore what religious privileges we enjoy (as a minor part of the state) we enjoy as favors granted, and not as inalienable rights; and these favors we receive at the expense of such degrading acknowledgements as are inconsistent with the rights of freemen.

The Baptists acknowledged that "the national government cannot destroy the laws of each state," but they hoped that "the sentiments of our beloved president . . . will shine and prevail through all these states and all the world, till hierarchy and tyranny be destroyed from the earth" (see appecix C). In contemporary political parlance, they were lobbying the president to use his bully pulpit to put pressure on Connecticut to grant the same religious freedoms that Jefferson himself had helped secure for Virginians.

On the same day he crafted his response to the Danbury Baptists, Jefferson wrote to his attorney general, Levi Lincoln, that "averse to receive addresses, yet unable to prevent them, I have generally endeavored to turn them to some account, by making them the occasion, by way of answer, of sowing useful truths and principles among the people."[42] The letter from the Danbury Baptists, specifically, gave Jefferson an excellent opportunity to blunt the Federalist critique that he was an atheist by portraying his well-known opposition to religious establishment as a commitment to religious freedom—one backed by one of the more theologically conservative denominations in the country.

Jefferson was also anxious to respond to criticism that, unlike Washington and Adams, he refused to call for national days of fasting and thanksgiving. As he told Lincoln, the letter "furnishes an occasion . . . which I have long wished to find, of saying why I do not proclaim fasting and thanksgiving, as my predecessors did."[43] In the initial draft of his letter to the Danbury Baptists, Jefferson mentioned fast days specifically, but he removed them on Lincoln's advice so as not to offend New England Republicans unnecessarily.[44] His final letter, which was also published in a Massachusetts newspaper, relies heavily on the "wall of separation" metaphor to convey both his support of religious liberty and his belief that meaningful liberty required the state's official neutrality:

> Believing with you that religion is a matter which lies solely between Man & his God, that he owes account to none other for his faith or his worship, that the legitimate powers of government reach actions only, & not opinions, I contemplate with sovereign reverence that act of the whole American people which declared that their legislature should "make no law respecting an establishment of religion, or prohibiting the free exercise thereof," thus building a wall of separation between Church & State.[45]

In this brief letter, Jefferson accomplished three specific political objectives: (1) he subtly invoked the Constitution to support his refusal to proclaim nondenominational fast days; (2) he reassured religious dissenters—who allied with him politically in spite of their grave misgivings about his personal religious beliefs—that he supported their most important political objective; and (3) he confined his attack on state establishment to a statement of personal disapproval, thus telegraphing to his fellow Republicans that he had no intention of doing anything official to interfere with the rights of states to do as they pleased.

In none of these points did Jefferson stray from the political beliefs he held throughout his career; from his authorship of the Virginia Statute for Religious Freedom on, he consistently argued for a strict separation between civil and ecclesiastical matters—not because he was hostile to religion but because he believed religious ideas should be left free to stand or fall on their own merits. In the field of religion, he writes in his *Notes on the State of Virginia*, "reason and persuasion are the only practicable instruments. To make way for these, free enquiry must be indulged."[46]

Like Madison, Jefferson drew a strong distinction between "religious toleration" and "religious freedom." The first of these had been famously advocated by John Locke in his 1689 *Letter concerning Toleration*. In this brief treatise, Locke argues passionately that England should tolerate nearly all varieties of Protestantism. He draws the line, however, at Roman Catholics and atheists, whom he saw as inherently dangerous to the civil state. In his own "Notes on Locke," Jefferson writes, "It was a great thing to go so far . . . but where he stopped short, we may go on."[47] Jefferson believed that, unlike religious toleration, genuine religious liberty is an unalienable right that all citizens have the power to claim on an equal basis.

In his discussions of religious liberty, Jefferson refused to draw any distinction between Christians, non-Christians, and nonbelievers. "The legitimate powers of government extend to such acts only as are injurious to others," he writes. "It does me no injury for my neighbor to say there are twenty gods, or no god. It neither picks my pocket nor breaks my leg."[48] For Jefferson, the notion that the United States was a "Christian nation" would have been utter nonsense. Being Christian (or any other religion) is not the sort of thing a nation can legitimately do, as it requires the state to act in a sphere in which it can have no legitimate interest.

One of the Right's most deceptive tactics is to frame the debate over the separation of church and state as a debate over supporting or opposing religion. Neither Jefferson nor Madison saw it that way. Rather, they believed the best way to support the growth and development of religion was to remove it entirely from the scope of government intervention and allow all religious beliefs to compete equally in the free market of ideas, where the best and truest opinions would ultimately rise to the surface. To a great extent, this is exactly what has happened. When the courts began to gravitate toward the Jeffersonian/Madisonian understanding of the First Amendment in the middle of the twentieth century, American religion experienced unprecedented growth, and America became, and remains, the most religious nation in the industrialized world.

The great irony here, of course, is that many conservatives believe in a small-government, free-market, laissez-faire approach to everything *but* religion. Major planks of the Right's platform—state-sponsored prayers in schools, religious displays in public buildings, official acknowledgment of America's Christian nature—amount to nothing less than state subsidies of a particular religion. They require the state to determine which forms of worship will, and which will not, be permitted in sponsored venues. And the writings of conservatives like David Barton and Tim LaHaye ultimately demonstrate that many on the religious right are unwilling to defend their ideas in the marketplace without government protection of their monopoly.

CHAPTER 5

STATES' RIGHTS/STATES' WRONGS: HOW THE RIGHT HIJACKED FEDERALISM

If it shall be found . . . that Congress will upon all proper occasions exercise the powers with a firm and steady hand, instead of frittering them back to the Individual States where the members in place of viewing themselves in their National character, are too apt to be looking—I say after this essay is made if the system proves inefficient, conviction of the necessity of a change will be disseminated among all classes of the People. Then, and not till then, in my opinion can it be attempted without involving all the evils of civil discord.
—George Washington to James Madison on the need for a Constitutional Convention

The entire purpose of the Constitution was to limit the power the federal government held over the states and the people.
—Senator Rand Paul,
The Tea Party Goes to Washington

Senator Paul's assertion that the only purpose of the Constitution was "to limit the power the federal government held over the states and the people" is not merely wrong, it is *exactly* wrong.[1] The purpose of the Constitution was to strengthen the power of the federal government. The original Articles of Confederation had created not a nation but a league of independent states much like the European Union. The Confederated States had become financially insolvent, commercially unviable, and militarily incompetent. The most visionary of the Founding Fathers—including George Washington, Alexander Hamilton, and James Madison—understood that the former colonies were heading toward either civil war with each other or conquest by one of the European powers that maintained a strong presence in the New World.

Under the pretense of revising the Articles of Confederation, Madison and Hamilton convinced the existing Congress to summon delegates from each state to the Federal Convention in Philadelphia in the summer of 1787. It was not called a "Constitutional Convention" at the time, nor could it have been, as the creation of a constitution far exceeded the delegates' mandate to assemble "for the sole and express purpose of revising the Articles of Confederation."[2] They were not supposed to alter the fundamental nature of the Confederation as a voluntary association of sovereign states. They were not tasked with writing a new constitution. They did not have the authority to reinvent the government.

But they reinvented the government.

The approval of the Constitution by thirty-nine out of the fifty-five delegates to the Federal Convention ranks as one of the greatest political accomplishments of the modern age. The delegates bridged gaps and negotiated compromises that would have derailed any other deliberative body ever assembled. They overcame radical differences in geography, lifestyle, religion, economic structure, and worldview to produce the remarkable document that has governed America for more than two hundred years. For all their accomplishments, however, they were still just thirty-nine people with a radical proposition and an uncertain future. Until it was ratified by the people in their state conventions, the Constitution was just so much ink and paper.

The Constitution initially faced a rocky path to ratification. The deliberations of the convention had been kept secret, and most people in the colonies expected no more than a few moderate amendments to the Articles of Confederation. Some of the most powerful and prestigious delegates had refused to sign the final document and wasted no time in rallying opposition to the proposed Constitution. Less than a week after the convention closed, anti-Constitution editorials began to appear in the major American papers, some signed by their authors but most written under pseudonyms such as "Cato" and "Brutus"—both named for republicans of ancient Rome who resisted the dictatorial advances of Julius Caesar.

The latter of these writers, "Brutus," was almost certainly the New York jurist Robert Yates, who left the convention early to protest the nationalistic character of the proceedings. The first essay by "Brutus" was published on October 18, 1787, one month after the conclusion of the Federal Convention. This essay lays out a fairly complete case against the Constitution and establishes the main arguments that would be repeated and developed throughout the ratification process, becoming the major debating points of those who opposed ratification in the state conventions:

1. that the Constitution creates a powerful and potentially tyrannical central government,
2. that it unwisely grants this government an unlimited power of taxation,
3. that it contains provisions such as the Necessary and Proper Clause that would allow the legislature to pass any law imaginable,
4. that it grants too much power to an unelected Supreme Court,
5. that it endangers liberty by permitting a standing army, and
6. that it substitutes a faceless centralized authority for the more personal, local government of the several states.[3]

Since the presidential election of 2008, and the subsequent emergence of the Tea Party, each of these issues (with the exception of number five) has surfaced as a major talking point of the American Right—whose fundamental gospel includes the doctrines that the current American government is tyrannical, that taxation is theft, that nearly all federal legislation exceeds the Constitution's mandate, that the Supreme Court is ruining the country, and that the only way to restore America's greatness is for the people to demand the federal government devolve power back to the states.

We must be very clear that, while these are the opinions of some of the Founding Fathers, they are *not* the opinions of the Founders who supported the Constitution but, rather, of the Founders who opposed it. The confusion between the two sets of opinions is inevitable, however, as both sets of Founders described their position with the word *federal*—a term whose definition was probably more contested than that of any other word in the Founding era.

THE FEDERALIST BAIT AND SWITCH

As a matter of definition, the term *federalism* can refer to any political arrangement in which constituent units share power with a larger central government, forming a federation of partially autonomous states. Federal systems can share power in a number of different ways, from the very weak central government of the European Union to the much stronger national governments of Germany and Australia. Since 1776, the United States has had some kind of federal system, though the actual division of power between the states and the federal government has fluctuated, with the federal government becoming generally more powerful over time.

Is this what the Founders wanted? Is the Right correct in asserting that the federal government since FDR has been a steady march of betrayal of federalist principles? Yes, no, and maybe. As with so many of the questions in this book, it depends on which Founder we are talking about. It also depends on which of the many possible definitions of *federalism* we use.

Originally, a Federalist was someone who supported the Articles of Confederation, which established a minimal federal apparatus to coordinate the interests of thirteen powerful state governments. The articles limited the federal government to a few clerical and ceremonial functions, with all other powers reserved to the states through the crucial Second Article. To understand the difference between the federalism of the Articles of Confederation and the federalism of the Constitution, we need only compare the Second Article of Confederation with its near relation, the current Tenth Amendment to the Constitution:

SECOND ARTICLE OF CONFEDERATION (1777)	TENTH AMENDMENT (1789)
Each state retains its sovereignty, freedom, and independence, and every power, jurisdiction, and right, which is not by this Confederation expressly delegated to the United States, in Congress assembled.	The powers not delegated to the United States by the Constitution, nor prohibited by it to the States, are reserved to the States respectively, or to the people.

The Tenth Amendment is substantially weaker than the Second Article of Confederation in its delegation of power to the states, and it allows more room for interpretation about the proper roles of the states and the federal government. This was quite intentional. In the debates over the Bill of Rights, Madison himself fought off two separate proposals by Anti-Federalist congressmen—South Carolina's Thomas Tucker and Massachusetts's Elbridge Gerry—to restore the language of the Articles of Confederation and insert the word "expressly" before the word "delegated" in the Tenth Amendment. Madison insisted that "it was impossible to confine a government to the exercise of express powers" and that "there must necessarily be admitted powers by implication, unless the constitution descended to recount every minutiae."[4]

In the early stages of the Constitution debate, those who wanted to retain the Articles of Confederation—with its strong states and weak central government—called themselves "federalists," or proponents of a federal (i.e., confederated) government. Those who supported a stronger union between the states—with a more powerful central government that could enforce laws, levy taxes, raise armies, and the like—were called "nationalists." But the latter term sounded too much like "monarchist" to the former colonists, so Alexander Hamilton, James Madison, and other nationalist leaders pulled one of the great fast ones of all time, which Jackson Turner Main explains in his well-known book *The Antifederalists*:

> It was a nice piece of misdirection by the Federalists. Originally the word "federal" meant anyone who supported the Confederation. Several years before the Constitution was promulgated, the men who wanted a strong national government, who might more properly be called "nationalists," began to appropriate the term "federal" for themselves. To them, the man of "federal principles" approved of "federal measures," which meant those that increased the weight and authority or extended the influence of the Confederation Congress. The word "antifederal," by contrast implied hostility to Congress. According to this definition, the antifederal man was opposed to any effort to strengthen the government and was therefore unpatriotic. Eventually the term became a general word of opprobrium applied by the Nationalists to anyone who opposed their designs.[5]

The Federalists who used to be nationalists set up shop in New York and began to craft responses to the Anti-Federalists who used to be federalists. The new Federalists determined to leave no accusation on the table. They would respond to every charge made by the opponents of the Constitution, and they would respond in such detail, with so much sheer bulk, that "Brutus" and the others would never be able to counter it all. Alexander Hamilton took primary responsibility for organizing the rebuttals, and he recruited James Madison and John Jay to join him in writing essays—which would later be called the Federalist papers—under the collective pseudonym "Publius." The Constitution that they defended preserved the best elements of the Articles of Confederation, including a division of power between the state and federal governments. But it also created a vigorous national government and endowed it with the right to make "all laws Necessary and Proper" to implement the powers delegated to it.[6]

Hamilton, Madison, and Jay did their job very well. In just over seven months, "Publius" wrote eighty-five essays of nearly two hundred thousand total words, dwarfing the production of any of their opponents and, in the process, creating the best explanation of the American Constitution ever produced. However, the strategic ambiguity they created around the meaning of the word *federalist* persists to this day. Because of this confusion, today's self-proclaimed constitutional conservatives have been able to get away with presenting—as the opinions of Hamilton, Madison, and Jay—the precise positions these Founders were actively trying to refute.

Nobody in the current political arena has misused the term *federalism* more than Mark Levin. In the "On Federalism" chapter of *Liberty and Tyranny*, Levin makes as strong a case as anybody has made in two hundred years for the kind of government established by the Articles of Confederation—a coalition of sovereign states bound together by a severely limited federal government. Levin, of course, calls this form of government "federalism" and its opposite "nationalism"—precisely the way the terms were defined before the Federal Convention.

But Levin falls right into the trap Hamilton and Madison set 230 years ago: he confuses this original definition of federalism with the very different position outlined in the Federalist papers. Consider his misinterpretation of Madison's *Federalist* no. 39, the Federalist essay most relevant to the discussion of both federalism and nationalism, which he presents as clear evidence that the Founders preferred a federalist government over a national one:

> In "*Federalist* 39," James Madison wrote, in part, "Each state, in ratifying the Constitution, is considered as a sovereign body, independent of all

others, and only to be bound by its own voluntary act. In this relation, then, the new Constitution will, if established, be a FEDERAL and not a NATIONAL constitution."

Of course, today, it is more national than federal.[7]

Levin's evidence here certainly seems persuasive. There it is in black and white: the father of the Constitution and one of the chief architects of American democracy said plainly that the new Constitution should be federal and not national. The great man even used all caps. How could America have lost its way and incorporated so many national elements into what was supposed to have been a federal system?

But that's not what Madison said. It's not even close. The whole point of *Federalist* no. 39 is to try to bridge the gap between nationalists and federalists by explaining how the Constitution creates a system that combines elements from both. The passage Levin quotes is part of a much longer, more complicated argument that explains both the federal and the national aspects of the Constitution. Levin simply chooses a small portion of this argument that deals with one aspect of the Constitution that is entirely federal (its procedure for ratification, which had to occur in at least nine states before a national government could be created and which was, therefore, federal by definition). In his final paragraph, Madison makes it very clear that the Constitution was designed as a mixture of the two models:

> The proposed Constitution, therefore . . . is, in strictness, neither a national nor a federal Constitution, but a composition of both. In its foundation it is federal, not national; in the sources from which the ordinary powers of the government are drawn, it is partly federal and partly national; in the operation of these powers, it is national, not federal; in the extent of them, again, it is federal, not national; and, finally, in the authoritative mode of introducing amendments, it is neither wholly federal nor wholly national.[8]

By presenting one part of a complex five-part argument as though it were a single assertion, Levin manages to completely reverse Madison's original meaning. It was the opponents of the Constitution who insisted that the government should be a federal compact among sovereign states. The Federal Convention was called precisely because this sort of federalism did not work. In *Federalist* no. 39, Madison rejects the premise that the Constitution does or should create a wholly federal government. But he does so with long, complicated, and learned arguments, making his words highly susceptible to the dishonest proof texting that has become a standard procedure for right-wing writers and radio hosts.

Make no mistake: Levin's selective quotation strategy is fundamentally dishonest. By treating the Federalist papers as a series of one-paragraph proof texts rather than as internally coherent arguments, he patently misrepresents what one of the most important Founding Fathers said about the Constitution. Academics and journalists who misrepresent sources to the extent Levin does in this chapter often lose their jobs. Radio hosts, of course, are held to less rigorous standards of citation integrity.

Still, it is a very strange way to treat an idea that one is pretending to take seriously.

FOUNDING FACTIONS: MADISON'S *FEDERALIST* NO. 10

Today's right-wing federalists believe—as the Anti-Federalists of 1787 (who were the federalists of 1785) believed—that state governments do almost everything better than the federal government does. In his federalist manifesto *Fed Up!*, for example, Texas governor Rick Perry included a long section titled "Why States Remain Liberty's Friend." His answers include "States allow us to live with people of like mind," "States promote mobility," and "States encourage civic virtue, independence, and self-reliance." People in Massachusetts, he assures us, are free to be represented by the likes of Ted Kennedy and Barney Frank if that's what they want, while sensible states like Texas can elect a governor who "goes jogging in the morning, packing a Ruger .380 with laser sights and loaded with hollow-point bullets."[9]

Nearly identical arguments have been advanced by Levin, Grover Norquist, Glenn Beck, and the Tea Party faithful across America—all of whom believe America cannot be truly free until the federal government returns most of its power to the individual states. Perhaps the strongest recent supporter of this position has been Tea Party (and Utah) senator Mike Lee, who argues in his book *The Freedom Agenda* that

> our Founding Fathers understood that every government becomes more susceptible to tyranny as it amasses more wealth and power. Any leader . . .

can become a tyrant, and likely will become a tyrant, unless his powers are carefully limited. The Founders also knew that, although local governments are capable of tyranny, the risk is less severe than it is at the national level. That's because local governments operate closer to the people, making them more responsive to the people's needs and desires.[10]

Lee is right about the views of the Founding Fathers who opposed the ratification of the Constitution. But he is wrong about the views of the Founding Fathers who supported the Constitution. Washington, Madison, Hamilton, and most of the other signers of the Constitution, while concerned about the dictatorial potential of national government, perceived a much greater threat to liberty in the actions of individual states and local governments. They knew these local bodies, in the name of responsiveness to the majorities within their jurisdictions, often deprived their other citizens of even the most basic civil and political rights. This, in fact, is the main point of the most widely read and cited of all the Federalist essays: James Madison's magisterial *Federalist* no. 10 (see appendix D).

Madison's primary objective in *Federalist* no. 10 is to rebut one of the arguments against the Constitution that had gained a lot of traction in the state of New York: that the territory of the United States was too large to be incorporated into a functional republic. The original source of this objection was the Baron de Montesquieu, one of the best-known political theorists of the eighteenth century, who argued in *The Spirit of Laws* that

> it is natural to a republic to have only a small territory, otherwise it cannot long subsist. In a large republic there are men of large fortunes, and consequently of less moderation; there are trusts too great to be placed in any single subject; he has interest of his own; he soon begins to think that he may be happy, great and glorious, by oppressing his fellow citizens; and that he may raise himself to grandeur on the ruins of his country.[11]

Montesquieu's views on large republics were first introduced into the ratification debate in a 1787 essay by Robert Yates writing as "Brutus." In the first of his sixteen Anti-Federalist essays, "Brutus" quotes Montesquieu and argues that the sheer size of the thirteen colonies, and the distances that must be traveled to any capital, will prevent any kind of effective representative government. "In a large extended country," he insists, "it is impossible to have a representation, possessing the sentiments, and of integrity, to declare

the minds of the people."[12] With the publication of "Brutus's" first essay, Montesquieu's views quickly became the starting point for most arguments against the Constitution.

By citing *The Spirit of Laws*, "Brutus" was quoting scripture against Madison and the Federalists. Montesquieu's ideas about the separation of powers had contributed significantly to the foundation of the proposed Constitution. It is largely on the French philosopher's authority that the delegates divided the government into three separate functions—legislative, executive, and judicial—and gave each branch ways to check the power of the other two. Because "Brutus's" arguments came from a source often cited by the pro-ratification Founders, they raised serious doubts among New York's educated elites.

When Madison teamed up with Hamilton and Jay to create "Publius," he understood that his first task must be to refute "Brutus," the most forceful and articulate of the Anti-Federalist writers active in the state of New York. It would not do to argue simply that a large republic would not trample individual rights. Such an argument would turn "Brutus's" negative into a neutral, but Madison had no intention to play for a draw. He wanted to win, and that meant showing that large republics could protect individual liberty in ways small republics could not. Using ideas he had initially worked out on the floor of the Federal Convention, Madison constructed his first *Federalist* contribution around the revolutionary proposition that only a strong national government could control what he called "the violence of faction."

For Madison, a "faction" was something like what we would call a "special-interest group" today—a collection of individuals, in either the majority or the minority, "who are united . . . by some common impulse of passion, or of interest, adverse to the rights of other citizens, or to the permanent and aggregate interests of the community." Among the potential factions in the United States, Madison mentions religious sects, supporters of paper money, and advocates for the equal division of property. He believed the tendency to form factions lay deep within human nature and that "as long as the reason of man continues fallible, and he is at liberty to exercise it, different opinions will be formed."[13]

Madison saw factions as a nonnegotiable, unpreventable byproduct of freedom. No truly free society can keep factions from forming or prevent them, once formed, from trying to advance their agendas at the expense of other people's rights. As long as a faction does not constitute a majority within a nation, the rule of the majority will ultimately keep it in check.

However, when a faction becomes a majority in a democratic society, it gains the ability to impose its will on a minority.

Madison believed permanent majority factions were the greatest danger of republican rule. Temporary majorities are necessary to pass legislation, but democracy works best when majorities continually form, dissolve, and re-form with different participants, thus ensuring that everybody is in the majority on some issues and in the minority on others. Largely because of the way Madison and other Founders set up the political system, most Americans experience just such an environment. Over the course of a normal lifetime, we all win some, and we all lose some. That's how the system was designed to work.

But imagine what a democratic government would be like for someone who never had a chance to win. It would not take long before such a person concluded that there was no reason to continue participating in the democratic process. This is precisely what America discovered in its recent war with Iraq. After toppling Saddam Hussein (the easy part of the job), the American military tried to create representative government in a country where one religious faction—Shia Islam—represented a permanent majority of 60–65 percent of the population. The minority Sunni population had very little incentive to participate in a government that consigned it to perpetual minority status, which, largely, is why American forces remained for many years after President Bush's rosy "Mission Accomplished" declaration in 2003.

In *Federalist* no. 10, Madison proposes a way to solve this problem and, in the process, offers a brilliant rebuttal to both "Brutus" and Montesquieu. The way to prevent a permanent majority from forming, he argues, is to make sure the republic is large enough to contain so many factions that none of them can ever stay in the majority for long.

> The smaller the society, the fewer probably will be the distinct parties and interests composing it; the fewer the distinct parties and interests, the more frequently will a majority be found of the same party. . . . Extend the sphere, and you take in a greater variety of parties and interests; you make it less probable that a majority of the whole will have a common motive to invade the rights of other citizens; or if such a common motive exists, it will be more difficult for all who feel it to discover their own strength, and to act in unison with each other.[14]

With this single masterstroke, Madison takes one of the Constitution's greatest perceived weaknesses and turns it into a powerful strength. A large republic such as the United States will contain so many different factions and interest groups that none of them will ever predominate. Temporary coalitions between different interests will arise to resolvle certain issues, but they will be continually forming and dissipating, making it almost impossible for a single faction to seize power long enough to damage the rights of the minority.

If we look closely, we can see that the majoritarian tyranny Madison feared is simply the flip side of the "responsiveness to the people" aspect of state sovereignty that conservatives often praise. Rick Perry's sunny dictum that "states allow us to live with people of like mind" should scare the socks off people who live in states where their minds (or bodies, or economic values, or religious beliefs) are unlike those of their neighbors. The Perry doctrine comes perilously close to declaring open season on such people's basic civil rights. "From marriage to prayer," he insists, "from zoning laws to tax policy, from our school systems to health care, and everything in between, it is essential to our liberty that we be allowed to live as we see fit through the democratic process at the local and state level."[15]

Though Governor Perry clearly has other political issues in mind, his words have an eerie resonance with the stance that most Southern states— including Texas—took against civil rights for African Americans for most of the twentieth century. On the issue of marriage, for example, the state of Texas had one of the nation's strictest laws against interracial marriage until the Supreme Court's *Loving v. Virginia* (1967) decision overturned all such laws in the United States. Schools, healthcare facilities, public transportation, and most other state-controlled services were similarly segregated throughout the South until the federal judiciary forced states to comply with the Fourteenth Amendment and grant basic civil rights to all people within their borders.

But we need not go back to the civil rights era to see the rights of minorities being invaded "through the democratic process at the local and state level." A Pew Research Center report released on August 30, 2011, documents thirty-seven challenges to proposed mosques and Islamic centers in the United States between 2008 and 2011, nearly all of which included some element of community discomfort with the Muslim religion. Most of these construction projects have been allowed to proceed, but often only with some pressure from the federal Department of Justice, which launched sixteen investigations of violations of the Religious Land Use and Institutionalized Persons Act between May 2010 and August 2011 alone.[16] Without some federal check on the power of state majorities to "live as we see fit," I suspect that American Muslims would have a difficult time securing the right to worship freely in many state and local jurisdictions.

Perry's assertion that states "allow us to live with people of like mind" posits a world that simply does not exist—a world in which every citizen of a particular state has made an affirmative decision to live among people who share his or her values. In such a world, people are not constrained to live in certain places by economic circumstances, family ties, job opportunities, healthcare needs, and other considerations. Those who don't like a certain political climate can simply move around until they find a more suitable one.

This is not how life works for most of us. We live where we live for all kinds of reasons, most of which have little to do with whether our governor packs heat on his morning jog. Conservatives live in Massachusetts, liberals live in Texas, Mormons live in Alabama, Catholics live in Utah, and everybody has certain fundamental rights that are not subject to the whims of the people around them. While majorities generally get their way on most political issues, they cannot get their way all the time, or our society would cease to be free. The Founding Fathers who supported the Constitution understood this clearly.

But Governor Perry is also making an argument about what the Founding Fathers supposedly believed. And in the manner of a true proof-text patriot, he closes out his "states allow us to live with people of like mind" argument with a quote from a bona fide member of the Founding generation:

> As one pro-states Revolutionary-era politician writing under the pseudonym of Agrippa said, "The idea of an uncompounded republic [with millions of] inhabitants all reduced to the same standards of morals, of habits, and of laws is in itself an absurdity, and contrary to the whole experience of mankind." Just as each individual is unique, so, too, do we come together to form unique communities with differing needs.[17]

To spell out what observant readers will probably have already guessed, "Agrippa"—also known as James Winthrop, a minor state official in Massachusetts—was one of the Constitution's most dedicated opponents.[18]

FEDERALISM'S SLAVERY PROBLEM

The problem of tyrannical majorities, which Madison diagnoses so compe-
tently in *Federalist* no. 10, was not satisfactorily addressed in his lifetime. The
Bill of Rights he helped to create in 1789 protected individual liberties but only
at the federal level. The process of applying the Bill of Rights to the states—
known as "incorporation"—began with the Fourteenth Amendment in 1868
and went on until 2010, when the Supreme Court's *McDonald v. Chicago* decision held states responsible for protecting the Second Amendment right to bear
arms.

The incorporation of the Bill of Rights has substantially altered the relationship between the states and the federal government—most people
believe for the better—by taking away the power of individual states to abro-
gate the inalienable rights of individuals in the name of majority rule. This is
such a clear and logical extension of Madison's own arguments in the Federal Convention and in the Federalist essays that we might wonder why he
didn't think of it himself.

As it turns out, though, he did. During the congressional debate on the
Bill of Rights, Madison did, in fact, propose an amendment to the Constitution that read "no state shall infringe the equal rights of conscience, nor the
freedom of speech, or of the press, nor of the right of trial by jury in criminal
cases."[19] He considered this "the most valuable amendment on the whole list"
and argued that "if there was any reason to restrain the government of the
United States from infringing on these essential rights, it was equally necessary that they should be secured against the state governments," which he had
already identified as the greatest potential threat to individual liberty.[20]

Madison was ultimately unable to secure passage of a constitutional
amendment that required the states to recognize individual liberties. To
understand why, we must now look at the eight-hundred-pound gorilla of the
early American republic: the institution of slavery, which was protected for
more than seventy-five years by the Constitution and by a definition of federalism that allowed white majorities to deny all civil and human rights to a
substantial portion of the population. Ending slavery in America required a
massive exercise of federal power, a nearly total (albeit temporary) nullifica-
tion of state and local sovereignty, and a fundamental renegotiation of the
division of powers between state and federal governments.

More than any other issue in American history, slavery demonstrates the validity of Madison's most important contribution to political theory: that small political bodies, such as states, pose a greater risk to freedom than large nations. And the problems with slavery and federalism trace directly back to the Federal Convention, where the division between free and slave states was so pronounced it almost prevented the formation of any union at all. Delegates from Southern states were under orders to protect slavery at any cost—and they did so. As Paul Finkelman describes in his invaluable study *Slavery and the Founders*, the Southern delegates secured the following five specific clauses in the Constitution that ensured that the compact it created would never be able to abolish slavery without fundamentally altering its structure.

- **Article I, Section 2.3:** *Representatives and direct Taxes shall be apportioned among the several States which may be included within this Union, according to their respective Numbers, which shall be determined by adding to the whole Number of free Persons, including those bound to Service for a Term of Years, and including Indians not taxed, three fifths of all other Persons.*

  This "three-fifths compromise," which established that three-fifths of a state's slaves would count in its population for the purpose of apportioning congressional representation, was an enormous victory for the Southern states; it dramatically increased their representation in both the House of Representatives and the Electoral College without requiring them to grant any political rights to enslaved people. Largely because of the electoral imbalance created by the Three-Fifths Clause, five of the first seven American presidents were slave owners, and the interests of slave states dominated both the legislative and the executive branches of government for the first half of the nineteenth century.

- **Article I, Section 9.1:** *The Migration or Importation of such Persons as any of the States now existing shall think proper to admit, shall not be prohibited by the Congress prior to the Year one thousand eight hundred and eight, but a tax or duty may be imposed on such Importation, not exceeding ten dollars for each Person.*

  This is commonly known as the Slave Trade Clause, which forbade Congress from banning the slave trade until 1808 and does not require it to do so afterward. It is important to note that this clause deals only with the importation of slaves from Africa and not with the sale of existing slaves or their children. Unlike other major slavery provisions of the Constitution, this clause did not represent a compromise between Northern and Southern interests but between the states in the Deep South, which favored continued slave trade, and Virginia and Maryland, which already had an excess of slave labor and looked forward to the internal monopoly a ban on future slave imports would give them.[21]

- **Article I, Section 9.4:** *No Capitation, or other direct, Tax shall be laid, unless in Proportion to the Census or Enumeration herein before directed to be taken.*

  This clause repeats the charge in Article 1, Section 2.3 that any direct, or per-head, tax levied by Congress be apportioned among the states by using the three-fifths ratio discussed in Section 2.3. Direct taxes in this sense were extremely rare in the United States before the ratification of the Sixteenth Amendment in 1913, which allowed Congress to collect taxes on incomes "without apportionment among the several States, regard to census or enumeration."

- **Article IV, Section 2.3:** *No person held to Service or Labour in one State, under the laws thereof, escaping into another, shall in Consequence of any Law or Regulation therein, be discharged from such Service or Labour, but shall be delivered up in Claim of the Party to whom such Service or Labour may be due.*

  The infamous Fugitive Slave Clause of the Constitution was adopted with relatively little debate, largely because the Northern delegates "failed to appreciate the legal problems and moral dilemmas that the rendition of fugitive slaves would pose."[22] Once in the Constitution, however, this clause provided strong constitutional support for the Fugitive Slave Acts of 1793 and 1850 and for the various Supreme Court decisions that invalidated the citizenship of escaped slaves.

- **Article V:** *. . . No Amendment which may be made prior to the Year one thousand eight hundred and eight shall in any Manner affect the first and fourth Clauses in the Ninth Section of the first Article.*

Article V, which establishes the procedure for approving amendments, is in many ways the most remarkable of all the Constitution's protections of slavery. Like much of what the Constitution says about slavery, it does not support the institution directly. The Framers excised all direct references to slaves and slavery to avoid offending Northern sensibilities. What this article does, however, is exempt the Slave Trade Clause and the Direct Tax Clause from the normal amendment procedure until 1808, thus making it impossible, even with a constitutional amendment, to stop the slave trade before the agreed-upon date. The only other provision Article V exempts from amendment is Article I, Section 3, which grants equal representation to each state in the Senate.

Taken together, these five provisions amount, in Finkelman's words, to "a strong claim to 'special treatment' for its [the South's] peculiar institution."[23] South Carolina's Charles Cotesworth Pinckney, one of the convention delegates most responsible for the Constitution's protections of slavery, acknowledged as much when he told his state's representatives that both the Constitution and the principles of federalism would protect slavery forever:

> We have a security that the general government can never emancipate them [slaves], for no such authority is granted and it is admitted, on all hands, that the general government has no powers but what are expressly granted by the Constitution, and that all rights not expressed were reserved for the several states.[24]

To any decent human being in the twenty-first century, Pinckney's assurances can be read only as an indictment of the kind of federalism that the Right now advocates as the cure for America's ills. But it should also be read as a vindication of Madison's main point in *Federalist* no. 10: that smaller political units such as states cannot protect liberty as well as large centralized governments because the homogeneity of these smaller units allows permanent majorities to invade the rights of minorities. The Anti-Federalists missed this point entirely, as do their philosophical descendants on the Far Right, who routinely accuse the federal government of "tyranny" while touting state sovereignty as the Founding Fathers' solution to nearly every political problem not solved by a massive tax cut.

The plain facts of slavery in America wreak havoc with the Far Right's ideological agenda. The Constitution's proslavery clauses cast doubt on the narrative of a collection of demigods meeting in Philadelphia to produce a lasting testament to liberty. And the clear role that state sovereignty played in perpetuating the slave industry confirms Madison's belief in the tyrannical potential of local governments. Some of the most morally offensive, historically unsupportable recent arguments from the Right have been those that have tried to minimize the support for slavery in the Founding era. As just one example of this phenomenon, consider this passage from the end of Glenn Beck's *Arguing with Idiots*, where he blatantly revises the three-fifths compromise in his clause-by-clause explication of the Constitution :

> By including the slave population in the census on a one-to-one basis, the South would have had all the representation it needed to outvote the North on the slavery issue . . . indefinitely. So, in order to keep representation of the South down (thereby keeping the elimination of slavery on the table), the Founding Fathers devised this counting method [the three-fifths compromise] to limit the power the South could wield, thus ensuring that one day this new nation would be able to abolish slavery.[25]

Where does one even begin to parse such nonsense? We might begin with the fact that the three-fifths decision was the slaveholding South's greatest victory at the convention, as it allowed them to increase their representation by nearly 50 percent without giving up anything. Or we could point out the profound unfairness of apportioning democratic representation on the basis of a population that does not have democratic rights. The strongest rebuttal, however, is simply to point out that "this new nation" did not abolish slavery through the political process—the Constitution itself closed off that option in a dozen different ways—but through a violent civil war that completely suspended the democratic process in the Southern states.

At some level, even Beck must realize the futility of his argument, as, in this same constitutional gloss, he skips the Fugitive Slave Clause entirely and misreads the Slave Trade Clause as applying to voluntary immigrants. Beck's only commentary on the Constitution's extraordinary, unamendable protection of the slave trade concerns the allowable ten-dollar tax on new slaves, which he treats as the price of admission to America: "That's right," he quips, "the Founders actually put a price tag on coming to this country:

$10 per person. Apparently they felt like there was a value to being able to live here. Not anymore. These days we can't ask *anything* of immigrants—including that they abide by our laws."[26]

Either Beck is unaware that the passage he refers to explicitly protects the slave trade and that the "price tag" is a tax on the lawful importation of human beings, or he knows this and is still willing to use this disgraceful part of our history to launch cheap shots against immigrants. In either case, Americans of any political persuasion should be terrified that millions of their fellow citizens rely on this man for their understanding of our Founding heritage.

The most recent right-wing arguments have expanded from merely trying to minimize the importance of slavery in the Constitution to asserting a dazzlingly incoherent revision of antebellum history: the suggestion that unconstitutional federal intervention against the rights of Northern states was responsible for both slavery and the Civil War. Perry, perhaps the strongest proponent of this silliness, argues as follows:

> Unwilling to give up a way of life inexcusably based on an abominable practice, southern states persuaded Congress—the federal government—to pass the Fugitive Slave Act of 1850, which *compelled* citizens of northern states to act against their conscience and help return escaped former slaves into bondage. Meanwhile, the federal Supreme Court got involved, striking down states' personal liberty laws and ruling in *Dred Scott v. Sanford* that . . . free states were not entitled to offer the rights of citizenship to former slaves. Thus, while the southern states seceded in the name of "states' rights," in many ways it was the northern states whose sovereignty was violated in the run-up to the Civil War.
>
> We can never know what would have happened in the absence of federal involvement because we cannot rewrite history. There was a major divide in the nation, and it is possible that war was inevitable.[27]

By characterizing the Civil War as something only "possibly" necessary to end the practice of slavery, Perry necessarily makes the counterassertion that it, *possibly*, was not—that, had the central government only given federalism a chance, the Northern states might, *possibly*, have brought slavery to its knees simply by granting citizenship to escaped slaves. It is also *possible*, of course, that the Federalism Fairy could have freed the slaves with magic dust. We can never know for sure because we just can't rewrite history. We can, however, read history, and when we do, we encounter a collection of actual facts that makes it impossible to accept Perry's fanciful narrative, no matter how comforting it may be.

The first uncomfortable fact is that, as we have already seen, the Constitution explicitly required the return of fugitive slaves in Article IV, Section 2. This was part of the compact between federal and state governments from the very beginning; therefore, under Perry's own definition of federalism, Northern states had no constitutional right to harbor escaped slaves—especially not under the "original intent" standard of constitutional interpretation that Perry puts forth as a requirement for federal legislators.

Furthermore, Perry's assertion that, according to the Dred Scott decision, "free states were not entitled to offer the rights of citizenship to former slaves," while technically true, does not constitute proof of federal encroachment on states' rights. What the Dred Scott decision actually says is that states can offer their own citizenship to whomever they choose, but only Congress has the right to grant citizenship in the United States. This position simply restates the requirements of Article I, Section 8.4 of the Constitution: states do not grant US citizenship, a fact that I suspect Governor Perry would rush to point out if New Mexico ever tried to naturalize all the undocumented immigrants within its borders and send them over to Texas with all the rights and privileges of US citizens.

My point here is not that the Fugitive Slave Act and the Dred Scott decision were good things. They were deplorable invasions of an oppressed minority's fundamental rights. But they were not, by any stretch of the imagination, the unconstitutional invasions of states' rights that Perry presents them as. Rather, they were the logical result of a Constitution that was designed to protect slavery; an understanding of federalism that protected the tyranny of the majority; and an environment that allowed irresponsible, poorly informed demagogues to inflame their audiences by denouncing any federal attempt to protect individuals as "tyranny."

But irresponsible, poorly informed demagogues have been with us always. In 1787, they nearly succeeded in preventing the ratification of the Constitution. "The day on which we adopt the present proposed plan of government," exclaimed one prominent Anti-Federalist just days after the Constitution's initial publication, "we may Justly date the loss of American liberty."[28] A writer known only as "Centinel" thundered that the Constitution was "a most daring attempt to establish a despotic aristocracy among freemen, that the world has ever witnessed."[29] And the irrepressible "Brutus" warned citizens that "if you adopt it, this only remaining asylum for liberty will be shut up, and posterity will execrate your memory."[30]

The overblown rhetoric that almost killed the Constitution in its infancy continues to be advanced today by the ideological heirs of "Brutus" and "Centinel." On August 2, 2010, Mark Levin announced on his radio show that "federalism is dead," that the Constitution "is in its last death throes," and that "we are living in a soft tyranny."[31] He meant it, of course, as an attack on President Obama and the Democrats—which is just the sort of irresponsible hyperbole required by twenty-first-century talk radio and eighteenth-century pamphleteering alike. But in a way, Levin was right. Federalism as Mark Levin and his fellow conservatives understand the term died on June 21, 1788, when New Hampshire became the ninth state to ratify the Constitution. Its chief executioners were George Washington, James Madison, Alexander Hamilton, and John Jay. And its demise made the United States of America possible.

But if the Right's definition of *federalism* is wrong, which definition is right? Under what terms did Hamilton, Madison, and the other Framers of the Constitution divide power between the states and the federal government? This turns out to be a very difficult question to answer, as the principal actors did not agree with each other about the proper division of power. This very question, in fact, led to the first major factional split in the new American republic—a split that involved most of the people we now revere as Founding Fathers.

After the Constitution was ratified, Hamilton, George Washington, John Adams, and others all continued calling themselves Federalists; under that name, they fought to increase the power of the federal government and decrease the power of the states. Madison, on the other hand, joined his long-time ally Thomas Jefferson to create the Democratic-Republican Party, which favored strong state governments and saw the federal government's role as one strictly limited to the specific powers enumerated in the Constitution. This division, and its enduring consequences for American politics, will be the subject of the next chapter.

CHAPTER 6

THE JEFFERSONIAN MYTH AND THE HAMILTONIAN BOGEYMAN

> When this government was first established, it was possible to have kept it going on true principles, but the contracted, English, half-lettered ideas of Hamilton, destroyed that hope in the bud. We can pay off his debt in 15 years; but we can never get rid of his financial system.
> —Thomas Jefferson on Alexander Hamilton

> If to national union, national respectability, public order, and public credit they are willing to substitute national disunion, national insignificance, public disorder, and discredit—then let them unite their acclamations and plaudits in favour of Mr. Jefferson.
> —Alexander Hamilton on Thomas Jefferson

Even by the raucous standards of late eighteenth-century political debate, Thomas Jefferson and Alexander Hamilton fought a lot. Their rivalry began soon after George Washington selected them as his two closest cabinet advisors—Jefferson as the first secretary of state and Hamilton as the first secretary of the Treasury. Washington could not have chosen two men who saw the meaning of the American Revolution more differently. In the years that followed, the terms *Jeffersonian* and *Hamiltonian* would come to define the two extreme poles of political thought in America.

The official story about the rivalry goes something like this: Hamilton, an immigrant from the West Indies, saw America as a potential economic superpower. He favored the interests of the merchants, manufacturers, and financiers, who he believed would become the backbone of the American commercial empire. Hamilton believed America should unite under a strong central government and become a major player on the world stage. Jefferson, on the other hand, was both a quintessential Virginia planter and a learned Enlightenment thinker. Jefferson saw himself as an advocate for common people and rural values. He saw Hamilton's nationalism and financial program as great threats to the agrarian way of life, which needed only plentiful land, low taxes, and a government that stayed out of the way. He believed in strong state governments and a limited national government, and he opposed most kinds of taxation, which he saw as a way to redistribute income from the poor to the rich.

The Jefferson-Hamilton rivalry has become part of both our national memory and our standard middle-school curriculum. Most Americans know (or at least once learned) that Hamilton and Jefferson both served in Washington's cabinet, that they fought bitterly, and that Thomas Jefferson "won" and became president, while Hamilton "lost" and got shot by Aaron Burr— somehow managing to get his picture on the ten-dollar bill in the process. We also understand that as we use history to frame our own political arguments, we are better off siding with Jefferson than with Hamilton. Though we aren't exactly sure why, we know Jefferson was the good guy.

But there are many ways of siding with Jefferson, as Joseph Ellis explains in *American Sphinx*: "Soon after his death in 1826, Jefferson became a touchstone for wildly divergent political movements that continued to compete for his name and the claim on his legacy."[1] So varied were his opinions that the term *Jeffersonian* has plausibly been adopted by Northern abolitionists, Southern secessionists, Midwestern populists, New York industrialists, New Deal liberals, John Birch conservatives, and twentieth-century student radicals. With the advent of Tea Party conservatism, we can add one more movement to this list, as the ultralibertarians in the Tea Party movement have raised the standard of Jefferson (and his ism) as the battle flag of limited government.

Perhaps the chief contemporary standard raiser has been the economist Thomas DiLorenzo—a Southern regionalist, an acknowledged secessionist, and an economics professor at Loyola University in Baltimore. DiLorenzo's 2008 book *Hamilton's Curse: How Jefferson's Arch Enemy Betrayed the American Revolution—and What It Means for Americans Today* (the title says it all) is probably the most sustained recent treatment of the Jefferson-Hamilton feud from the ultralibertarian point of view.

Hamilton's Curse falls somewhere between economic history and biblical archetype: The American people once lived in a paradisaical state of small-government bliss under the gentle reign of a just and constitutionally limited deity (Jefferson). All was well until the evil serpent (Hamilton, of course) beguiled the nation into eating of the fruit of big government. The only remedy, DiLorenzo insists, is a return to prelapsarian (Jeffersonian) innocence:

> The only way to end the Hamiltonian curse of centralized monopoly on government is for Americans to once again embrace the Jeffersonian philosophy of government—to recognize that that government is best which governs least; that the citizens of the free and independent states are sovereign; and that they, along with their state and local representatives, are the best hope for the protection of liberty against the despotic proclivities of the central state.[2]

Though they have been a standard part of American public discourse for two centuries, simplistic views like DiLorenzo's are fundamentally flawed because they attempt to separate ideologies from the cultural forces that produced them. This is always a bad idea. In the case of Jefferson and Hamilton, it is a *really* bad idea, as it entirely fails to account for the historical context of late eighteenth-century America, which shaped both men's opinions.

In the remainder of this chapter, I will examine three of the most important controversies involving Hamilton and Jefferson that occurred during George Washington's first term, during which both men served in the cabinet. Though they would later disagree on other issues—and revise and reform their opinions—these three debates drew the initial boundary lines between the Hamiltonian party that kept the name "Federalist" and the Jeffersonian party that eventually took the name "Republican." As we shall see, the official story takes us only so far in understanding the rivalry between two of America's most influential Founding Fathers—and not far at all in applying their ideas to the issues and debates of our own time.

GOVERNMENTS AND FREE MARKETS:
THE BOND-DISCRIMINATION CONTROVERSY

Hamilton and Jefferson were at odds with each other before they ever met. As the American minister to France from 1785 to 1789, Jefferson had not taken part in the Federal Convention or the ensuing battle for ratification. When he arrived back in the United States in September of 1789, he was met with a letter from Washington appointing him secretary of state, but he did not arrive in the capital until March of 1790. Hamilton, who was appointed at the same time but began serving immediately, had a six-month head start for his agenda. As Hamilton began to advance his financial program, James Madison, who was serving in the House of Representatives, emerged as his primary opponent. And because Madison and Jefferson were political allies and close correspondents, Jefferson began his cabinet service as an opponent of Hamiltonianism.

The issue that drove the first wedge between Hamilton and Madison—and alienated Hamilton and Jefferson before they ever began working together—involved the proper way for the government to pay its internal creditors. As a result of the Revolutionary War, the federal government owed $54 million and the individual states owed $25 million, for a total of $79 million (about $2 billion in 2010).[3] About $42 million of this was in the form of government bonds that had been issued to Americans as payment for services during the war. Hamilton wanted to settle this debt by paying the full value of the bonds, plus interest, to the current bondholders, many of whom had purchased the bonds from their original owners.

Hamilton's position would not even be questioned today; it is standard practice throughout the world to pay the full value of securities to those who own them. Nobody would seriously suggest that a government or business should try to track down the original owner of a bond to work out a profit-sharing agreement with the current holder. But that is exactly what a number of people wanted to do in 1790. Hamilton's position was controversial because many of the bonds had been issued as payment to soldiers and suppliers during the Revolutionary War, who had sold them for pennies on the dollar—despite Washington's continual exhortations that they keep them. Many people felt a sentimental desire to make sure the soldiers and poor farmers were compensated for their sacrifices during the war even if they had sold their bonds.

The cause of the original bondholders was championed in Congress by James Madison, who argued that "there must be something radically wrong in suffering those who rendered a bonafide consideration to lose 7/8 of their dues, and those who have no particular merit towards their country to gain 7 or 8 times as much as they advanced."[4] The government, Madison argued, should pay only part of the face value of the bond (the highest market rate plus interest) to the current bondholder, with the remainder being paid to the original recipient of the bond. "Madison sought no total reduction in the payments due from the government," explains biographer Ralph Ketchum. "Rather, he proposed a *redistribution* of the payments, to benefit those who had suffered from the government's earlier defaults, and to scale down the profits of the speculators who had gathered the depreciated certificates."[5]

Hamilton had anticipated just such a proposal in his original report, in which he responds that any discrimination against the legitimate purchasers of the bond would be "highly injurious, even to the original holders of public securities; as ruinous to public credit." It would be, he argues, "inconsistent with justice" because it would breach a contract and violate the rights of "a fair purchaser." And it would defeat the very purpose of issuing the bonds, as "the intent, in making the security assignable, is, that the proprietor may be able to make use of his property, by selling it for as much as it *may be worth in the market*, and that the buyer may be *safe* in the purchase."[6]

The House of Representatives overwhelmingly agreed with Hamilton, and Madison's proposal was defeated on February 22, 1790, by a vote of thirty-six to thirteen. Thomas Jefferson was en route from Monticello when the vote was taken, but when he arrived in New York City a week later, he quickly became incensed at what his Treasury colleague had done. This controversy, as he later wrote in his "Anas," set him on a course of opposition to Hamilton's financial programs:

> In the bill for funding & paying these [bonds], Hamilton made no difference between the original holders, & the fraudulent purchasers of this paper. . . . Immense sums were thus filched from the poor & ignorant, and fortunes accumulated by those who had themselves been poor enough before. Men thus enriched by the dexterity of a leader, would follow of course the chief who was leading them to fortune, and become the zealous instruments of all his enterprises.[7]

The debt-discrimination debate drew the battle lines that would define the next generation of American politics. As Ron Chernow explains in his biography of Hamilton, "the funding debate shattered the short-lived political consensus that had ushered in the new government. For the next five years, the political spectrum in America was defined by whether or not people endorsed or opposed Alexander Hamilton's programs."[8] As Jefferson settled into the cabinet, he replaced Madison as the public face of anti-Hamiltonianism.

As important as it was to the development of the political system, this first skirmish had much more to do with the ends of government than the means. The Hamiltonian and Jeffersonian positions here did not focus, as they often did, on defining the proper limits of government power. In this instance, in fact, Hamilton was the one who wanted to allow the market to operate freely; Jefferson, never a fan of financial markets, wanted the government to step in and redistribute wealth. It was only in the ultimate goal of protecting ordinary citizens from the machinations of wealthy financiers that Jefferson's position can even be called "Jeffersonian," as neither he nor Madison had any scruples at all about pitting the power of the government against the forces of the free market.

ENUMERATED AND IMPLIED POWERS: THE NATIONAL BANK CONTROVERSY

No principle is more important to the conservative political critique than the doctrine of "enumerated powers," or the assertion that the Framers of the Constitution limited the federal government to eighteen specific functions—which are all laid out in Article I, Section 8 of the Constitution—with all other powers reserved to the states by the Tenth Amendment. This doctrine is a cornerstone of a number of recent books by such figures as Mark Levin, Mike Lee, Rick Perry, and Rand Paul—and of the cramped version of federalism that the Right now embraces. Roger Pilon, vice president for legal affairs at the Cato Institute, defines this doctrine succinctly in the Cato publication *The Purpose and Limits of Government*:

> It was the doctrine of enumerated powers that was meant to constitute the principal defense against overweening government. Since all power began with the people, the people could limit their government simply by giving

it, through the Constitution, only certain of their powers. That, precisely, is what [the Founders] did, through enumeration, thus making it clear that the government had only such powers as were found in the document.[9]

Fringe conservatives speak and write as though the Founders universally embraced the doctrine of enumerated powers. They did not. It was, rather, one of the most hotly disputed issues of the Founding era. Thomas Jefferson was the strongest supporter of the doctrine. Madison invoked it frequently, but not consistently, throughout his career. Most of the other Founders rejected it in favor of the competing doctrine of "implied powers": the belief that the Constitution authorizes Congress to exercise any power necessary to accomplish its enumerated responsibilities—even if such power is not specifically mentioned in the Constitution.

According to its adherents, the doctrine of implied powers proceeds naturally from Article I, Section 8 of the Constitution. The final enumerated power in this section is "to make all Laws which shall be necessary and proper for carrying into Execution the foregoing Powers, and all other Powers vested by this Constitution in the Government of the United States or any Department or Officer thereof." This phrase, usually called the "Necessary and Proper Clause," has been one of the most controversial passages in the Constitution from the very beginning of the American republic. Opinion about the clause is as sharply divided today as it was at the Federal Convention, when it was written, and during the presidency of George Washington, when it became the focus of much of the conflict between Jefferson and Hamilton.

At a minimum, the Necessary and Proper Clause makes Article I, Section 8 much harder to interpret than it would have been if the list had stopped at seventeen. Its inclusion in the final draft contributed to the decision of three delegates—George Mason, Elbridge Gerry, and Edmund Randolph—to leave the convention without signing the Constitution, as they feared it conveyed almost unlimited power to the federal government.[10] When this clause became a major line of Anti-Federalist attack, Madison defended it vigorously in *Federalist* no. 44. "No axiom is more clearly established in law, or in reason," he writes, "than that wherever the end is required, the means are authorized; wherever a general power to do a thing is given, every particular power necessary for doing it is included."[11]

Madison argued forcefully for implied powers in the Federalist essays, and again during the congressional debates, when he defeated two proposals to add the word "expressly" before "delegated" in the Tenth Amendment's statement that "the powers not delegated to the United States by the Constitution . . . are reserved to the states." He did not understand at the time that his own arguments would pave the way for a major political conflict that would pit him against his one-time friend and ally Alexander Hamilton.

Hamilton wanted a national bank modeled after the highly influential Bank of England, which was chartered in 1694 and made possible the formidable war machine that America faced during the Revolution. Hamilton felt the banking structure of the United States could not adequately address the financial needs of the new nation. A national bank, he argued, would make credit widely available to business interests and would help create a national currency that could standardize transactions in the states—which were using as many as fifty different international currencies at the time.

The industrial areas of the North were ecstatic about the bank proposal, which would apply the power of government to the biggest economic problem of the day: the lack of reliable sources of credit. The primarily agricultural Southern states, however, were opposed to the whole business of banks, national or otherwise. These states had no need of elaborate credit systems or even of paper currency, and they were highly suspicious of financial markets that seemed to generate wealth through incomprehensible paper transactions. "Real wealth," for the majority of Southerners, was measured in land, slaves, and tobacco.

Madison and Jefferson, both Virginians, emerged as the primary opponents of the national bank proposal. When it passed in Congress, both urged Washington to veto it as an unconstitutional exercise of federal power. Washington was deeply concerned about the constitutional implications of the bank. He understood very clearly that his decision would set a precedent for the future and that his two top advisors were on different sides of the fence. With characteristic thoughtfulness, Washington asked both Jefferson and Hamilton to prepare a report on the constitutionality of a national bank (see appendix F).

Jefferson prepared a relatively brief summary for Washington based on speeches Madison had given on the House floor. He based his opinion squarely on the doctrine of enumerated powers, asserting that this doctrine is "the foundation of the Constitution" and that "the incorporation of a bank, and the powers assumed by this bill, have not . . . been delegated to the United States." Though Jefferson concedes that the bank might have positive effects, he insists this would not justify exceeding the authority granted in the

Constitution. "It would," he argues, "reduce the whole instrument to a single phrase, that of instituting a Congress with power to do whatever would be good for the United States; and, as they would be the sole judges of the good or evil, it would be also a power to do whatever evil they please."[12]

Jefferson does not discount the Necessary and Proper Clause of Article I, Section 8. He insists, however, that a bank was not necessary to do any of the things the Constitution authorized Congress to do, such as collecting taxes to pay debts, borrowing money, or regulating commerce. It might make exercising such responsibilities more convenient, but Jefferson insists that "the Constitution allows only the means which are '*necessary*,' not those which are merely 'convenient' for effecting the enumerated powers. If such a latitude of construction be allowed to this phrase as to give any non-enumerated power, it will go to every one, for there is not one which ingenuity may not torture into a *convenience* in some instance *or other*."[13]

In a report six times longer than Jefferson's, Hamilton lays down the foundations of the doctrine of implied powers, insisting that "implied powers are to be considered as delegated equally with express ones." Actually, Hamilton divides federal power into three categories. In addition to implied and express powers, he also introduces the notion of "resulting powers," or powers that were the logical result of the exercise of enumerated powers. "It will not be doubted that if the United States should make a conquest of any of the territories of its neighbours," he argues, "they would possess sovereign jurisdiction over the conquered territory." The sovereignty would result not from the constitutional delegation of power but from "the whole mass of powers of the government & from the nature of political society."[14]

Hamilton devotes most of his report to rebutting Jefferson's interpretation of the Necessary and Proper Clause. He blasts Jefferson's definition of the term "necessary." "It is essential to the being of the National government," he writes, "that so erroneous a conception of the meaning of the word *necessary*, should be exploded." To be necessary, something does not have to be absolutely indispensible. "Neither the grammatical, nor popular sense of the term requires that construction. According to both, *necessary* often means no more than *needful, requisite, incidental, useful*, or *conducive to*." He insists that "to understand the word as the Secretary of State does, would be to depart from its obvious & popular sense, and to give it a *restrictive* operation: an idea never before entertained. It would be to give it the same force as if the word *absolutely* or *indispensably* had been prefixed to it."[15]

Contemporary fringe conservatives such as Thomas DiLorenzo have attacked Hamilton mercilessly for having "invented the myth that the Constitution somehow grants the government 'implied powers.'"[16] But this ignores the fact that most of the Constitution's Framers agreed with Hamilton—including George Washington, who accepted Hamilton's report and rejected Jefferson's. Hamilton's arguments for the bank were also accepted by most of the seventeen delegates to the Federal Convention who served as members of the First Congress. Despite Madison's intensive floor campaign against it, fourteen of the seventeen voted in favor of the national bank. When we also consider that the same Congress that ratified the Tenth Amendment voted nearly three to one in favor of the national bank, we get a pretty strong affirmation that the Framers were more open to the idea of implied powers than today's conservatives are willing to admit.[17]

When looking at their presidential tenures, we must count both Jefferson and Madison among those Founders who felt comfortable with the idea of implied powers—or, if they remained uncomfortable with the notion, they did not allow their discomfort to stand in the way of invoking the doctrine to defend their executive actions. Jefferson invoked this principle more blatantly than any president before him—and, arguably, since—when he purchased the Louisiana Territory from Napoleon. Jefferson originally intended to seek a constitutional amendment authorizing the purchase, realizing that the Constitution did not grant the president or the Congress the power to acquire land. However, when the Federalists in Congress suddenly converted to strict constructionism and vowed to block an amendment, Jefferson settled for simply asking for Congress's permission. To Madison, he wrote, "The less we say about the constitutional difficulties respecting Louisiana, the better, and what is necessary for surmounting them must be done *sub silentio*."[18]

The irony of Jefferson's sudden embrace of implied powers was not lost on John Quincy Adams, who described the Louisiana Purchase as "an assumption of implied power greater in itself and more comprehensive in its consequences, than all the assumptions of implied power in the twelve years of the Washington and Adams Administrations put together." He continued his critique by insisting that "through the sixteen years of the Jefferson and Madison Administrations, not the least regard was paid to the doctrines of rejecting implied powers, upon which those gentlemen had vaulted into the seat of government, with the single exception that Mr. Madison negatived [vetoed] a bill for applying public money to the public internal improvement of the country."[19]

For Adams, though, the final irony in the bank battle occurred in 1816, when James Madison signed legislation creating the Second Bank of the United States. Madison, who had allowed the First Bank's charter to expire in 1811, experienced such a severe financial crisis after the War of 1812 that he was forced to support the very measure he and Jefferson "had stubbornly contended as unconstitutional, because *express* power was not given to the Congress to incorporate banks."[20]

AMERICA ON THE WORLD STAGE: THE NEUTRALITY DEBATE

In his "Anas," or his memoirs of his time in Washington's cabinet, Thomas Jefferson complains bitterly that, in the aftermath of the French Revolution, a Federalist politician compared Jeffersonian Republicans to French revolutionaries, "thus daring to identify us with the murderous Jacobins of France."[21] He wrote these words in 1818, long after his retirement from public life and long after the horrors of the Reign of Terror had become part of the world's history. In the early 1790s, however, Jefferson and his Republicans regularly compared French revolutionaries to American patriots. Most Americans agreed, proud to think their own revolution had inspired an imitation in one of the world's most powerful nations.

The French Revolution became an American foreign-policy issue in April of 1793, when Americans learned the revolutionary government of France had declared war on England and other European powers. War between France and England had significant implications for the United States, as both countries had significant territorial and commercial interests in the Americas. If the United States were to enter the war on the side of France—as many Americans wanted—French privateers would be able to use American ports, and even American volunteers, to harass British ships. But such actions would bring about reprisals from the British, who remained, by a large margin, the United States' most important trading partner.

Hamilton pushed hard for an official statement of neutrality, and Washington agreed. Jefferson conceded that neutrality was the only rational position for a young country without a standing army, but he did not want to alienate the French with a specific statement. He understood, as Hamilton and Washington did, that a statement of neutrality would effectively favor Britain, as there were many in the country who wanted to help the French and would be deterred by such a proclamation, while there was very little interest in helping the British. Jefferson felt it was enough for the United States to avoid any statements or policies that favored one side over the other.

Both Hamilton and Washington felt an official proclamation would be necessary, though Washington did agree to avoid the word "neutrality." Thus, on April 22, 1793, Washington released a statement, under both his and Jefferson's signatures, directing American citizens to "adopt and pursue a conduct friendly and impartial toward the belligerent powers." The proclamation further stipulated that Americans should "avoid all acts and proceedings whatsoever, which may in any manner tend to contravene such disposition," concluding that "prosecutions [will] be instituted against all persons, who shall . . . violate the law of nations, with respect to the powers at war, or any of them."[22]

Less than a week before issuing the neutrality proclamation, Washington received Edmond-Charles Genet, the new French minister to the United States, in Philadelphia. Citizen Genet, as he called himself, attracted large crowds in the United States and worked diligently to undercut American neutrality. Specifically, he enlisted Americans to convert captured British merchant ships into French privateering vessels—precisely the activity the proclamation was designed to prohibit. Genet succeeded in stirring up significant opposition to Washington's proclamation, much of it coming through the *National Gazette*, an opposition newspaper Jefferson and Madison secretly set up to counter Hamilton's influence in the Washington administration.

As the neutrality proclamation blossomed into a full-fledged political carnival, it helped sharpen the boundaries of the two factions that had already started to form. At stake were both the meaning of the American Revolution and the future of the American republic. Would America become something like England—a trade-oriented constitutional system in which the executive, though elected, wielded much the same power as a king? Or would it become, like post-Revolution France, a truly classless society in which all "citizens" had an equal claim to sovereignty?

On one side were Alexander Hamilton, George Washington, and the Federalists, who saw themselves as the inheritors of a British-style system in which a benevolent elite ruled within a constitutional system for the benefit of the common people, who would grow rich through manufacture and trade. On the other side were Thomas Jefferson, James Madison, and the Republicans, who held that people had both the ability and the right to govern themselves and that a federal government was, at best, a necessary evil. Republicans believed the Federalists were crypto-monarchists who were laying the foundations to convert the presidency into a hereditary monarchy. Federalists believed Republicans were anarchists who were willing to tear society apart in the name of a flawed utopian vision.

By the end of 1793, both sides had pegged their ideological positions to their own distinctive interpretations of the French Revolution, and these entrenched positions structured both sides' responses to the unfolding narrative from France. When stories of mass executions in Paris filtered in, Republicans regretted the excesses but pronounced them necessary to the higher goals of liberty. Of the executions, Jefferson writes, "These I deplore as much as anybody. But I deplore them as I should have done had they fallen in battle." In fairly typical hyperbole that he would later regret, he goes on to argue that "the liberty of the whole earth was depending on the issue of the contest" and that "rather than it should have failed, I would have seen half the earth desolated."[23]

Federalists, on the other hand, took every reported atrocity as a warning against the perils of mob rule and, by extension, Jeffersonian Republicanism. As early as 1790, John Adams predicted—quite correctly, it turned out—that the Revolution would lead to "great and lasting calamities," including violence, chaos, and the rise of a dictator.[24] For his part, Hamilton used the Reign of Terror to score quick political points. Seizing on Jefferson's earlier statements of support, he regularly compared the American Republicans to their French brethren. If Jefferson and his American Jacobins were allowed to succeed, Hamilton insisted, there would be guillotines along the Potomac as soon as the new capital opened for business.

We can look back now and see that the Jeffersonians were wrong about France. Jefferson understood this toward the end of his life, when he wrote to John Adams that "your prophecies . . . proved truer than mine" and that "the destruction of 8 or 10 millions of human beings has probably been the effect of these convulsions."[25] At the time, however, the truth was much harder to divine. Under ideal conditions, news took seven to eight weeks to reach America from Europe. Most of the news coming from the French Revolution came through England first, which both increased the delay and decreased the accuracy. It would take years for Americans to sort out the significance of this faraway revolution.

In 1793, most Americans still supported the French Revolution enthusiastically. The neutrality debate of that year was as much about the correct rationale for foreign-policy decisions as it was about the proper European nation to emulate. Hamilton admired the British and distrusted the French, and he also knew the vast majority of America's trade was with England and would be for a long time to come. America would gain much by closer ties with the British Empire and would sacrifice much if those ties were severed. And Hamilton believed the only rational basis for foreign-policy decisions was national self-interest, which, measured in economic terms, lay clearly with the British Empire and with the Proclamation of Neutrality.

Jefferson, on the other hand, felt America should stand by France in its struggle for liberty in the same way that France had stood by America during its revolution. He saw the two countries united by a common love of liberty—an ideological kinship that went beyond mere commercial self-interest. In a letter to Madison, he referred to Hamilton and other Federalists as members of "the confederacy of princes against human liberty," and, on the eve of Washington's declaration, he wrote that "a proclamation is to be issued, and another instance of my being forced to appear to approve what I have condemned uniformly from its first conception."[26]

When the gloves finally came off, however, the major ideological differences between Jefferson and Hamilton were subordinated to a question of constitutional process: Did the president of the United States have the constitutional authority to declare neutrality? One of the powers specifically delegated to Congress is the declaration of war, but the text of the Constitution says nothing about declarations of peace. Jefferson wrote to Madison, "As the Executive cannot decide the question of war on the affirmative side, neither ought to do so on the negative side."[27] Any neutrality proclamation, he insisted, should be issued by Congress.

On its face, the argument about congressional power was a red herring on Jefferson's part. When Washington asked his cabinet whether to take the matter to Congress, Jefferson and Hamilton both agreed that a congressional declaration would raise unnecessary alarm.[28] Washington was not trying to bypass congressional authority as much as he was trying to prevent calling too much attention to an issue that might not turn out to be very important.

He had every reason to think the heavily Federalist Congress would have supported the neutrality proclamation had he and Hamilton brought it forward—which in fact they did in June of 1794, when Congress passed the Neutrality Act, which codified the principles in Washington's proclamation.

But there was much more at stake, and both Hamilton and Jefferson knew it. By issuing an executive order, complete with the threat of penalties for noncompliance, Washington had exercised a legislative power. Because Washington's presidency would set precedents for future administrations, his seemingly innocent declaration of neutrality would empower all future presidents to legislate through executive directives—something Jefferson opposed at the time, though both he and Madison would eventually exercise similar executive prerogatives during their own presidential administrations.

As the debates in Congress and in Washington's cabinet became more intense, Hamilton went public. On June 29, 1793, he published the first of seven essays under the pseudonym "Pacificus." In this essay, Hamilton lays out and attempts to refute the major Jeffersonian objections to the neutrality proclamation. In response to the argument that only Congress could declare war *or* peace, Hamilton takes a strict-constructionist position, arguing that the only power granted to Congress was to declare war and that it is "the duty of the Executive to preserve Peace till war is declared."[29] In making this argument, Hamilton labels both war and peace as inherently executive powers "subject only to the *exceptions* and *qualifications* which are expressed in the instrument [the Constitution]."[30] Declarations of war, he concludes, are specifically transferred to the legislative branch by the Constitution. Declarations of neutrality, on the other hand, remain with the executive.

Hamilton also addresses the common belief that the neutrality proclamation violated America's treaties with France and ignored the gratitude America owed for "the succors rendered us in our own revolution."[31] To the first argument, Hamilton responds that the change in French government had yet to be officially recognized by the United States and that "until the new Government is *acknowledged*, the treaties between the nations . . . are of course suspended." He further characterizes America's treaties with France as part of a purely defensive alliance and France's conflict with Britain and other European states as an offensive war.[32]

In the fifth "Pacificus" essay, Hamilton takes on the most sentimental objection to Washington's proclamation: that America had a moral obligation to help France as a repayment for the considerable French assistance to America during the Revolutionary War. France, Hamilton insists, had acted only in its own self-interest as England's greatest European rival. "The dismemberment of this country from Great Britain was an obvious, and a very important interest of France," he writes. "It cannot be doubted, that it was both the determining motive and an adequate compensation, for the assistance afforded us."[33] All nations, Hamilton insists, act out of self-interest rather than gratitude to other nations, and America should do the same—which, for the secretary of the Treasury, meant normalizing relations with its largest trading partner.

Rather than refuting Hamilton himself, Jefferson asked Madison to do so. "Take up your pen," he prodded, "there is none else who can and will enter the lists with him."[34] Madison responded by producing five periodical essays under the name "Helvidius." In these essays, Madison characterizes the followers of "Pacificus" as "foreigners and degenerate citizens among us, who hate our republican government, and the French revolution."[35]

The major target of Madison's attack in the first "Helvidius" paper is Hamilton's assertion that war and peace—and the treaties, generally—are executive powers unless specifically decreed to be otherwise. Madison insists on a strict division between the power to make laws and the power to enforce laws. To argue that the president can issue any statement that has the force of law is to say "that the executive department naturally includes a legislative power. In theory, this is an absurdity—in practice a tyranny."[36]

The idea that making treaties and declaring war are inherently executive powers is so alien to the laws of nations, Madison argues, that it could only come from one place: "The power of making treaties and the power of declaring war, are *royal prerogatives* in the *British government*, and are accordingly treated as Executive prerogatives by *British commentators*."[37] And this, for Madison, was the smoking gun that proved, as he and Jefferson had argued all along, that Hamilton and his allies were closet monarchists with an unholy attraction to all things British.

It would not be fair to say that either Madison or Hamilton twisted the meaning of the Constitution to serve their ideological agendas. The Constitution really is silent on the power to declare neutrality in a time of war, and both Madison and Hamilton came to reasonable conclusions based on inference and analogy. It would be absurd, however, to treat their debate over this issue as an abstract philosophical dispute about the separation of powers.

There were much more immediate political interests in play. If the Jeffersonian preference to favor France had been better served by an increase in presidential power, and the Hamiltonian preference to support England had required a weaker executive, Jefferson and Hamilton would have found—as both did on other occasions—very different procedural arguments to support their overall ideological agendas.

UNDERSTANDING THE JEFFERSON-HAMILTON RIVALRY TODAY

Modern conservatives like Thomas DiLorenzo, who hold Thomas Jefferson up as the author of liberty and denigrate Hamilton as an enemy of the people, see only a very small part of the ongoing conflict between two great men. Both of them loved their country and contributed to it in different ways. As the principal author of the Declaration of Independence, Jefferson created the philosophy that guided the American Revolution. As the principal author of the Federalist papers, Hamilton did more to ratify the Constitution than any other person. To suggest that either of them was "un-American" is just silly. America as we know it today would never have come into being without both of their contributions.

Yet they disagreed, constantly and fundamentally, about the most important issues of their day. And, though their opinions were not always consistent over time (Jefferson the president had a very different perspective from Jefferson the secretary of state), their basic positions during Washington's first term can be represented in something like parallel structure. The following chart represents a quick look at the major issues of contention between Hamilton and Jefferson.

ISSUE	JEFFERSON	HAMILTON
1. Federalism/ States' Rights	Jefferson saw the United States as a collection of individual sovereign states that each gave limited powers to the federal government to act in their collective interest. He believed any power not delegated specifically to the federal government by the Constitution could only be exercised by the states.	Hamilton saw the United States as a single great nation destined to stretch from coast to coast. He saw the states largely as administrative districts within the Union and believed the federal government, through the doctrine of implied powers, could exercise any powers not prohibited to it by the Constitution.
2. Financial Markets	Jefferson saw pure, market-based economics as a way to enrich the few at the expense of the many. He had a radical distrust of banks and financial institutions, and he supported policies, such as discrimination in bond payments, that interfered with market operations in order to protect the interests of the poor.	Hamilton had faith in the natural operations of financial markets. He believed the wealthy were better suited than the poor to drive economic progress, and he favored policies that, in effect, helped the rich get richer.
3. Business and Commerce	Jefferson believed the United States would be primarily an agricultural nation for the foreseeable future. He felt Hamilton's support of manufacturing and trading interests jeopardized the purer, more authentic way of life represented by farming.	Hamilton believed the United States would eventually become a powerful nation through manufacturing and commerce. He favored policies that would support the exploitation of America's natural resources and would facilitate trade with other nations.
4. Taxation	Jefferson saw taxation as a moral issue. Taxing the people more than necessary	Hamilton saw taxation as a purely practical issue. Excessive taxation was

	was a form of tyranny. He believed federal taxes should be kept at the absolute minimum necessary for the government to exercise the powers delegated to it by the Constitution.	unproductive and suppressed incentives to succeed. He felt taxes should generally be as high as people would bear while remaining productive. In his Federalist essays he argued for a virtually unlimited federal taxing power, to be checked by political rather than constitutional limitations.
5. The Judiciary	Jefferson believed the unelected judiciary posed a serious threat to democracy. He did not believe the Supreme Court had the power to overturn an executive or judicial action. He saw the increase in judicial activity under Supreme Court justice John Marshall as a danger to freedom.	Hamilton saw a strong judiciary as a bulwark against majoritarian tyranny. In *Federalist* no. 78, he explained the power of judicial review, by which federal courts can overturn unconstitutional legislative and executive actions.
6. Religion	Jefferson rejected the divinity of Jesus Christ while accepting him as the greatest moral teacher who ever lived. He took strong stands against most expressions of religion in the public square and believed in a "wall of separation between church and state"	Hamilton was a professing Christian who saw religion as a useful extension of the government. He favored many public expressions of religion. During the presidential campaign of 1800, he continually painted Jefferson as an atheist.
7. National Defense	Jefferson believed that human beings were inherently good and that disputes between nations were best handled through trade rather than through	Hamilton believed nations could only protect their interests by having a strong military force. He advocated both a standing army and a standing navy, and he

	force. He was a strong opponent of both a standing army and a standing navy, as he believed having military force available increased the chances of going to war. State militias, he felt, were all the protection the United States required.	believed one of the greatest advantages of having sufficient force available was in never having to use it. The threat of force, he felt, was an important part of international diplomacy.
8. Foreign Policy	In the debate over the neutrality proclamation, Jefferson argued for a foreign policy based on American values, natural law, and historical obligations. He believed supporting France in its conflict with the European nations fit these criteria.	Hamilton based foreign-policy decisions on a strict calculation of American interests, with little regard for either historical alliances or American values. In the neutrality debate, he favored an effectively pro-British policy because the British, as America's largest trading partner, were more important to American interests than the French were.

This chart makes it easy to see that Hamilton and Jefferson fought about many of the same political issues we fight about today. But though the issues are the same, the ideological combinations are not. Most Tea Party conservatives would agree with the positions detailed in the shaded areas in the chart, thus agreeing with Jefferson on issues 1, 4, and 5 and with Hamilton on issues 2, 3, 6, 7, and 8. Liberals would largely take the inverse positions. Both Jeffersonian and Hamiltonian positions have become part of the fabric of American political discourse, but they have not done so in ways either Jefferson or Hamilton could have predicted.

In 1789, when Hamilton and Jefferson began their famous feud, America was resource rich but infrastructure poor. Hamilton—who believed the future lay in manufacturing and commerce—wanted to use the government's resources to create a business-friendly climate that would encourage trade, and he did so with the near-unanimous support of the business community. Jefferson, on the other hand, had no use for commerce, finance, or complicated market economics. He believed America's future, like its past, lay with the hardworking common farmers. He wanted nothing to do with Hamilton's plans to tax farm products in order to enrich bankers and speculators, and he felt the best way to protect the way of life he cherished was to keep as much power as possible in the hands of the individual states, especially Virginia.

But we live in a very different world now. Small farms account for a vanishingly small portion of the American gross domestic product, and financial institutions are well established and have no need of government support. What this all adds up to is that Jeffersonian means (small government, low taxes, limited government borrowing) are no longer the best way to achieve Jeffersonian goals (distributing income more evenly, protecting the common person from corporate irresponsibility). Similarly, Hamiltonian means (government intervention, high taxes) are anathema to Hamiltonian ends (improving the climate for business, securing the loyalty of the monied classes). Any coherent political position in America today is, therefore, going to have both Jeffersonian and Hamiltonian elements. Liberals want to employ Hamiltonian intervention to reduce income inequality—a very Jeffersonian goal. Conservatives, on the other hand, advocate a return to Jeffersonian principles of government to restore the pro-business environment Hamilton spent his career creating.

Rather than poring through their speeches and letters to determine who was right and who was wrong, or creating proof texts to show that Hamilton and Jefferson both supported whatever contemporary ideology we happen to favor, we should acknowledge that both of their positions are legitimate examples of "what the Founders said." In the spectrum of positions represented by Hamilton and Jefferson, we can find the basis for most of the mainstream positions (and a fair number of not so mainstream ones) in America today. Rather than picking sides and declaring ourselves Jeffersonians or Hamiltonians, we should acknowledge that both of these great men, however much they may have hated each other, were honorable patriots who loved their country and profoundly influenced its development.

The most important lesson we can take from the Hamilton-Jefferson feud is simply that people can have wildly different opinions about important issues and still be good Americans. George Washington, one of the most remarkable leaders in America's history, understood this very well, which was why he usually listened to both Hamilton's and Jefferson's opinions before coming to his own conclusions. As we struggle to create our own compromises and consensuses about such questions as the role of state governments, the correct levels of taxation, and the place of religion in the public square, we should do so secure in the knowledge that, wherever we end up, some of the Founders will be there waiting for us—and some of them will not.

CHAPTER 7

GROVER NORQUIST AND THE TAX PLEDGE VERSUS ALEXANDER HAMILTON AND GOOD GOVERNMENT

> How is it possible that a government half supplied and always necessitous, can fulfill the purposes of its institution, can provide for the security, advance the prosperity, or support the reputation of the commonwealth? How can it ever possess either energy or stability, dignity or credit, confidence at home or respectability abroad? How can its administration be anything else than a succession of expedients temporizing, impotent, disgraceful?
> —Alexander Hamilton, *Federalist* no. 30

> I'm not in favor of abolishing the government. I just want to shrink it down to the size where we can drown it in the bathtub.
> —Grover Norquist

Americans don't like taxes. We owe our existence as a nation to the fact that the British figured this out too late. When the British Parliament tried to collect taxes from the colonists to help pay for the Seven Years' War, our forebears came up with the now famous slogan "No taxation without representation." In the name of liberty, they refused to pay the new taxes, boycotted British products, and dumped tea in the Boston Harbor before kicking the tax collectors, and the rest of the British, out for good.

As it turned out, the colonists didn't much care for taxation *with* representation either. The Articles of Confederation did not give Congress the power to collect taxes directly from the people, though it could make assessments to the individual states. In theory, the states had to pay any reasonable assessment. In practice, they almost never did, leaving the confederation government no way to pay its expenses or retire its massive war debt. And the states did not fare much better. State tax assessments were often met with strong resistance, the most famous example being Shays' Rebellion in Massachusetts (1786–1787), which dramatically accelerated the calls for a new Constitution. When the Federal Convention met in Philadelphia in the summer of 1787, their most pressing objective was to create a national government that had the ability to raise its own revenue. And that is exactly what they did.

As Anti-Federalists quickly pointed out, the Constitution sets very few limitations on the government's ability to impose taxes. Writing as "Brutus," Robert Yates devoted three periodical essays (nos. 5, 6, and 7) to the objection that the Constitution allows the federal government a virtual monopoly on taxing powers. "Every source of revenue is under the controul of the Congress," he laments in his seventh essay.[1] Patrick Henry was even harsher in his speech at the Virginia ratifying convention:

> What does this Constitution say? The clause under consideration gives an unlimited and unbounded power of taxation. . . . This Constitution can counteract and suspend any of our laws that contravene its oppressive operation; for they have the power of direct taxation, which suspends our Bill of Rights; and it is expressly provided that they can make all laws necessary for carrying their powers into execution; and it is declared paramount to the laws and constitutions of the States.[2]

Both "Brutus" and Henry objected to the Constitution's provision for direct taxation. At the time of the convention, nearly all government revenue was generated by indirect taxes—most commonly, import tariffs collected at the water's edge and passed on to consumers as increased prices for foreign goods. The Constitution (Article I, Section 2.3) allowed the federal government a monopoly on import tariffs and also permitted it to collect both excise taxes on specific goods and all direct taxes (such as head taxes or property taxes), as long as they were levied on each state proportionately by population. (The Sixteenth Amendment did not grant Congress the power to tax income, as many believe; Congress has always had this power. The Sixteenth Amendment merely abolished the apportionment requirement.)

Madison provided a lengthy rebuttal to Henry's objections at the same Virginia ratification convention. The power of direct taxation "was essential to the salvation of the Union," he argued. "It appears to me necessary, in order to secure that punctuality which is necessary in revenue matters. Without punctuality individuals will give it no confidence; without which it cannot get resources." Madison believed that the potential for an attack on the United States would alone justify granting the government the power of direct taxation, "or run the risk of a national annihilation."[3] With ratification, Madison and the other supporters of the Constitution secured for the new national government an almost unlimited authority to levy and collect taxes.

But having the constitutional authority to do something is not the same as having the political power to get away with it, and taxes were no more popular under the Constitution than they had been under the Articles of Confederation (or, for that matter, under the British). The majority of the government's revenue came from tariffs until well into the nineteenth century. And, in fact, the first time the new federal government exercised its theoretically unlimited taxing power, it caused the prolonged armed uprising we now call the "Whiskey Rebellion."

As armed uprisings go, the Whiskey Rebellion was a fairly mild affair. When Congress passed an excise tax on distilled spirits in 1790, many farmers—who converted their corn to alcohol for easy transport and sale—simply refused to pay. Tax collectors in rural areas were treated with contempt and, on occasion, with violence. In 1794, the tax protest became a rebellion when five hundred farmers in western Pennsylvania burned down the house of a local tax inspector. Soon after, more than six thousand armed men marched through Pittsburgh in protest of the tax. The federal government responded by federalizing troops from four state militias—in Pennsylvania, New Jersey, Virginia, and Maryland—and assembling an army of more than thirteen thousand soldiers to put down the resistance and arrest the leaders for treason. The rebellion collapsed immediately, and, though Washington eventually pardoned the instigators, he established once and for all that the government was willing to enforce its laws—especially its tax laws.

Most historians see the Whiskey Rebellion as an important event in the development of executive authority in the new republic. By acting decisively to put down an armed rebellion, Washington enhanced the credibility of the federal government and demonstrated his intention to enforce the rule of law. In the bizarre universe of twenty-first-century right-wing radio, however, the

Whiskey Rebellion has become a myth in which noble, Constitution-loving Americans stood up to oppressive taxation and forced the federal government to its knees. Here is how Glenn Beck describes this bit of our history:

> In 1791, a tax on whiskey was imposed to help pay for the Revolutionary War. . . . By 1794, the tension created by this tax gave rise to an armed rebellion, which was quickly extinguished by a U.S. Army force of over 13,000, led by President George Washington himself. No shots were ever fired.
>
> This is a perfect illustration of what eventually happens when the federal government becomes oppressive and nonresponsive to the will of the people. In 1803, the government got the message and repealed the whiskey tax . . . will they get the message this time?[4]

In a perfect world, or even a reasonably consistent one, Glenn Beck would have some explaining to do after writing a passage like this. He would have to explain how he could so blithely justify an action that George Washington, his own personal hero, considered an act of treason. He would also have to tell us why he would choose to use words like "oppressive and nonresponsive to the will of the people" about a government consisting primarily of the Founding Fathers he insists all modern leaders should emulate. And he would have to explain why he would have opposed a tax designed to help pay off the massive national debt.

Among the hard Right, however, Beck appears to be the sane one when it comes to protesting taxes. Others speak frankly of armed tax rebellion in a present context. In a 2009 radio interview, for example, Representative Michele Bachmann responded to the proposal for cap-and-trade legislation with an unapologetic call for armed rebellion. "I want people in Minnesota armed and dangerous on this issue of the energy tax because we need to fight back. Thomas Jefferson told us, having a revolution every now and then is a good thing, and the people—we the people—are going to have to fight back hard if we're not going to lose our country."[5]

Bachmann's quotation from Thomas Jefferson, which has become a favorite of the Tea Party movement, comes from a letter Jefferson wrote while in France to his friend William Smith. In the letter, Jefferson addresses Shays' Rebellion and its impact on the Constitution. Specifically, Jefferson thought the Constitution gave too much power to the chief executive—especially the power to be reelected perpetually. He believed the delegates had been "too much impressed by the insurrection of Massachusetts," causing them to strengthen executive power imprudently. Jefferson dismissed the importance of Shays' Rebellion with the now famous sentence, "The tree of liberty must be refreshed from time to time with the blood of patriots & tyrants."[6]

The Tea Party activists who regularly put this quote on banners (usually adding something like "and she is very thirsty" for emphasis) should, minimally, recognize that Jefferson was wildly out of step with the Constitution and its Framers. From a safe distance in Paris, Jefferson ridiculed men like James Madison and George Washington for taking Shays' Rebellion seriously, and he faulted all the Framers for creating an executive whose tenure in office was not strictly limited to a single term, a flaw in the Constitution that he saw as nearly fatal. Happily, Jefferson managed to overcome his objection to multiple presidential terms in time to run for reelection in 1804.

I do not believe either Glenn Beck or Michele Bachmann—or the many followers who echo their words—really mean what they clearly say: that they would like to see an armed tax revolt against the federal government. When pressed, both acknowledge that they mean terms like *blood*, *tyrant*, *armed*, and *dangerous* metaphorically. And, to be fair, martial rhetoric has always been part of mainstream political discourse in America. But at the fringes of the fringe, these are not metaphors at all. In the dark underbelly of the tax protest movement—where the income tax is illegal and the federal government is a dictatorship—so-called patriots speak regularly of the "Second Amendment solution" to America's ills. To be on the safe side, they have been stockpiling guns and ammunition for years.

During the 2010 campaigns, this rhetoric slipped briefly into mainstream politics through Tea Party–backed candidates like Sharron Angle in Nevada, who refused to renounce "Second Amendment remedies" to the problem of liberal Democrats in Congress, or Texas Republican Stephen Broden, who pointedly remarked that the option of violent revolution was "on the table" if Republicans did not win control of government.[7] These extremist candidates were not simply musing about possibilities; they were speaking in code to America's most rabid antigovernment tax protesters and saying "We're on your side."

Though both Broden and Angle won surprise victories in their Republican primaries, neither won the general election. Angle's nomination, in fact, allowed Senate Majority Leader Harry Reid to win reelection in a year when most political analysts expected him to lose. But it does not bode well for America that antigovernment extremists could win major-party nominations for congressional seats without renouncing violent revolution against the very government they were trying to become a part of. Americans of all political persuasions should denounce such fundamentally anti-American rhetoric, as George Washington denounced the Whiskey Rebellion, as "a treasonable opposition . . . propagating principles of anarchy."[8]

HAMILTONIAN GOOD SENSE AND THE TAXPAYER PROTECTION PLEDGE

Most tax protesters in America today are not armed rebels or dangerous kooks. Most, in fact, are respectable citizens who (like most of us) would like to share less of their income with the government. They believe that taxation is out of control and that the federal government has exceeded its constitutional authority to raise funds and regulate commerce. Their weapon of choice is political pressure, and their chief spokesperson is the Washington, DC, superlobbyist Grover Norquist, the president of Americans for Tax Reform.

In 1986, Norquist created the "Taxpayer Protection Pledge," which politicians sign to promise that they will never, ever, under any circumstances, increase the federal tax burden on the American people. The pledge for members of the House of Representatives goes like this:

> I, _____, pledge to the taxpayers of the _____ district of the state of _____, and to the American people that I will: ONE, oppose any and all efforts to increase the marginal income tax rates for individuals and/or businesses; and TWO, oppose any net reduction or elimination of deductions and credits, unless matched dollar for dollar by further reducing tax rates.[9]

As of October 2011, 238 representatives and forty-one senators had signed the pledge, all but three of them Republicans. Norquist has been clear that there will never be an exception to justify a tax increase and that any signer who breaks the pledge will suffer severe political consequences.

The Taxpayer Protection Pledge has now become official Republican orthodoxy. In the summer of 2011, largely because of this pledge, Republican members of Congress came within hours of allowing the United States to default on its debts rather than accept a budget plan that would have included huge cuts in discretionary and entitlement spending coupled with modest increases in revenue. In August of the same year, every single candidate for the Republican presidential nomination said in a debate that he or she would oppose a theoretical deficit-reduction plan that cut ten dollars in government spending for every one dollar of tax increases. The Republican Party appears to have locked the door to any increase in taxes for an entire generation.[10]

There is no fiscally responsible justification for such a stance, and most mainstream Republicans know it. Just a few months earlier, in March 2011, the House Republicans on the Joint Economic Committee released a detailed report on deficit reduction that concluded the ideal strategy would include 85 percent spending cuts and 15 percent revenue increases—a ratio of less than six to one.[11] And after the Republican presidential field rejected a hypothetical deal almost twice as favorable as the House Republicans' best-case scenario, Virginia Republican Frank Wolf took to the House floor to castigate Norquist for his influence on American politics. "Everything must be on the table," he said, "and I believe how the 'pledge' is interpreted and enforced by Mr. Norquist is a roadblock to realistically reforming our tax code. Have we really reached a point where one person's demand for ideological purity is paralyzing Congress to the point that even a discussion of tax reform is viewed as breaking a no-tax pledge?"[12]

But Wolf is a political anomaly. As one of only six Republican representatives who has refused to sign the Taxpayer Protection Pledge, he is free to follow his own instincts and consider proposed tax increases on their merits. The overwhelming majority of Republicans do not have this luxury. They have been painted into a corner by the promise that they signed. They know that if they were to vote in favor of any tax increase at all, they would face the wrath of a powerful and well-funded lobby that would brand them liars and cheats and would spare no expense to defeat them in their next primary election.

Nobody can fault Grover Norquist for trying to tie members of Congress to his agenda; that's what lobbyists do. Members of Congress, however, are not doing their jobs by allowing themselves to be tied. The power to cut or raise taxes is one of the most important responsibilities the Constitution assigns to the legislative branch of government. Elected officials who sign the Taxpayer Protection Pledge as candidates, therefore, come into office having already abdicated one of their most important legislative responsibilities.

It is a great tribute to Alexander Hamilton's genius that, before the Constitution was even ratified, he understood the importance leaving the government's hands free in the matter of taxes. As we have already seen, Anti-Federalists fumed about the lack of structural restraints on the taxing power, and they insisted on an amendment to check that power within the text of the Constitution itself. In a sustained counterattack consisting of seven essays (*Federalist* nos., 30–36), Hamilton rejects such arguments as shortsighted and potentially fatal. In *Federalist* no. 34, he argues that we can never safely limit the federal government's ability to collects taxes:

> We must bear in mind that we are not to confine our view to the present period, but to look forward to remote futurity. Constitutions of civil government are not to be framed upon a calculation of existing exigencies, but upon a combination of these with the probable exigencies of ages, according to the natural and tried course of human affairs. Nothing, therefore, can be more fallacious than to infer the extent of any power, proper to be lodged in the national government, from an estimate of its immediate necessities. There ought to be a CAPACITY to provide for future contingencies as they may happen; and as these are illimitable in their nature, it is impossible safely to limit that capacity.[13]

Hamilton makes it very clear that the decision to raise or to not raise taxes—one of the most consequential votes a legislator can ever make—must be based in contemporary reality and not subject to prior restraint. Like Madison, he stresses the need for self-defense in an emergency, but he also speaks to the needs of "remote futurity"—by which he means, of course, us. More than any other Founder, Hamilton understood that the United States would not always be what it was in the 1780s—a rural, agricultural society with vast resources but little industrial infrastructure. He knew the future was unforeseeable, and he understood that the Constitution had to be flexible enough for future generations to mold it to their needs and circumstances.

As an example of the need for unlimited taxing potential, Hamilton brings up the "poll tax." A poll tax, or a fixed levy on every citizen, was the closest thing Hamilton could imagine to the modern income tax, and he freely confesses that he despises the very idea. "I should lament to see them introduced into practice under a national government," he writes in *Federalist* no. 36. But he steadfastly refused to rule them unconstitutional. "As I know nothing to exempt this portion of the globe from the common calamities that have befallen other parts of it," he writes, "I acknowledge my aversion to every project that is calculated to disarm the government of a single weapon, which in any possible contingency might be usefully employed for the general defense and security."[14] Hamilton's Federalist essays operate from an indisputably sound management principle: don't limit your options when you don't have to.

Compare Hamilton's common-sense approach to that of the Taxpayer Protection Pledge—a unilateral declaration by a legislator to limit the government's capacity to raise revenues. While any single vote against raising taxes can be justified as a proper exercise of a legislator's discretion, a blanket refusal to consider exercising an important legislative power cannot. There is no way anybody can determine in advance that there will never, ever come a time when tax increases will be in the best interests of the country. No conscientious public servant should sign an oath that presumes otherwise.

THE UNSTARVED BEAST

The fiscal strategy that animates Norquist and his allies is called "starving the beast." According to this theory—which was developed by fiscal conservatives in the 1970s and became an important part of Ronald Reagan's tax cutting strategy in the 1980s—government will spend any money it has access to. No matter how high taxes go, it will never be enough because politicians will want to please their constituents by spending more money. Government spending is out of control, they say, and the only way to stop it is to shut off the supply of money and create a fiscal crisis that will force cuts in spending.

One of the most prominent of the early beast starvers was economist Bruce Bartlett. After starting his career as an advisor to Ron Paul in 1976, Bartlett soon became a staff economist to Jack Kemp and worked on the Kemp-Roth tax bill, which became the basis for the Reagan tax cuts in 1981. He served as an economic advisor to both Reagan and George H. W. Bush. Since the administration of George W. Bush, however, Bartlett has become a severe critic of the "starve the beast" ideology he once embraced. In a 2010 essay for *Forbes*, Bartlett calls it "the most pernicious fiscal doctrine in history" and blames it for much of the current economic turmoil.[15]

As Bartlett explains, starving the beast doesn't work because it ignores basic political reality. Tax cuts and spending increases are politically popular and therefore easy to enact. Tax increases and spending cuts are politically unpopular and therefore difficult to enact. In a representative democracy, politicians will always have much higher incentives to cut taxes than they will to cut spending. Major tax cuts, therefore, do not lead to spending cuts but to high deficits:

> Starve the beast was a theory that seemed plausible when it was first formulated. But more than 30 years later it must be pronounced a total failure. There is not one iota of empirical evidence that it works the way it was supposed to, and there is growing evidence that its impact has been perverse— raising spending and making deficits worse. In short, STB is a completely bankrupt notion that belongs in the museum of discredited ideas, along with things like alchemy.[16]

Bartlett is not alone. Very few serious analysts on either the left or the right now believe tax cuts will ever force spending cuts. And as unpopular as tax increases are, they are still more popular than the massive cuts to Social Security and Medicare that would be required to balance the budget without them—which means political pressure will force tax increases long before a majority of the people in the country accept the de facto elimination of entitlement programs. The math is not even difficult: tax cuts lead to budget shortfalls, which lead to higher deficits, which, eventually, lead to tax increases. This is the gerbil wheel that American fiscal policy has been running on for more than thirty years.

Some evidence suggests that starving the beast is even worse than useless in controlling spending. In a well-known 2006 paper, conservative economist William Niskanen, chair of the libertarian Cato Institute, concludes that "the 'starve-the-beast' hypothesis is not consistent with the facts" and that "reducing the current tax burden of federal spending has much the same effect as a price control, increasing the amount demanded relative to that supplied from current revenues."[17] Starving the beast, in other words, actually leads to an increase in federal spending by making the services the government provides seem cheaper than they really are. As Bartlett explains, "If higher spending never leads to higher taxes, which Norquist has virtually guaranteed as long as Republicans have veto power over tax increases, then higher spending is essentially a free lunch."[18]

If starving the beast does help control spending, we should now have some evidence of the fact. Since the second Bush administration, Republicans have been remarkably effective in bringing down the tax burden and keeping it low. As chart 7.1 demonstrates, the federal tax burden as a percent of the gross domestic product has been trending downward since 2001 and is now at its lowest since 1950.

CHART 7.1.

Tax Burdens, Federal Expenditures, and Surplus/Deficit as Percentages of GDP (1948–2011)

Fiscal Year	Federal Receipts as % of GDP (Tax Burden)	Individual Income Tax as % of GDP	Corporate Income Tax as % of GDP	Federal Expenditures as % of GDP	Surplus or Deficit as % of GDP	National Debt as % of GDP
1948	16.2	7.5	3.8	17.1	4.6	98.2
1949	14.5	5.7	4.1	20.5	0.2	93.1
1950	14.4	5.8	3.8	22.7	-1.1	94.1
1951	16.1	6.8	4.4	20.7	1.9	79.7
1952	19.0	8.0	6.1	25.8	-0.4	74.3
1953	18.7	8.0	5.7	26.8	-1.7	71.4
1954	18.5	7.8	5.6	25.7	-0.3	71.8
1955	16.5	7.3	4.5	24.7	-0.8	69.3
1956	17.5	7.5	4.9	23.9	0.9	63.9
1957	17.7	7.9	4.7	24.7	0.8	60.4
1958	17.3	7.5	4.4	26.3	-0.6	60.8
1959	16.2	7.5	3.5	27.3	-2.6	58.6
1960	17.8	7.8	4.1	26.2	0.1	56.0
1961	17.8	7.8	4.0	27.4	-0.6	55.2
1962	17.6	8.0	3.6	27.8	-1.3	53.4
1963	17.8	7.9	3.6	27.7	-0.8	51.8
1964	17.6	7.6	3.7	27.7	-0.9	49.3
1965	17.0	7.1	3.7	26.5	-0.2	46.9
1966	17.3	7.3	4.0	27.0	-0.5	43.5
1967	18.4	7.6	4.2	28.9	-1.1	42.0
1968	17.6	7.9	3.3	30.3	-2.9	42.5

Fiscal Year	Federal Receipts as % of GDP (Tax Burden)	Individual Income Tax as % of GDP	Corporate Income Tax as % of GDP	Federal Expenditures as % of GDP	Surplus or Deficit as % of GDP	National Debt as % of GDP
1969	19.7	9.2	3.9	29.5	0.3	38.6
1970	19.0	8.9	3.2	29.5	-0.3	37.6
1971	17.3	8.0	2.5	30.1	-2.1	37.8
1972	17.6	8.1	2.7	30.1	-2.0	37.1
1973	17.6	7.9	2.8	28.7	-1.1	35.6
1974	18.3	8.3	2.7	29.0	-0.4	33.6
1975	17.9	7.8	2.6	32.0	-3.4	34.7
1976	17.1	7.6	2.4	32.0	-4.2	36.2
TQ	17.7	8.4	1.8	31.8	-3.2	35.0
1977	18.0	8.0	2.8	30.8	-2.7	35.8
1978	18.0	8.2	2.7	30.2	-2.7	35.0
1979	18.5	8.7	2.6	29.5	-1.6	33.2
1980	19.0	9.0	2.4	31.3	-2.7	33.4
1981	19.6	9.4	2.0	31.5	-2.6	32.5
1982	19.2	9.2	1.5	32.8	-4.0	35.3
1983	17.5	8.4	1.1	33.3	-6.0	39.9
1984	17.3	7.8	1.5	31.6	-4.8	40.7
1985	17.7	8.1	1.5	32.5	-5.1	43.8
1986	17.5	7.9	1.4	32.5	-5.0	48.2
1987	18.4	8.4	1.8	32.0	-3.2	50.4
1988	18.2	8.0	1.9	31.6	-3.1	51.9
1989	18.4	8.3	1.9	31.5	-2.8	53.1
1990	18.0	8.1	1.6	32.5	-3.9	55.9
1991	17.8	7.9	1.7	33.5	-4.5	60.7
1992	17.5	7.6	1.6	33.4	-4.7	64.1
1993	17.5	7.7	1.8	32.4	-3.9	66.1
1994	18.0	7.8	2.0	31.8	-2.9	66.6
1995	18.4	8.0	2.1	31.6	-2.2	67.0
1996	18.8	8.5	2.2	31.0	-1.4	67.1
1997	19.2	9.0	2.2	30.1	-0.3	65.4
1998	19.9	9.6	2.2	29.5	0.8	63.2
1999	19.8	9.6	2.0	29.0	1.4	60.9
2000	20.6	10.2	2.1	28.8	2.4	57.3
2001	19.5	9.7	1.5	29.2	1.3	56.4
2002	17.6	8.1	1.4	30.4	-1.5	58.8

Fiscal Year	Federal Receipts as % of GDP (Tax Burden)	Individual Income Tax as % of GDP	Corporate Income Tax as % of GDP	Federal Expenditures as % of GDP	Surplus or Deficit as % of GDP	National Debt as % of GDP
2003	16.2	7.2	1.2	31.3	-3.4	61.6
2004	16.1	6.9	1.6	30.9	-3.5	63.0
2005	17.3	7.5	2.2	31.1	-2.6	63.6
2006	18.2	7.9	2.7	31.2	-1.9	64.0
2007	18.5	8.4	2.7	30.9	-1.2	64.6
2008	17.6	8.0	2.1	32.6	-3.2	69.7
2009	15.1	6.6	1.0	37.1	-10.1	85.2
2010	15.1	6.3	1.3	35.4	-9.0	94.2
2011	15.4	7.3	1.2	35.4	-8.7	98.7

Source: Office of Management and Budget, Historical Tables, http://www.whitehouse.gov/omb/budget/Historicals.

*TQ stands for "Transitional Quarter," which occurred between July and September of 1976, when the federal government switched from a July–July fiscal year to a September–September fiscal year.

We can see several things clearly in these figures. First, in 2009–2010 the total federal tax burden on Americans was lower than it had been since the end of World War II. This is not a trivial point, as it invalidates the implicit narrative at the heart of the Tea (Taxed Enough Already) Party's meteoric rise. According to that narrative, taxes have been going up and up for years, finally reaching a crisis point that required concerned citizens to take to the streets in protest. But this narrative is pure fiction. When Tea Party tax protests began in early 2009, the tax burden was lower than it had been in sixty years.

The data also show a strong relationship between tax cuts and deficit spending, and no relationship at all between tax cuts and spending cuts. The largest tax cuts in modern history were passed in 1981 under Ronald Reagan and in 2001 and 2003 under George W. Bush. After each tax cut, government revenues fell, but government spending did not, leading to higher deficits. Concerns about deficit spending led to large tax increases in 1982 and 1984 (Reagan), 1990 (Bush), and 1993 (Clinton). But only under Clinton did government spending as a percentage of the GDP decrease after a tax increase, leading to the only balanced budgets since 1969.

Finally, the figures show something most people already know perfectly well: that, since the recession in 2008, both deficit spending and the cumulative debt have reached near-historic proportions. The only time in modern history that the debt was higher as a proportion of the GDP was from 1948 to 1950, when the country was still paying off debt from World War II. And it is projected to go even higher. The Office of Management and Budget projects that the national debt will soar to 107.8 percent of the GDP by 2014—approaching the all-time high of 121.7 percent in 1946.

Most conservatives attribute the skyrocketing debt to Barack Obama's bailout and stimulus packages, which increased government spending dramatically. Most liberals attribute it to the Bush tax cuts of 2001 and 2003, which reduced government revenues significantly. Both are correct. Between 2008 and 2009, the federal deficit increased from 3.2 percent of the GDP to an unprecedented 10 percent. Increased expenditures and decreased tax revenues both contributed, and, as analysts across the political spectrum agree, both significant tax increases and dramatic cuts to entitlement spending will be necessary to solve the debt problem.

The economists who now support addressing the debt with a mix of tax hikes and spending cuts are hardly the tax-and-spend liberals that the Right likes to vilify. Niskanen and Bartlett were primary architects of the "Reagan Revolution," along with Martin Feldstein, Reagan's chief economic advisor, who also now advocates a mixed approach.[18] They all remain committed to supply-side economics and limited government, but they are also good at math. And the math says trying to cut enough spending to eliminate our debt would completely wreck the economy.

We have reached one of those times Alexander Hamilton foresaw in his Federalist essays: a time when it makes no economic sense to tie our own hands with a blanket opposition to taxation. The total tax burden is at a sixty-year low. Economists and analysts from across the political spectrum believe the debt crisis can only be solved with both entitlement reforms and tax increases, and, by a margin of almost two to one, the American people agree.[19] Under normal political assumptions, a modest tax increase at this point in history would have broad bipartisan support. However, as Bartlett points out, normal political assumptions no longer seem to matter. "There is no possibility that Republicans are prepared to actually legislate a tax increase," he writes. "Grover Norquist won't let them."[20]

ALEXANDER HAMILTON AND THE
NATIONAL DEBT

Most Tea Party conservatives agree on at least two points: (1) that we must reduce the runaway federal deficit and bring down the national debt; and (2) that we must not, under any circumstances, increase taxes. Deficits and taxes are bad things, they insist, and we must get rid of them both.

While it is certainly true that deficits and taxes are unpleasant, it is also true they are not the same thing; therefore, by the rules of basic logic, they cannot both be the *worst* thing. Sometimes we will have to choose between lowering one and lowering the other. For the past few years, the standard Republican talking point has been, "We don't have a revenue problem; we have a spending problem." Unless we repeal the laws of mathematics, however, this is just nonsense. Deficits occur when expenditures exceed revenues. Even if we have not yet reached the point where the debt cannot be addressed without higher taxes, it is mathematically certain that such a point exists. Why, then, would a conscientious legislator promise never to increase revenues? Alexander Hamilton could well have been describing the modern Tea Party movement when he wrote, in an article for the *National Gazette*, that "a certain description of men are for getting out of debt; yet are against all taxes for raising money to pay it off. . . . They are alike opposed to what creates debt, and to what avoids it."[21]

Hamilton, of course, understood the problem clearly. When he became America's first Treasury secretary in 1789, the national debt threatened to stifle the economy for decades. The $79 million war debt constituted about 42 percent of the nation's gross domestic product—much less than today's debt, but much more constricting at a time when the country had no standardized money supply and was chronically short of hard currency. Hamilton knew that defaulting on the debt would dry up credit completely. To become a great nation, America would have to pay its bills.

One of Hamilton's first official acts as a new cabinet member was to submit the *Report on Public Credit* to Congress, which he did in January of 1790. In this document, Hamilton attempts to educate legislators, many of whom had no experience with banking and finance. More important, though, he lays out his entire financial program—bond consolidation, assumption of state debts, a national bank, a tax on distilled spirits, and all the rest—making it clear that all his proposals form part of a single, coherent plan to address the most pressing issue of the day.

Hamilton begins his report with a strong defense of what, to him, was an obvious fact: that "exigencies are to be expected to occur, in the affairs of nations, in which there will be a necessity for borrowing."[22] This was perhaps the greatest lesson Hamilton learned from the British Empire during the American Revolution. With a highly centralized national economy, expansive taxing powers, and excellent credit, the British could assemble a formidable war machine almost instantly and sustain it almost indefinitely. Hamilton did not feel America could be either safe or prosperous without the same ability.

If the United States would sometimes have to borrow money, Hamilton reasons, it should make sure to borrow on the best terms possible—which meant it would need to establish and maintain good credit. "When the credit of a country is in any degree questionable," he writes, "it never fails to give an extravagant premium . . . upon all the loans it has occasion to make. Nor does the evil end here; the same disadvantage must be sustained upon whatever is to be bought on terms of future payment."[23]

To the chagrin of many Southern politicians, who harbored deep suspicions of banks and finance, Hamilton crafted a plan to improve America's credit over time rather than trying to pay off the debt immediately. Unlike Jefferson and the Republicans, Hamilton felt carrying a modest debt—and creating a process for making regular payments on it—would be good for the country; it would establish credit with European investors, and it would give Americans a safe place to put their money and draw reasonable interest rates. Transferrable bonds would also give Americans a government-backed currency that could facilitate economic transactions. On several occasions, Hamilton wrote that a national debt, if properly structured and financed, would become "a national blessing."[24]

The first step to turning the national debt into a national blessing was to assure creditors that they would be paid according to accepted procedures, which led to the discrimination controversy discussed in the previous chapter. Next, Hamilton had to get all the debt in one place. About a third of the national debt, $25 million, was owed by the individual states to different creditors at different terms—which meant there were thirteen different debtors whose actions could impact the credit of the whole nation. Hamilton wanted to have the federal government assume the states' war debts—which

Madison and others opposed largely because Virginia had made more progress than most states in paying back its debts, and assumption would reward less responsible states at the expense of frugal ones.

The assumption debate threatened to undo the nation in the first year of the new contitutional government. The Virginia delegation, especially, refused to move an inch toward assumption, and Hamilton did not believe his economic program could function without it. However, it was resolved by none other than Thomas Jefferson, whose discomfort with Hamilton's program had yet to crystallize into formal opposition. In June of 1790, Jefferson invited Hamilton and Madison to his home for dinner. There, the three men arrived at one of the great compromises in American history: Madison agreed not to oppose Hamilton's assumption plan, and, in return, Hamilton agreed to support locating the permanent capital of the United States at a site along the Potomac River, near Virginia, rather than in New York or Philadelphia, as most Northerners preferred.[25]

The great lesson we learn from Hamilton's first year in office is that fiscal responsibility requires political courage. Both the bond nondiscrimination plan and the assumption proposal were wildly unpopular in Hamilton's day, just as tax increases and entitlement cuts are unpopular today. In making the case for his proposals, Hamilton permanently alienated one of his closest political allies, James Madison, with whom he had collaborated to write the Federalist papers. The compromise that Hamilton helped craft worked directly against his own state's most important political agenda, which was to keep the nation's capital in New York City. For Hamilton, however, nothing was more important than placing America on solid financial footing—even if it meant moving the capital to the banks of the Potomac.

The most controversial part of Hamilton's report was a new tax. Nobody wanted new taxes, but Hamilton needed a source of revenue that could be attached to the national debt to ensure regular payment. Hamilton calculated the necessary payments at nearly $3 million a year. This sum, he argues, could be obtained "from the present duties on imports and tonnage, with the additions, which . . . may be made on wines, spirits, including those distilled within the United States."[26] Hamilton thought carefully about the first federal excise in American history. He avoided basic necessities, chose products both the medical community and the clergy had an interest in suppressing, and earmarked all funds produced by the tax to service the national debt. Even Madison, who had become the chief congressional critic of Hamilton's program, supported the tax.[27]

Despite several difficult legislative battles and the rocky reception of the distilled-spirits tax, Hamilton's overall program was a resounding success. When Hamilton left the Treasury Department in 1795, the entire national debt had been restructured, government revenues were sufficient to service the debt, and American credit was placed on solid footing. For more than two hundred years, the credit of the United States of America was equal to that of any other nation in the world—a state of affairs that lasted until August 5, 2011, when Standard & Poor's downgraded America's credit rating for the first time in history.

The cause of America's first downgrade was not the size of the debt but the volatility of the political situation. In the weeks preceding the downgrade, Republicans in Congress refused to raise the statutory debt ceiling—something that had been approved routinely under Reagan (eighteen times), Clinton (eight times), and the younger Bush (seven times). Raising the debt limit does not allow the president or Congress to authorize new expenditures; it merely allows the government to pay for expenses already incurred. By refusing to authorize an increase, congressional Republicans were signaling their willingness to allow the United States to default on its financial obligations—a decidedly un-Hamiltonian approach to American credit. Standard & Poor's responded:

> We lowered our long-term rating on the U.S. because we believe that the prolonged controversy over raising the statutory debt ceiling and the related fiscal policy debate indicate that further near-term progress containing the growth in public spending, especially on entitlements, or on reaching an agreement on raising revenues is less likely than we previously assumed and will remain a contentious and fitful process.[28]

Standard & Poor's, in other words, downgraded America's credit rating because it does not completely trust our political process to reach the compromises necessary to reduce the debt—compromises that will require both "containing the growth in public spending" *and* "reaching an agreement on raising revenues." Previously, S&P had declined to lower America's rating because it believed the Bush tax cuts would expire. But in 2011, it wrote that its new projection "now assumes that the 2001 and 2003 tax cuts, due to expire by the end of 2012, remain in place. We have [S&P has] changed our [its] assumption on this because the majority of Republicans in Congress continue to resist any measure that would raise revenues."[29]

Finally, the report makes absolutely clear that the decision to downgrade

America's credit was influenced by the statements from members of the Tea Party Caucus, which openly threatened to allow a default if their demands for spending cuts, with no tax increases, were not met. "The political brinksmanship of recent months," S&P writes, "highlights what [S&P sees] as America's governance and policymaking becoming less stable, less effective, and less predictable than what [S&P] previously believed. The statutory debt ceiling and the threat of default have become political bargaining chips in the debate over fiscal policy."[30]

This is as direct a statement as S&P could have made against the arrogant, irresponsible way that the once-uncontroversial debt-ceiling issue was turned into a hostage situation by a group of legislators determined to press one way of addressing the debt (entitlement cuts) while steadfastly refusing to consider the other (tax increases). Soon after the S&P report came out, House Majority Whip Eric Cantor issued a memo to his Republican caucus, telling them, "There will be pressure to compromise on tax increases. We will be told that there is no other way forward. I respectfully disagree."[31]

Cantor got it wrong. It is not political pressure that motivates those who want to increase revenues to prevent default; it is moral pressure, the obligation to do one's job well even if it means taking unpopular positions. Political pressure will always be against raising taxes—especially for Republicans who have signed the badly named Taxpayer Protection Pledge. In exactly the same way, major entitlement reform will remain politically unpalatable to Democrats for a very long time. There is simply no way America will be able to reduce its national debt until members of both political parties follow Hamilton's lead and place fiscal responsibility ahead of political expedience—or even political survival.

When Hamilton was confronted with a stifling debt and a recalcitrant Congress, he put all his political capital on the line and led his contemporaries to two important conclusions: first, that America should protect its good credit, and second, that the political decision to pay off a significant debt includes a commitment to new revenues. To secure these objectives, Hamilton risked everything. He championed two deeply unpopular fiscal measures (bond consolidation and debt assumption), provoked an armed rebellion over the tax on distilled spirits, and earned the eternal enmity of the eighteenth century's great antitax champion, Thomas Jefferson. In return, he, with the tireless support of President George Washington, set America on the fast track to economic prosperity.

The violence to Hamilton's intentions currently being inflicted in the name of "the Founding Fathers" is both real and consequential. There is an increasingly good chance that "constitutional conservatives" will destroy Hamilton's greatest achievement, the good credit of the United States, by ignoring one of his most important pieces of advice: never rule out the possibility of new taxes.

CHAPTER 8

COURTING DISASTER: THE DUMB RIGHT-WING ATTACK ON THE FEDERAL JUDICIARY

> Most importantly, the framers did not intend to grant general authority to the judiciary to rule on the constitutionality of legislative acts.
> —Mark Levin, *Men in Black*

> The complete independence of the courts of justice is peculiarly essential in a limited Constitution. By a limited Constitution, I understand one which contains certain specified exceptions to the legislative authority. . . . Limitations of this kind can be preserved in practice no other way than through the medium of courts of justice, whose duty it must be to declare all acts contrary to the manifest tenor of the Constitution void.
> —Alexander Hamilton, *Federalist* no. 78

In his quest for the 2012 Republican presidential nomination, Newt Gingrich declared war on the federal judiciary. As president, he told reporters, he would refuse to enforce Supreme Court decisions he disagreed with, he would impeach federal judges for the content of their decisions, and he would send federal marshals to arrest judges and force them to explain their decisions before Congress. "Are we forced for a lifetime to keep someone on the bench who is so radically anti-American that they are a threat to the fabric of the country?" Gingrich asked reporters on December 17, 2011.[1] When asked to name such a judge, Gingrich pointed to Texas judge Fred Biery, who in

June 2011 issued a ruling against public prayers at high school graduations that was overturned almost immediately on appeal.[2]

The reaction came quickly—and not just from the Left. Conservative firebrand Ann Coulter called the idea of subpoenaing judges "outrageous," and Bill O'Reilly of Fox News labeled it "frightening."[3] Bert Brandenberg, director of the nonpartisan Justice at Stake campaign, called it a "constitutional disaster." One by one, establishment Republicans and serious constitutional conservatives lined up against the former House Speaker on this issue; they understood very well that the fight he wanted to pick was both bad politics and bad history.

Nobody need think that Gingrich was speaking from deeply held convictions. He may or may not actually believe a president has the right to haul Supreme Court justices before Congress in chains, but he clearly understood that to have a chance at the nomination, he had to lock in the support of at least one major Republican constituency. Both fiscal conservatives and the Christian Right were spoken for, leaving angry paleoconservatives as his best bet. And there is nothing angry paleoconservatives hate more than the Supreme Court. As they see it, the court is a self-appointed cabal of liberal activists who delight in subverting the Constitution. The subtitle of Mark Levin's 2005 book *Men in Black* says it all: "How the Supreme Court Is Destroying America."

In the collective understanding of the extreme Right, the Supreme Court has been destroying America for quite some time. The court's long crusade against all things holy got underway in 1793 with the *Chisholm v. Georgia* decision, which ruled that the State of Georgia could be sued in federal court by a citizen of another state. The public outrage over *Chisholm v. Georgia* led to the ratification of the Eleventh Amendment, which took from the court the power to hear lawsuits against an individual state without that state's consent. Since then, things have just gotten worse as the court has kicked God out of schools, set murderers free on technicalities, and walked in lockstep with the liberal statist agenda to turn America into a fascist state.

Politicians have been complaining about Supreme Court decisions for more than two hundred years. President Obama channeled the spirits of Thomas Jefferson and Andrew Jackson in his 2010 State of the Union address when he publicly castigated the court's conservative majority for its *Citizens United v. Federal Election Commission* decision, which allows unlimited political spending by corporations and unions. "With all due deference to separation of powers," Obama said, "last week the Supreme Court reversed a century of law that I believe will open the floodgates for special interests—including foreign corporations—to spend without limit in our elections. I don't think American elections should be bankrolled by America's most powerful interests, or worse, by foreign entities. They should be decided by the American people."[4]

What Obama did not do, however, is flatly refuse to enforce the Citizens United decision in the way Gingrich suggests a president should. Presidents have been criticizing Supreme Court decisions for many years, but, generally, their opposition has been political rather than constitutional. This has not always been the case; some early presidents—Thomas Jefferson and Andrew Jackson, to name two—despised judicial interference so much that they simply refused to enforce Supreme Court decisions they disagreed with. According to legend, Jackson once greeted one of the Marshall Court's decisions in favor of American Indians with the retort, "John Marshall has made his decision; now let him enforce it!"

Fortunately for the rule of law, no president has taken such a position since the end of the Civil War. If they had, the courts would have had very few courses of action available to them. The Framers intentionally created the judiciary to be, in Alexander Hamilton's words, "beyond comparison the weakest of the three departments of power."[5] Gingrich and others often quote this line as proof that the Framers did not mean to give the courts the authority to overturn legislative actions. "None of the Founding Fathers," writes Gingrich in a recent book, "expected the courts ever to have the arrogance to reach into the legislative and executive branches and begin writing law and redefining America. In fact, the Founding Fathers believed the judicial branch was the weakest branch."[6]

But this is not what Hamilton meant. By "weakest," he was talking not about constitutional authority but about coercive power. Unlike the legislature, which controls the purse strings, or the executive, which controls the military, the judicial branch of government cannot compel anybody to follow its dictates:

> The Executive not only dispenses the honors, but holds the sword of the community. The legislature not only commands the purse, but prescribes the rules by which the duties and rights of every citizen are to be regulated. The judiciary, on the contrary, has no influence over either the sword or the

purse; no direction either of the strength or of the wealth of the society; and can take no active resolution whatever. It may truly be said to have neither FORCE nor WILL, but merely judgment; and must ultimately depend upon the aid of the executive arm even for the efficacy of its judgments.[7]

As Hamilton so clearly understood, the Supreme Court has authority but very little power. Consider, for example, the way public schools were desegregated in the 1950s and 1960s. In theory, American schools were desegregated by the Supreme Court's *Brown v. Board of Education* decision in 1954. In practice, desegregation required substantial executive effort. In Little Rock, Arkansas, President Eisenhower had to federalize the Arkansas National Guard and send in the 101st Airborne to escort nine black students to a city high school. The Supreme Court had the constitutional authority to declare school segregation unconstitutional, but it had no power to enforce its decision. This is what Hamilton means by "the weakest branch."

The Supreme Court has a great deal of power today, but only because the other branches of government—and the majority of the American people—recognize it as the legitimate final authority on what the Constitution means. This does not mean most people agree with the court's decisions all or even most of the time. Most people who follow the Supreme Court can rattle off a pretty long list of decisions they disagree with. Modern liberals loathe the Citizens United decision, for example, while most contemporary conservatives detest the 2005 *Kelo v. City of New London* decision, which expanded the right of local jurisdictions to exercise eminent domain to seize private property. And both sides can point to many other decisions they similarly despise.

Most Americans, however, ultimately respect the process by which an independent federal judiciary determines the constitutionality of state and federal legislation. We grump and growl when things don't go our way, but we don't really think the country would be well served by turning judges into pawns of the other branches of government. For the extreme right wing, however, this is not the case. Newt Gingrich and Mark Levin are prominent examples of modern extremists who regularly seek to undermine the independence of the judiciary and strip from it the authority to interpret the Constitution. Predictably, they want to do so in the name of "honoring the intentions of the Founding Fathers." And, just as predictably, they get almost everything the Founders said completely wrong.

WHY THE JUDICIARY MUST REMAIN INDEPENDENT

The judiciary has always been a target for political frustration because it is the only branch of government that can't be voted out of office. Congress can change hands every two years, presidents can be dumped every four years, but Supreme Court justices serve for life. This is not to say that justices are not political; nobody who has ever watched a judicial confirmation hearing could believe that. But they are not subject to the immediate political pressures that drive the other two branches. Supreme Court justices often sit for thirty years or more, ensuring that the political perspectives of previous electorates retain some hold on the government today. No matter how much we might want to, we can't quite change everything by throwing a national hissy fit. And this is precisely how the system was designed to work.

Most of the delegates to the Federal Convention, while committed to the republican principle, were nonetheless suspicious of too much democracy. They did not want to give people the ability to undo their society completely in a moment of collective pique, so they built in safeguards against runaway populism. Three of the most important of these safeguards were the indirect election of senators, the selection of the president by the Electoral College, and the independence of the federal judiciary.

The first two of these safeguards are no longer in place. The Seventeenth Amendment changed the Constitution to require direct election of senators, and, since the mid-nineteenth century, all states have used popular-vote tallies as the basis for assigning presidential electors. These have been welcome adjustments to the Constitution. The indirect selection of senators and presidents relied on a notion of natural aristocracy that, while held by many of the Founders, no longer makes sense today. But we would be foolish to ignore all the Framers' advice about slowing the pace of change. As Madison wrote in *Federalist* no. 63,

> there are particular moments in public affairs when the people, stimulated by some irregular passion, or some illicit advantage, or misled by the artful misrepresentations of interested men, may call for measures which they themselves will afterwards be the most ready to lament and condemn. In these critical moments, how salutary will be the interference of some temperate and respectable body of citizens, in order to check the misguided

career, and to suspend the blow meditated by the people against themselves, until reason, justice, and truth can regain their authority over the
public mind?[8]

The judiciary is now the only part of government capable of checking the
power of an enthusiastic majority. A single party can capture both of the
other branches of government very quickly; this happened between 2006 and
2008, when the House, the Senate, and the presidency went from Republican
to Democratic control over the course of two elections. But this cannot
happen with the Supreme Court, where justices serve for life. Consequently,
Barack Obama started his presidency with a Democratic House and a filibuster-
proof majority in the Senate but, with only two of the nine Supreme Court
justices having been nominated by a fellow Democratic president, a judicial
minority that could not prevent the Citizens United decision Democrats so
despise.

The appointment of judges "during good behavior" to an indefinite term
of office is the constitutional mechanism designed to ensure the independence of the judiciary. In *Federalist* no. 78 (see appendix E), Hamilton praises
the term of judicial appointment for life as "one of the most valuable of the
modern improvements in the practice of government" and as "the best expedient which can be devised in any government, to secure a steady, upright,
and impartial administration of the laws."[9] One of the most disturbing and
constitutionally untenable proposals to come from the Far Right in recent
years, then, has been the suggestion that Supreme Court justices and other
federal judges should be removed from office for the content of their judicial
decisions. Levin, for example, insists—without a shred of textual evidence—
that "the framers intended impeachment to be a practical limitation of the
scope of judicial conduct." He asserts that "knowingly doing harm to the
Constitution, in my view, is not the sort of 'good behavior' the framers envi-
sioned justifying continuance in office."[10]

Levin plays a dangerous game here by trying to attach the term "good
behavior" to the decisions a judge reaches in his or her official capacity—
precisely the definition the Constitution rejects. This is not what the Framers
meant by the term. It does not reflect the eighteenth-century understanding
of a "good behavior" appointment, nor has it ever been accepted by subsequent policy makers in any of the three branches of government. By making
such a suggestion, Levin seriously damages his claim that he is an "origi-

nalist" in his interpretation of the Constitution, as does Newt Gingrich when he writes,

> Americans can also insist that judges who consistently ignore the Constitution and the legitimate powers of the other two coequal branches of the federal government fall short of the constitution's "good behavior" clause. Thus the Ninth Circuit judges who found the words "one nation under God" unconstitutional could be considered unfit to serve and be impeached.[11]

This is just plain wrong. The Constitution tells us exactly what it means by "good behavior" and by its opposite. In Article II, Section 4, the Constitution stipulates that civil officers of the United States "shall be removed from Office on Impeachment for, and Conviction of, Treason, Bribery, or other high Crimes and Misdemeanors." Period. This sets the bar for impeachment very high. To qualify, a judge or other official must be guilty of an actual, indictable crime; there is no other rational way to read the text.

At the Pennsylvania ratifying convention, the issue of impeaching judges for judging actually did come up. When James Wilson, one of the most active delegates at the convention on judicial issues, explained how judicial review would work, somebody shouted out that any judge who ruled a legislative act unconstitutional would be impeached. The suggestion that "judges [would] be impeached, because they decide an act null and void," Wilson responded, "was made in defiance of the Constitution! What house of representatives would dare to impeach, or senate to commit judges for the performance of their duty?"[12]

When politicians are on the stump, they can fire up the base by pledging to get rid of judges who are destroying the Constitution. But, of course, everyone says the other side is destroying the Constitution. And almost all judges, whatever their political dispositions, honestly believe they are interpreting the supreme law of the land to the best of their abilities. Determining who should be impeached for their opinions—rather than for their crimes—requires a purely political judgment that can only end with the subordination of the judiciary to one of the other branches of government. There is not a word or phrase in the Constitution that would even begin to support such a baldly political transfer of power from one branch to another. Exactly none of the Constitution's Framers supported the use of impeachment as a political tool.

One of the Founding Fathers who was not a Framer, however, did see judicial impeachment the way Gingrich and Levin do. In 1800, Thomas Jefferson came into the presidency with commanding majorities in both houses of Congress—only to find the Federalists had stacked the judiciary with enough judges to control it for the next twenty years. Jeffersonian Republicans immediately set out to diminish the influence of the courts. They eliminated judgeships, refused to implement judicial orders, and, on two occasions, resorted to the ultimate weapon of impeachment. In the process, they helped to define the scope of judicial power for the next two centuries.

The first judge to be impeached was John Pickering of the United States District Court in New Hampshire. Pickering was a dedicated Federalist and a determined opponent of Jefferson's politics. He was also mentally insane, an alcoholic, and a perpetual no-show on the bench. In 1803, the Republicans finally decided to impeach him. The impeachment trial focused entirely on his alcoholism and dereliction of duty, though everybody knew there was a political subtext, as Pickering had issued several decisions unfriendly to the Republicans. He was convicted by the Senate on a straight party-line vote of nineteen to seven, above the two-thirds majority required by the Constitution to impeach an official of the United States. With the Pickering case, Jefferson and the Republicans established that they were willing and able to use their political power to get rid of judges who opposed them.[13]

The second impeachment trial, however, did not go as well for Jefferson. Under Chief Justice John Marshall, the Supreme Court began to exercise more power than Jefferson felt it should. The most vulnerable of the Federalist justices was Samuel Chase, who frequently harangued Republicans from the bench and was not above issuing questionable rulings to make sure they lost in court (at this time, Supreme Court justices also served as trial judges in other jurisdictions). When Chase publicly criticized Jefferson in his instructions to a grand jury in Baltimore, the president felt he had endured enough. He worked behind the scenes to initiate impeachment proceedings against Chase, which the House of Representatives began in 1804.

It was the first great show trial in American history, and Jefferson lost big. It did not help that the presiding officer, Vice President Aaron Burr, had become one of Jefferson's most dangerous enemies (nor did it help that Burr had recently been indicted for murder in two states for killing Alexander Hamilton in a duel). But the star witness was Chase himself, who argued that, according to the Constitution, he could be impeached "only if he were

found guilty of an indictable offense within the strictures of criminal law."
He then proceeded to show a far greater command of both criminal and constitutional law than any of his accusers.[14] Each of the eight articles of
impeachment failed, one of them unanimously. Republicans controlled a
supermajority in the Senate and would have won any political vote. In the
end, however, Jefferson's own party refused to use a constitutional remedy
to solve a political problem.

Samuel Chase was acquitted of "high crimes and misdemeanors" on
March 1, 1805. No Supreme Court justice has been impeached since. Thirteen federal judges have been impeached since 1805, all of them charged
with actual criminal misconduct. In his book *Grand Inquests*, the late Chief
Justice William H. Rehnquist dates the meaningful independence of the federal judiciary to the Chase verdict:

> The acquittal of Samuel Chase by the Senate had a profound effect on the
> American Judiciary. First, it assured the independence of federal judges
> from congressional oversight of the decisions they made in the cases that
> came before them. Second, by assuring that impeachment would not be used
> in the future as a method to remove members of the Supreme Court for their
> judicial opinions, it helped to safeguard the independence of that body.[15]

World history gives us a number of examples—none of them good—of
what happens when the judiciary loses its independence. This was certainly
the case in post-Revolution France, when the Revolutionary Tribunal became
the primary instrument of mobocracy during the Reign of Terror. It was also
true in most Communist countries during the Cold War, where judges acted
as an enforcement arm of the Communist Party, and it remains true in today's
most violent and oppressive dictatorships. Without a doubt, Americans must
sometimes endure inconveniences and errors because our judges do not have
to answer to any nonjudicial authority. But this pales in comparison to what
we would have to endure if they did.

MARK LEVIN V. THE FRAMERS ON JUDICIAL REVIEW

Mark Levin is no fan of judicial review, the power by which the Supreme Court and other federal courts rule on the constitutionality of state and federal laws. Unlike most conservatives—who merely disagree with how the court has used judicial review in recent years—Levin disapproves of the Supreme Court having such power at all and insists that "the framers did not intend to grant general authority to the judiciary to rule on the constitutionality of legislative acts."[16] Such an attack on the principle of judicial review fits nicely into the right wing's current political agenda, but it does not fit the historical facts.

Most textbooks trace the concept of judicial review back to the Supreme Court's *Marbury v. Madison* decision in 1803, generally and justly considered one of the most important cases in the court's history. The plaintiff, William Marbury, was appointed to a minor judicial position (a part-time justice of the peace in the District of Columbia) in the waning hours of John Adams's presidential term and then prohibited from taking office when Jefferson stopped the outgoing mail in the Capitol. Ostensibly, the case was about whether the court could force Jefferson—and, by extension, his secretary of state, James Madison—to acknowledge Marbury's appointment and allow him to take his job. What was really at stake, though, was the right to interpret the Constitution.

Jefferson and the Republicans argued that each of the three branches of government had equal power to determine the meaning of the Constitution within its own sphere of authority. Under Jefferson's interpretation of the Constitution, a judicial appointment was not official until the notification letter was sent, so, by stopping the mail, he felt he had prevented the appointment. The Federalists begged to differ. Chief Justice John Marshall believed the Constitution itself gave the courts the exclusive right to determine the constitutionality of a legislative or executive action. Though the docket said "*Marbury v. Madison*," everybody understood it was really Marshall versus Jefferson.

Conventional wisdom held that Jefferson could not lose. Either Marshall would rule in favor of Jefferson and acknowledge the right of each branch to interpret the Constitution for itself, or, more likely, he would rule in favor of Marbury, and Jefferson would refuse to carry out the order. If the latter occurred, the power of the judiciary would be broken, and Jefferson would establish forever that the president could ignore the Supreme Court with impunity. Had either result actually occurred, America would have become a very different country than it is today.

But John Marshall won one of the greatest political battles in history by refusing to give Jefferson anything to fight against. He ruled that Marbury had a right to the position but that the Supreme Court could not enforce that right because the Judiciary Act, under which Marbury sued, was itself unconstitutional. This delivered a crushing blow to Jefferson without giving him any possible way to fight back. Though Jefferson was itching for a fight and would certainly have won any conflict with the Supreme Court, there was nothing in the decision he could attack. Technically, Jefferson won the case, but Marshall established the right of judicial review for all subsequent Supreme Court justices.

According to right-wing mythology, the *Marbury v. Madison* decision was an unconscionable power grab by Marshall and the Supreme Court. Mark Levin calls it "the counter-revolution of 1803" and contends that it patently reversed the Framers' original intent:

> Marshall's Federalist Party had lost the presidency and Congress, but Marshall was determined to fight back. And so the doctrine of judicial review was born. Yes, the Constitution is indeed the supreme law of the land. But now the court, by its own fiat, would decide what is or is not constitutional. The Constitution's structure, including the balance of power between the three branches, was now broken.[17]

This is a serious mischaracterization of history. *Marbury v. Madison* is the Supreme Court's most important decision not because it *created* judicial review but because it *settled the argument over* judicial review that had been going on since the creation of the Constitution. The Federalist Founding Fathers—George Washington, John Adams, Alexander Hamilton, and, for the most part, James Madison—had always believed the Constitution provided the judiciary with the exclusive power to void unconstitutional laws. The Anti-Federalists felt this power was too dangerous, and they opposed it vociferously. And Jefferson believed, as we have already seen, that the Constitution allowed each branch of government to interpret the Constitution for itself.[18]

Jefferson, like Levin, held that the power of judicial review was not mentioned specifically in the Constitution. This is absolutely true, but it does not invalidate the procedure. Unlike Article I, which enumerates a detailed collection of powers assigned to the legislative branch of government, Article II (the executive) and Article III (the judiciary) enumerate very few of the powers associated with either the presidency or the Supreme Court. Article II simply invests the president with "the executive power," and Article III grants the court "the judicial power," assuming a general understanding of the meaning of those terms. If the term *judicial power* as it was understood in the eighteenth century included the power to void unconstitutional laws, then attributing this power to the Supreme Court follows inevitably from a close reading of the text. On the other hand, if Marshall really did invent the power of judicial review on the spot in 1803, then Levin is right, and we have a big problem.

But, of course, Marshall did no such thing. Judicial review has always existed in America. In colonial times, British judges regularly voided laws they held to be in violation of the laws of England. Between 1776 and 1789, judges in the various states continued to strike down laws that, in their opinion, violated the state constitutions. The Framers of the Constitution were well acquainted with the practice of judicial review, and their conversations in the convention about the judiciary clearly assumed it would continue under the new Constitution much as it always had.

In his original Virginia Plan, Madison proposed a much stronger role for the judiciary than one confined to judicial review. He wanted to make the federal judiciary a partner with the president in determining which legislation to approve and which to veto. This would have given the Supreme Court the power to reject legislation for any reason at all.[19] Levin seizes on this proposal—and the convention's rejection of it—as proof that the delegates had the opportunity to give the courts the power to strike down laws and chose not to. "In the final analysis," he writes, "if the framers had wanted to empower the judiciary with a legislative veto, they could have done so. They did not."[20] But this is not how the debate actually played out. The judicial negative was brought forward several times during the convention; when it was, nearly all the floor speakers—both those in favor of the resolution and those opposed to it—assumed the judiciary would already have the ability to strike down laws on constitutional grounds. The debate concerned whether to give it a second veto on substantive grounds.

The first debate over the judicial veto occurred on June 4. Elbridge Gerry opposed the resolution right out of the gate, arguing that the judiciary already had a significant check on the legislature through judicial review and did not need another. According to Madison's own record of the convention,

> Mr. Gerry doubts whether the Judiciary ought to form a part of it [the Council of Revision], as they will have a sufficient check ag[ainst] encroachments on their own department by their exposition of the laws, which involved a power of deciding on their Constitutionality. In some states the Judges had actually set aside laws as being ag[ainst] the Constitution. This was done too with general approbation.[21]

With Gerry in the lead, the convention voted eight states to two to give the veto solely to the executive, without judicial participation. Madison brought the issue up again two days later, but it was again defeated, this time by a margin of seven to three. But Madison was persistent and brought it up again on July 21 and once more on August 15.

In the July 21 debate, the judicial veto was reintroduced by James Wilson of Pennsylvania, whom Washington would later appoint as one of the original six justices of the Supreme Court. Wilson argued that the veto was necessary even though the courts would have the power to declare laws unconstitutional:

> The Judiciary ought to have an opportunity of remonstrating ag[ainst] projected encroachments on the people as well as on themselves. It had been said that the Judges, as expositors of the Laws, would have an opportunity of defending their constitutional rights. . . . But this power of the Judges did not go far enough. Laws may be unjust, may be unwise, may be dangerous, may be destructive; and yet may not be so unconstitutional as to justify the Judges in refusing to give them effect.[22]

In this opinion, Wilson was opposed by the fervent antinationalist Luther Martin, who argued that

> a knowledge of Mankind, and of Legislative affairs cannot be presumed to belong in a higher [degree] to the Judges than to the Legislature. And as to the Constitutionality of laws, that point will come before the Judges in their official character. In this character, they have a negative on the laws. Join them with the Executive in the Revision and they will have a double negative.[23]

George Mason of Virginia responded to Martin that the power to set aside an unconstitutional law was not a sufficient check on the legislature:

> It has been said . . . that if the Judges were joined in this check on the laws, they would have a double negative. . . . He [Mason] would reply that in this capacity they could impede in one case only, the operation of laws. They could declare an unconstitutional law void. But with regard to every law however unjust oppressive or pernicious, which did not come plainly under this description, they would be under the necessity as judges to give it a free course.[24]

The judicial veto was defeated every time it was introduced. But both its supporters and its opponents acknowledged that it was something different from the normal power of judicial review. The record of the Federal Convention simply does not support Levin's assertion that "the framers did not intend to grant general authority to the judiciary to rule on the constitutionality of legislative acts." It would be more accurate to say that the Framers did not specifically enumerate the power of judicial review because it was already included in *judicial powers* as they understood that term.

The argument for judicial review becomes even stronger when we look at the state ratifying conventions, as Saikrishna Prakash and John C. Yoo do in their seminal 2003 article, "The Origins of Judicial Review." "In at least seven state ratifying conventions," they write, "leading delegates openly declared that the Constitution authorized judicial review of federal legislation. In none of these conventions did anyone deny that the courts could refuse to enforce unconstitutional federal statutes. Nor did anyone ever admit that they were unfamiliar with or unaware of judicial review."[25] In the Connecticut convention, for example, Oliver Ellsworth (a convention delegate himself) specifically attached judicial review to the Constitution's delegation of *judicial power* to the federal judiciary:

> This Constitution defines the extent of the powers of the general government. If the general legislature should at any time overleap their limits, the judicial department is a constitutional check. If the United States go beyond their powers, if they make a law which the Constitution does not authorize, it is void; and the judicial power, the national judges, who to secure their impartiality are to be made independent, will declare it to be void.[26]

During the ratification debate, Anti-Federalists and Federalists alike assumed the courts would have the power of judicial review. This was one of the major attacks on the Constitution by Robert Yates ("Brutus") during the New York debates. Yates (who had also been a delegate to the convention) felt the unelected judiciary would come to exercise dictatorial power because "there is no power provided in the constitution, that can correct their errors, or controul their adjudications."[27] Quite tellingly, Mark Levin's attack on judicial review quotes four long passages from "Brutus" and only one brief passage from Hamilton's response in *Federalist* no. 78, which lays out clearly the power the Constitution gives to the Supreme Court to rule on the constitutionality of legislative actions. In a passage Levin ignores, Hamilton writes,

> The interpretation of the laws is the proper and peculiar province of the courts. A constitution is, in fact, and must be regarded by the judges, as a fundamental law. It therefore belongs to them to ascertain its meaning, as well as the meaning of any particular act proceeding from the legislative body. If there should happen to be an irreconcilable variance between the two, that which has the superior obligation and validity ought, of course, to be preferred; or, in other words, the Constitution ought to be preferred to the statute.[28]

During the Federal Convention and the state ratification debates, judicial review was clearly seen as part of the *judicial power* the Constitution conveyed to the judicial branch of government. For some, this was a good thing, and for others, it was a bad thing; but it was a thing everybody acknowledged. After the Constitution was ratified, judicial review formed a normal and uncontroversial part of the judiciary's job description. A federal court declared an act of Congress unconstitutional in 1792, and the Supreme Court first reviewed the constitutionality of a federal law (which they ruled in favor of) in their 1796 *Hylton v. United States* decision. At the time, nobody claimed the courts lacked the power of judicial review.

It was not until Thomas Jefferson became president that the constitutionality of judicial review was subject to dispute. Jefferson was a committed Republican who believed all elected officials should be accountable to the people. Appointed judgeships offended his political sensibilities—especially when they were appointed by his political enemies. The *Marbury v. Madison* decision did not enact a revolution; it prevented one. And John Marshall did not create the power of judicial review; he preserved it from an attack by a popular president determined to neutralize the court's effectiveness as a political opponent.

CONCLUSION

An old saying holds that the Supreme Court is not last because it is right; it is right because it is last. And that's about the size of it. Somebody has to go last. The rule of law requires that we be governed by knowable, settled interpretations of our most important legal document. Somebody, therefore, has to have the final responsibility for saying what the Constitution means. Where law is concerned, even an incorrect interpretation is better than a moving target.

Most of the Framers took it for granted that the federal judiciary would make the final ruling on a law's constitutionality. Jefferson disagreed, but he failed to offer a plausible alternative. His proposal to allow each branch of government to determine what the Constitution means within its own sphere of operation could not have worked. Just imagine what would happen if Congress and all the executive officers in the country (e.g., police officers, governors, FBI agents) believed that guns should be heavily regulated and that the Constitution did not prevent this, while all the judges in the country believed the right to bear arms was sacrosanct. Every day, thousands of gun owners would be arrested for possessing guns, booked into jail, charged, and then set free by judges who did not believe gun control laws were constitutional. Somebody has to have the power to render a final judgment. In the American constitutional system, that responsibility falls to the judicial branch.

Does this mean that judges never make bad decisions? Of course not. Any group or individual with the ultimate responsibility for interpreting the Constitution will make mistakes. Had this power been granted to the legislature or the president, constitutional decisions would be subject to much greater political pressure—and therefore much more manipulation—than they are today. Ultimate interpretive authority over the Constitution is a tremendous responsibility. Wherever it resides, it will present dangers and possibilities for abuse, but it has to reside somewhere. In the American system, it resides with an independent judiciary, where, not without problems, it has protected the Constitution for more than two hundred years. And during all this time, the courts have been continually attacked by extremists who would destroy the independent judiciary for the sake of their own agendas.

The right wing's antijudicial rhetoric assumes constitutional interpretation is easy—something anybody with a high-school degree and a few simple decision rules could undertake in his or her spare time. This assumption is not entirely incorrect. The vast majority of cases before American courts do not involve difficult constitutional issues. Precisely because they are not difficult, these cases never come before the federal judiciary.

The small fraction of cases that do come before federal judges—and the fraction of those that come before the Supreme Court—do so precisely because they are not easy. They require a delicate balancing act among competing constitutional claims and a profound understanding of history and law. Levin's assumption that Left-leaning justices like Stephen Breyer and Ruth Bader Ginsburg are sitting in their offices actively plotting ways to destroy the Constitution is both offensive and silly. Like their more conservative colleagues, these are honorable, knowledgeable public servants who revere the Constitution and have spent their professional lives studying it. When the Supreme Court issues a ruling—even one we disagree with profoundly—we owe some level of deference to the justices' expertise and to the process they represent.

What is really at stake in the antijudicial rhetoric of people like Newt Gingrich and Mark Levin is the right to treat a political disagreement as a moral failure. If the Constitution really does give the Supreme Court the final authority to interpret its meaning—as George Washington, John Adams, Alexander Hamilton, and nearly all the delegates to the Federal Convention believed—then the worst that can be said about a court decision is that it is wrong. If the Constitution does indeed authorize a procedure for its own interpretation, then, by definition, no Supreme Court decision can be unconstitutional. However, if Thomas Jefferson is correct, and the *judicial power* delegated to the Supreme Court really does not include judicial review, then anybody's interpretation of the Constitution is as valid as anybody else's. Presidents are free to ignore judicial decisions they don't like, and legislators are free to impeach judges for the "high crime" of disagreeing with them.

Fortunately, Jefferson's opinion remains as much in the minority among constitutionalists today as it was among his fellow Founding Fathers. Jefferson never reconciled himself to the outcome of *Marbury v. Madison*, but the decision was widely praised by both Federalists and moderate Republicans. Even the ultra-Republican Philadelphia *Aurora* acknowledged that Marshall "calmed the tumult of faction" and stood "a star of the first magnitude."[29] Most of the living Framers praised the ruling, and even James Madison, who suffered a political defeat with the decision, later acknowledged that judicial review "must be admitted to be a vital part of the system."[30]

Unlike most Communist nations and third-world dictatorships, the United States does not punish judges for the decisions they make in their official capacity as decision makers. Sometimes that means we really, really disagree with the Supreme Court. Occasionally, we may even amend the Constitution to reverse its decisions, as Americans did in 1795, with the ratification of the Eleventh Amendment in order to overturn *Chisholm v. Georgia*. As we have seen throughout our history as a nation, however, the benefits of an independent judiciary far outweigh its costs. Though we may disagree with their judgments, we must still respect the right of judges to judge. That is part of what it means to live under the rule of law.

CHAPTER 9

WHY AMERICA, THE CONSTITUTION, AND GOD WILL (PROBABLY) SURVIVE

I'm tired of people putting down this country. I'm tired of people pretending that this is still pre-slavery, pre-segregation, pre-internment. . . . I'm sick and tired of people ignoring the enormous progress we've made in this country. . . . Stop putting down my country.
—Mark Levin, February 23, 2008

Federalism is dead. The Constitution . . . is in its last death throes. And we are living in a soft tyranny.
—Mark Levin, August 2, 2010

In February 2008, future First Lady Michelle Obama caused a small firestorm when she said in a televised interview, "For the first time in my adult lifetime, I'm really proud of my country."[1] The reaction from the Right was swift and merciless. She was portrayed as an angry leftist, an ungrateful child of privilege, and an unregenerate America hater. Nobody rang this bell more loudly than Mark Levin, who took to the airwaves in high dudgeon and shouted, "I'm tired people putting down this country. I'm tired of people pretending that this is still pre-slavery, pre-segregation, pre-internment. That we're in a depression. I'm sick and tired of people ignoring the enormous progress we've made in this country. . . Stop putting down my country."[2]

From his merciless pounding of Mrs. Obama, one might suspect that Mark Levin doesn't like people criticizing America. One would be wrong. Mark Levin doesn't like liberals criticizing America. Conservatives, on the other hand, and especially conservatives named Mark Levin, can criticize their country as viciously as they please. They can rant for hours about the

171

awful place their country has become. They can call present-day America a "failed state," a "fascist dictatorship," and a "soft tyranny"—just as long as they blame everything on the liberals.

With the election of Barack Obama in 2008, the baldly anti-American rhetoric from the "patriotic" right wing intensified to become one of the great political ironies of the modern age. The day of Obama's election, Glenn Beck let it be known that the "Constitution was hanging by a thread."[3] Rush Limbaugh later accused the American people of voting for "torture . . . tyranny . . . dictatorship" when they voted for Obama.[4] Mark Levin himself, in his most recent bestseller, *Ameritopia: The Unmaking of America*, makes it very clear that America has been damaged goods for longer than most Americans have been alive.[5]

As Levin sees it, America has not been America for nearly a hundred years and has been fundamentally broken for nearly eighty. In the "real" America—the one the Founding Fathers supposedly created—the federal government was a bit player in American life. More power resided with the states, but even that was quite limited. Nobody had utopian dreams of an equal society, but everybody was free. And government knew its place. Since the beginning of the nineteenth century, "the federal government has become unmoored from its origins," and, "as a result, America today is not strictly a constitutional republic." We are a post-constitutional, democratic utopia, existing "behind a Potemkin-like image of constitutional republicanism."[6]

For Levin, Beck, and others, the primary architect of "America's unmaking" was Woodrow Wilson, who, as president from 1913 to 1921, unleashed Progressivism upon an unsuspecting nation. Wilson's parade of horribles includes income tax, the direct election of senators, child labor laws, woman suffrage, and Prohibition. Levin argues that as an academic, and later as a president, Wilson "sought to supplant the basic character of American society and the nation's founding with a supreme central government."[7]

Wilson's treachery became a fait accompli with the ascension of Franklin D. Roosevelt, who destroyed the last vestiges of limited government. "Whereas the Founders broke from tyranny," Levin proclaims, "Roosevelt broke from the Founders." By the end of Roosevelt's time in office, the presidency had become the seat of benevolent dictatorship, and Roosevelt himself was the author of a new Constitution that was "eerily similar in certain significant respects to the former Soviet Union's list of Fundamental Rights."[8] Beck agrees with Levin's assessment of both presidents. In *Arguing with Idiots*, in a fanciful list of the "Top Ten Bastards of All Time," Beck ranks Woodrow Wilson as number one and Franklin Roosevelt as number three—with Adolf Hitler coming in at number six.[9]

This sort of historical revisionism has consequences. It portrays nearly half of our nation's history as a long decline now reaching its nadir. And it idolizes the America of the late nineteenth and early twentieth centuries—a nation of massive income disparities, oppressive monopolies, expendable workers, and regional kleptocrats. In this supposedly better society, women were not permitted to vote and African Americans were barred from the basic protections of citizenship. The real per capita GDP (adjusted for inflation) was seven times less than in 2010, and, proportionally, about four times as many people lived in poverty as do today.

For Levin and Beck, the society that addressed these problems through its government was something less than real America—a nation that had become unmoored from its foundations and started down the road to tyranny. This shadow of America then won World War II and dismantled fascism in Europe. Not-quite-America, with its newly empowered central government, went on to become the world's greatest superpower and the bastion of freedom during the Cold War. By acting as a nation rather than a loose confederacy of independent states, this broken country created the interstate highway system—the most remarkable civil engineering project in history. It sent men to the moon and mapped the human genome. It virtually eliminated hunger within its borders and brought millions of its older citizens out of poverty. It ended segregation and incorporated all of its citizens into the social contract. Its colleges and universities became the envy of the world, and its industries drove the international economy for sixty years.

The country that did all these things is the only America most Americans today have ever known. This is the country patriots are talking about when they say they love their country. Yet for Levin and many others on the right, the America that did all these things (most of which could not have been accomplished without the strong central government they reject) is broken, destroyed, and unmade. All our nation's accomplishments since 1913 should appear in the historical records with an asterisk: "*Note: The country that did this was not really America but a flawed and broken shadow on its way to becoming a failed state."

In the Far Right's rule book, of course, only conservatives are allowed to make such criticisms. When those on the left make identical statements, they are met by the full force of right-wing radio. Just imagine what would have happened in 2008 if Michelle Obama had gone on television and said that America had become a "dictatorship," that the Constitution was "hanging by a thread," or that George Bush's undeclared war in Iraq had resulted in our becoming a "post-constitutional society." Can anybody doubt that Levin, Beck, and Limbaugh would have rushed to the airwaves to accuse her of anti-American treachery? Given how they reacted when Mrs. Obama admitted to lacking pride in her country for twenty years, how should we respond when right-wing conservatives say America has been fundamentally broken for nearly a century?

Here's how: Mr. Levin and Mr. Beck, I'm sick and tired of *you* putting down my country.

FAITH IN THE FOUNDERS

America's political destruction, which many on the right see as eminent (and some believe to have already occurred), is just as mythic as the enlightened golden age that supposedly produced the Constitution. This sense of impending doom situates the American narrative in a familiar pattern of biblical history. According to this story, America begins with the Founding era's prelapsarian innocence. After a fall from grace (that occurred under either Wilson or Roosevelt—opinion is divided here), America spent years in the wilderness. Ronald Reagan was sent in the 1980s to teach us the Good News, and we believed for a time. But then we fell away. Now we await the apocalypse.

Those who advance such narratives usually do so in the name of the Founding Fathers. We have abandoned their path and must return or face extinction, they say. But their arguments actually display contempt for the Founders and the system they created. Implicit in the assertion that the constitutional system is being (or has been) destroyed is the assumption that the system wasn't designed very well to begin with. By its own rhetoric, the Right assumes the Founders never considered that the federal government might try to overpower the states (the Founders did, in fact), or that people might start asking their government for more services than they were willing to pay for (they knew that as well), or that one branch of government might try to increase its power at the expense of the other two (they had it covered).

The Founding Fathers did a better job designing America than the Right is willing to admit. They understood both human nature and institutional behavior, and they designed a government capable of withstanding the worst excesses of both. Only those bad at history believe our generation's problems are the worst things America has ever faced. Over the past 230 years, our nation has faced and overcome worse security threats, financial crises, and political turmoil than we have seen in our lifetimes, and this is largely due to the system the Founders created.

To understand how this system has endured for so long, we need to resist the urge to see it as something it was never intended to be—namely, as a way to find answers to all our pressing political questions. We should see it, rather, as something we can use to create our own answers, to move forward as a political body even when we are deeply divided and cannot seem to reach agreement. Should we adopt universal healthcare? Should we continue to raise our debt ceiling? Can we control the deficit without raising taxes? The Founding Fathers had an excellent answer for all these questions: "Use the process we gave you and figure it out for yourselves."

Those who look to the Constitution for a checklist of approved political opinions miss almost everything about the point. That's not what constitutions do, and it's not what the Framers intended. They understood perfectly that they were creating a structure that would have to apply to situations and circumstances they could not foresee. When the Committee of Detail created the first full draft of the Constitution, for example, Edmund Randolph insisted that delegates "insert essential principles only; lest the operations of government should be clogged by rendering these provisions permanent and unalterable."[10]

Constitution, as Harvard Law School professor Laurence Tribe points out in a recent article, "is a verb, not a noun." It "*constitutes* us as a people—*e pluribus unum*—and draws all of our cross-generational debates into a project set in motion by, and unfolding through, its written and unwritten dimensions."[11] Supreme Court justice Stephen Breyer calls this aspect of the Constitution "active liberty." In a book of the same name, Breyer insists the primary purpose of the Constitution is "to create a framework for democratic government—a government that, while protecting individual liberties, permits citizens to govern themselves, and to govern themselves effectively. Insofar as a more literal interpretive approach undermines this basic objective, it is inconsistent with the most fundamental original intention of the Framers themselves."[12]

To the Far Right, of course, these are fighting words. Any hint that the Constitution could require subjective interpretation—or even that the Founders did not provide the answers to most of our contemporary questions—will earn the everlasting enmity of every right-wing radio host in America. In the Far Right's dramatis personae, there are only two schools of constitutional interpretation, which Levin defines in the first chapter of *Men in Black*. Either a person is an "originalist," who looks "to the text of the Constitution and the intent of the framers when deciding a constitutional question," or an "activist," who "consider[s] the Constitution a document of broad principles and concepts, one that empowers them to substitute their personal beliefs, values, and policies for those enumerated in the Constitution."[13]

As nice as it would be to live in a world of simplistic distinctions like these, the world we actually inhabit is considerably more complicated. Judges have to deal with a lot more factors than either law professors or radio hosts do; furthermore, judges' interpretations actually have consequences. Their judgments, therefore, do not lend themselves nearly as well to abstract theories of interpretation. All federal judges ground their rulings in the text of the Constitution (though they certainly don't all agree on their interpretations). Similarly, all judges bring their own values and perceptions to their judgments; human beings cannot do otherwise. Somewhere between Levin's two philosophies of judicial interpretation lie nearly all the interpretations that actually matter.

Perhaps an even greater objection to Levin's formulation is that his two core interpretive strategies—relying on "the text of the Constitution and the intent of the framers" and considering "their personal beliefs, values, and policies"—are not even real opposites. In many, if not most, instances, the text and its authors intend for us to use our own personal beliefs, values, and policies to make our own decisions about things. That's what *self-government* means. Consider the following phrases from the Constitution:

- Each House may determine the Rules of its Proceedings, punish its Members for disorderly behavior, and, with the Concurrence of two thirds, expel a Member. (Article I, Section 5)

- The Congress shall have Power To lay and collect Taxes, Duties, Imposts and Excises, to pay the Debts and provide for the common Defence **and general Welfare** of the United States. (Article I, Section 8)

- . . . to make all Laws which shall be **necessary and proper** for carrying into Execution the foregoing Powers, and **all other Powers** vested by this Constitution in the Government of the United States, or in any Department or Officer thereof. (Article I, Section 8)

- He [the President] shall from time to time give to the Congress Information of the State of the Union, and recommend to their Consideration such Measures **as he shall judge necessary and expedient**. (Article II, Section 3)

- The Congress shall have Power to dispose of and make **all needful Rules and Regulations** respecting the Territory or other Property belonging to the United States. (Article V, Section 4)

- The right of the people to be secure in their persons, houses, papers, and effects, against **unreasonable searches and seizures**, shall not be violated. (Amendment IV)

- . . . nor shall private property be taken for public use, **without just compensation**. (Amendment V)

- In all criminal prosecutions, the accused shall enjoy the right to a **speedy** and public trial, by an **impartial** jury of the state and district wherein the crime shall have been committed. (Amendment VI)

- **Excessive** bail shall not be required, nor **excessive** fines imposed, nor **cruel and unusual** punishments inflicted. (Amendment VIII)

- Congress shall have power to enforce this article by **appropriate** legislation. (Amendment XIII, repeated in Amendments XIV, XV, XIX, XXIII, XXVI)

Each of these phrases contains words that require subjective interpretation. Which laws are "necessary and proper" for Congress to pass? Which rules and regulations would be "needful" in a US territory? When does a search become "unreasonable"? How much compensation is "just" when the government takes somebody's land for public use? How much bail is "excessive"? What constitutes a "cruel and unusual" punishment? Phrases like these invite and require us to interpret key parts of the Constitution according to our own values and understandings.

Even when we can pinpoint beliefs in the Founding era that differ substantially from those common today, it does not follow that we should suspend our own judgment in deference to the eighteenth century. Archoriginalist Antonin Scalia clearly made this point in a famous 1998 lecture at the University of Cincinnati College of Law. "What if some state should enact a new law providing public lashing, or branding of the right hand, as punishment for certain criminal offenses?" Scalia asked. "Even if it could be demonstrated unequivocally that these were not cruel and unusual measures in 1791 . . . I doubt whether any federal judge—even among the many who consider themselves originalists—would sustain them against an Eighth Amendment challenge." Scalia finally concluded, "I cannot imagine myself, any more than any other federal judge, upholding a statute that imposes the punishment of flogging."[14]

Clearly, not everything in the Constitution can be read with this degree of interpretive license. Some passages are so clear that no reasonable person could dispute their meaning. When Article I, Section 3 says that "the Senate of the United States shall be composed of two Senators from each State," that means that each state gets two senators. Period. There are no interpretive tricks that can get our state three senators or another state one. Other terms, such as *due process of law* (Amendment XIV), were originally ambiguous but have been refined by more than two hundred years of practice and precedent to the point where there is now widespread agreement on their meaning. Even the elastic passages are not infinitely elastic. They can bear a range of interpretations, but they cannot mean absolutely anything. Living under the rule of law means accepting interpretive constraints when such constraints actually do exist.

The Framers designed the Constitution primarily to allow the people living under it to govern themselves. Nothing was more important to their vision than self-government, and nothing was more alien to their understanding than a system that would enforce a historical worldview on people trying to solve contemporary problems. As Laurence Tribe concludes in his article, we can avoid this, while still honoring the original meaning of the Constitution, when "all but the most mechanical of the Constitution's provisions [are] understood at a sufficiently high level of abstraction and generality . . . that the task of putting flesh on the Constitution's bones of 'liberty' and 'equality' remains inescapably our own."[15]

THE LEGACY OF THE FOUNDING FATHERS

Facile checklists of Founder-approved positions—from the Left or the Right—ultimately dishonor the Founders' accomplishments by reducing the democratic process to a simple clerical function. The current books and broadcasts of the American Right reference a virtual encyclopedia of opinions that the Founders would or would not have had about twenty-first-century issues. With no sense of irony, right-wing commentators and politicians tell us exactly what the Founding Fathers would have thought, collectively, about healthcare, same-sex marriage, affirmative action, environmental regulation, school prayer, the debt ceiling, and campaign-finance reform. We don't have to go through the hard work, debate, and compromise the Founding Fathers went through when they tackled their own issues. We simply have to figure out what they would have wanted us to do in a given situation (talk radio can help us here) and then do it.

But what they would have wanted us to do is govern ourselves. No theme is more important to the Founding era than self-governance. It is the main point of the Declaration of Independence, the Constitution, the Federalist papers, and the lives of the Founding Fathers themselves. They did not fight a war and construct a republic so that, two hundred years later, their descendants would try to govern the country through historical telepathy. Those who see the Founders' system as small government, low taxes, few regulations, and no entitlement programs are just as wrong as those who see it as big government, progressive taxation, federal regulation, and a basic right to healthcare. Through the practice of meaningful self-government, we can arrive at either of these extremes—or at any of the many points between them—while remaining completely faithful to the Founders' legacy.

In this concluding chapter, it is worth revisiting some of the remarkable aspects of the system the Founding Fathers set up in 1787 and argued about for most of their lives. It is a system that thrives on debate and, by directing disagreement to a positive conclusion, permits human beings with wildly different points of view to create a society and govern themselves. Here are some of the most noteworthy features of this system, which we can see in both the lives of the Founders and the Constitution they created:

The structure of government accounts for both individual human nature and organizational behavior. Everything about the Founders' system assumes that both people and organizations will usually follow their own interests. As Madison famously states in *Federalist* no. 51, "If men were angels, no government would be necessary. . . . In framing a government which is to be administered by men over men, the great difficulty lies in this: you must first enable the government to control the governed; and in the next place oblige it to control itself."[16]

By design, we are supposed to disagree with each other frequently and passionately. Many of the Founding Fathers saw majoritarianism as a greater threat to the liberty of the people than monarchy. In the hands of a stable majority, democracy becomes a dangerous weapon against those who believe otherwise. Since human interests can never be brought into alignment or placed under government control, an effective society must multiply interests and ensure that "society itself will be broken into so many parts, interests and classes of citizens, that the rights of individuals . . . will be in little danger from interested combinations of the majority."[17]

Just as people must be prevented from consolidating their opinions, government entities must be prevented from consolidating their powers. Through their reading of Montesquieu, the Framers understood that, for government to control itself, power needed to be separated into distinct and independent branches. And they understood that each of these branches would regularly try to empower itself at the expense of the others. This understanding gave rise to the elaborate system of checks and balances, whose constant aim, Madison explains, "is to divide and arrange the several offices in such a manner as that each may be a check on the other—that the private interest of every individual may be a sentinel over the public rights."[18]

Over time, both the judiciary and the executive branches of government have become more powerful in relation to the legislative branch. However, Congress has not exactly been reduced to a collection of figureheads, or to an impotent rubber stamp on a president's designs. Each of the three main branches of government remains powerful in its own right. Often, these branches come into conflict with each other. These conflicts produce the gridlock and stalemate that have become standard elements of American government. But we misunderstand the system when we assume that grid-lock and stalemate are signs of dysfunction; they are, rather, a pretty good indication that everything is going according to plan.

All power flows from the people, but different powers flow from the people in different ways. Nothing mattered more to the Founders than creating a government of the people. This was the basis of both the Declaration of Independence and the Revolutionary War, and it was (and remains) the fundamental genius of the American system. But power can flow from the people in a variety of ways, some purely democratic and others at a substantial remove from the electorate. The Framers understood that pure democracy was unworkable in a large country, but they also understood that in a republic there will always be a tension between the need to preserve liberty and the need to ensure stability. As Madison writes in *Federalist* no. 37:

> The genius of republican liberty seems to demand on one side not only that all power should be derived from the people, but that those intrusted with it should be kept in dependence on the people, by a short duration of their appointments; and that even during this short period the trust should be placed not in a few, but a number of hands. Stability, on the contrary, requires that the hands in which power is lodged should continue for a length of time the same.[19]

To balance these different needs, the Constitution created four different categories of elected official, each chosen in different ways for different periods of time: (1) representatives were to be chosen every two years by the direct election of their districts; (2) senators were to be selected for a six-year term by state legislatures, who were, in turn, elected by popular vote (this was changed by the Seventeenth Amendment in 1913); (3) presidents were to be chosen every four years by electors, whose method of selection was left up to each state; and (4) Supreme Court justices were appointed by presidents and confirmed by the Senate before taking a lifetime appointment on the bench. The result of these staggered terms is a blend of instant democracy and long-term stability—much of which has been on display in America over the past few election cycles.

In this system, the majority will always get its way eventually, but it will not always get its way immediately. The people can vote a new party into the House of Representatives every two years, and sometimes they can even switch enough votes in the Senate to do the same. But the Supreme Court will only change orientation if people keep electing presidents and senators of the same party for twenty or thirty years. Practically, this means that government policies can change radically, but not instantly, to accommodate the will of the people. A popular desire for radical change must be sustained through several election cycles in order to break through the Constitution's mechanisms for safeguarding stability.

For an example of how this works, consider FDR's famous court-packing scheme. When the Supreme Court struck down many of Roosevelt's initial New Deal proposals, the president responded by trying to increase the number of justices on the court so that he could appoint a majority. The plan met deep opposition from the public and Congress, and it failed miserably. But, as Justice Breyer notes, Roosevelt "ultimately won by being in office long enough to appoint eight of the nine justices on the Court."[20] What he could not do by fiat, he accomplished through sheer longevity. As people returned him to office again and again—fully aware of his domestic agenda—the popular will was translated into judicial interpretations in favor of the New Deal. This was not (as many on the right believe) a subversion of the Constitution; it was exactly how the process was designed to work.

It is much easier to prevent something from happening than it is to make anything happen. The American system makes it very easy to prevent things from happening. A president can veto any piece of legislation for any reason. Five Supreme Court justices can declare a law or executive action unconstitutional and strike it down. Forty senators can prevent a vote on any legislative action simply by threatening a filibuster. From any rational perspective, it is amazing that anything gets done in Washington at all.

And yet, things do get done. Legislation is passed, executive orders are signed, and America continues to solve—however imperfectly—its most pressing problems. We continue to move forward, despite our disagreements, precisely because the legislative gauntlet creates a powerful incentive for compromise. Anybody who can prevent something from passing must be accommodated, somehow, in the final product. As a result, those who propose initiatives must determine what they want most and what they are willing to give up in order to get it.

This "compromise imperative" made the Constitution possible in the first place. The great compromises of the Federal Convention, such as the plan that created the current bicameral legislature, happened only when it became clear that the convention would break up without a compromise. The common desire for a Constitution made it possible to bridge differences that seemed impossible to reconcile at the beginning of the convention. This same drama is reenacted in every session of Congress, as people with very different interests, perspectives, and constituencies come together—sometimes only briefly—to move their agendas forward before factional pressures split them apart again.

We often hear that there needs to be more civility and cooperation in government. I disagree. Our system was not designed for civility or cooperation; it was designed for compromise, which is a very different thing. People who cooperate usually share the same objectives and find ways to supplement each other's efforts as they strive toward the same goals. People who compromise with each other, on the other hand, often have very different objectives in mind. They collaborate on means, not ends, and when the collaboration is over, they go their separate ways. And this is as it should be. Bipartisanship is highly overrated. We should not want political enemies cooperating with each other too much, lest they find ways to do it at our expense. Our whole system of government has been designed to keep factions fighting with each other most of the time. When the lion lies down with the lamb, they are probably both up to no good.

The government works best when people understand it and participate in it meaningfully. In *Democracy in America*, published in 1835, Alexis de Tocqueville, America's first great international publicist, explains the role participation plays in America's participatory democracy. "The American learns about the law by participating in the making of it," Tocqueville writes. "He teaches himself about the forms of government by governing. He watches the great work of society being done every day before his eyes and, in a sense, by his hand."[21] Tocqueville took seriously what too many Americans accept only metaphorically: that the people are the government.

As Tocqueville saw it, voting was the beginning, not the end, of democratic participation in America. People voted throughout Europe, but the Americans Tocqueville knew were embedded in the political process in a way Europeans at the time were not. Schools educated students to be citizens, which is very different from training students to be subjects, and people integrated political discussions into the fabric of their daily lives. Tocqueville's

Americans saw the government as an extension of themselves—a mechanism that, in Justice Breyer's words, "helps a community of individuals democratically find practical solutions to important contemporary problems."[22]

One of the most disturbing aspects of recent right-wing rhetoric has been its tendency to portray the American government as something separate from the American people. We do not govern ourselves according to this formulation; "they" govern "us"—and rarely in a good way. This lets "us" off the hook too easily. If government is something done to us by others, then "we" did not cause the national debt by using the democratic process to demand more services from our elected officials than we were willing to pay for. "They" caused it by trashing the Constitution and giving our hard-earned money to "special-interest groups," which, like the government, are entirely separate from the body politic. It is all very convenient. And it is all very wrong.

Both Jefferson and Tocqueville understood the principle to which the signers of the Declaration of Independence pledged "our Lives, our Fortunes, and our sacred Honor." We are the government. Even when the other team wins (and, if the democracy is functioning correctly, nobody's team will win all the time), we are still the government. Presidents, legislatures, and judges exist as extensions of the popular will. The constitutional process allows us to act through them to accomplish—through deliberation, debate, and compromise—our objectives. When America faces problems, we face problems we created. To address these problems, we need to empower government to implement our solutions.

Finis

Senator Daniel Patrick Moynihan famously quipped, "Everyone is entitled to his own opinion, but not his own facts." The senator was being naive about the nature of both facts and entitlements. In a free country, we are all entitled not only to our own facts but also to our own narratives that we can use to beat up our ideological opponents. Historical facts convert nicely into rhetorical big sticks. By themselves, facts are both innumerable and meaningless. They acquire meaning when they are culled out of the primal-fact soup and situated in the narratives we call "history." The moral of any historical narrative depends on the facts we select, the facts we omit, and the plot of the story we are trying to tell. In any sustained debate about "what the Founding

Fathers meant," both sides are usually armed with perfectly legitimate facts to which, they believe, the other side should humbly bow.

But there are also plenty of nonfacts in these debates. One such nonfact is the assumption that the Founding Fathers constituted an ideologically coherent group of people who spoke with one voice about the important issues of their day. Taken as historical individuals, the major statesmen of the Founding era—Alexander Hamilton, Thomas Jefferson, George Washington, Benjamin Franklin, John Adams, and James Madison—make very bad battering rams. They were too distinct as individuals to be grouped into a single source of collective opinion, and they disagreed with each other too passionately to be invoked as a corrective to our contemporary political divisions.

When an entire structure of assumption and argument is based on a patent nonfact, the result is not history but myth. Myth is a powerful and necessary component of the human psyche. We need the moral clarity it provides, and we crave the connections to a better past that it promises. The myth of an ideologically coherent group of Founders has been particularly important in America for more than a hundred years. This myth has endowed generations of Americans with the sense that they belong to something truly remarkable, and it has provided politicians with a powerful rhetorical ground to contest. Nobody wants to be against the Founding Fathers.

It is not surprising, or even particularly disturbing, that many on the American Right now use a mythical version of America's Founding as a weapon against their political opponents. Most coherent ideological factions in American history have done the same. What is both surprising and disturbing, though, is that the rest of us are letting them get away with it. Too often, those of us to the left of the Tea Party greet the opinions of the Far Right with only ridicule and contempt. This is a bad strategy, as it merely confirms the "we are victims of the liberal elite" narrative that is nearly as important to talk radio as commercial interruptions are. Meaningful engagement, which the Founders themselves never shied away from, is the best response to the Right's often incoherent version of America's past.

The rhetorical ground of America's Founding is too important to concede. The power to define the past is also the power to determine the future, and the greatest antidote to a mythical narrative is a historical one. The lives of the Founding Fathers provide the raw material for much more interesting narratives than the Right is willing to tell. They were not a unified collection of disinterested patriots who collaborated to create a nation from the mind of God. But they were remarkable, passionate men who—largely through their disagreements—created a system that allows flawed, self-interested people to grope their way toward meaningful solutions and govern themselves.

In contesting the Right's mythic narrative of the past, we necessarily reject its grossly pessimistic vision of the future. The Right's false dilemma—either we undo much of what we have accomplished since the presidency of Woodrow Wilson, or we descend inexorably into the gaping jaws of tyranny—crumbles into nonsense when deprived of its foundational mythology. In its place is a future whose contours are limited only by our vision. If we have not fallen away from the truth, as some conservatives suggest, then we need to stop trying to get back to our mythical past and get busy constructing our actual future.

America has not yet seen its best days. The Founding Fathers did their job well, and the system they created remains as robust an engine for liberty and human progress as the world has ever seen. The American Right is doing its part to create the contention and conflict that make our democracy function. Liberals, centrists, and moderate conservatives need to step up to the plate and take their turns, to subject the Right's arguments and historical narratives to rigorous analysis and meaningful rebuttal. In the process, we must wrest the narratives of the Founding Fathers away from narrow ideologues of any persuasion and restore them to their rightful place as the common heritage of all Americans.

AN ACT FOR ESTABLISHING RELIGIOUS FREEDOM IN VIRGINIA

BY THOMAS JEFFERSON, 1777 (DRAFTED), 1779 (PROPOSED), 1786 (APPROVED WITH REVISIONS)

Virginia, the largest and most populous of the American colonies, was initially established as an Anglican colony and remained so until the time of the Revolution. By 1776, however, the majority of Virginians were not Anglicans but members of less centralized Protestant sects, such as Baptists and Presbyterians. But the Church of England remained the official, tax-supported religion of the colony—a status powerful Anglicans in the state were reluctant to surrender.

Soon after writing the Declaration of Independence, Thomas Jefferson returned to Virginia and was elected to serve in the House of Delegates. Many of his colleagues in the legislature wanted to curb the power of the established church, but Jefferson wanted to go much further. In 1777, he began to draft legislation that would make the state officially neutral on questions of religion. Such legislation would ensure equal treatment under the law for Catholics, Protestants, Jews, and even those with no religious beliefs at all. Jefferson proposed this legislation soon after he was elected governor of Virginia in 1779, but it was defeated in favor of more gradual, less radical measures to extend religious tolerance to non-Anglican Protestants.

By 1786, however, the mood of the Virginia legislature had changed significantly. At the time, Jefferson was serving as the American minister to France, but his closest ally, James Madison, remained in Virginia and served in the House of Delegates. When Patrick Henry proposed a nondenomina-

tional religious tax, Madison not only opposed the measure, he reintroduced Jefferson's Religious Freedom Bill, which passed by a wide margin. On his tombstone, Jefferson listed his authorship of the Virginia Statute for Religious Freedom, his authorship of the Declaration of Independence, and his founding of the University of Virginia as the three most significant accomplishments of his lifetime.

SECTION I.

Well aware that the opinions and belief of men depend not on their own will, but follow involuntarily the evidence proposed to their minds; that Almighty God hath created the mind free, and manifested his supreme will that free it shall remain by making it altogether insusceptible of restraint; that all attempts to influence it by temporal punishments, or burthens, or by civil incapacitations, tend only to beget habits of hypocrisy and meanness, and are a departure from the plan of the holy author of our religion, who being lord both of body and mind, yet chose not to propagate it by coercions on either, as was in his Almighty power to do, but to extend it by its influence on reason alone; that the impious presumption of legislators and rulers, civil as well as ecclesiastical, who, being themselves but fallible and uninspired men, have assumed dominion over the faith of others, setting up their own opinions and modes of thinking as the only true and infallible, and as such endeavoring to impose them on others, hath established and maintained false religions over the greatest part of the world and through all time: That to compel a man to furnish contributions of money for the propagation of opinions which he disbelieves and abhors, is sinful and tyrannical; that even the forcing him to support this or that teacher of his own religious persuasion, is depriving him of the comfortable liberty of giving his contributions to the particular pastor whose morals he would make his pattern, and whose powers he feels most persuasive to righteousness; and is withdrawing from the ministry those temporary rewards, which proceeding from an approbation of their personal conduct, are an additional incitement to earnest and unremitting labours for the instruction of mankind; that our civil rights have no dependence on our religious opinions, any more than our opinions in physics or geometry; that therefore the proscribing any citizen as unworthy the public confidence by laying upon him an incapacity of being called to offices of trust and emolument, unless he profess or renounce this or that religious opinion, is depriving him injuriously of those privileges and advantages to which, in common with his fellow citizens, he has a natural right; that it tends also to corrupt the principles of that very religion it is meant to encourage, by bribing, with a monopoly of worldly honours and emoluments, those who will externally profess and conform to it; that though indeed these are criminal who do not withstand such temptation, yet neither are those innocent who lay the bait in their way; that the opinions of men are not the object of civil government, nor under its jurisdiction; that to suffer the civil magistrate to intrude his powers into the field of opinion and to restrain the profession or propagation of principles on supposition of their ill tendency is a dangerous fallacy, which at once destroys all religious liberty, because he being of course judge of that tendency will make his opinions the rule of judgment, and approve or condemn the sentiments of others only as they shall square with or differ from his own; that it is time enough for the rightful purposes of civil government for its officers to interfere when principles break out into overt acts against peace and good order; and finally, that truth is great and will prevail if left to herself; that she is the proper and sufficient antagonist to error, and has nothing to fear from the conflict unless by human interposition disarmed of her natural weapons, free argument and debate; errors ceasing to be dangerous when it is permitted freely to contradict them.

SECTION II.

We the General Assembly of Virginia do enact that no man shall be compelled to frequent or support any religious worship, place, or ministry whatsoever, nor shall be enforced, restrained, molested, or burthened in his body or goods, nor shall otherwise suffer, on account of his religious opinions or belief; but that all men shall be free to profess, and by argument to maintain, their opinions in matters of religion, and that the same shall in no wise diminish, enlarge, or affect their civil capacities.

SECTION III.

And though we well know that this Assembly, elected by the people for the ordinary purposes of legislation only, have no power to restrain the acts of succeeding Assemblies, constituted with powers equal to our own, and that therefore to declare this act irrevocable would be of no effect in law; yet we are free to declare, and do declare, that the rights hereby asserted are of the natural rights of mankind, and that if any act shall be hereafter passed to repeal the present or to narrow its operation, such act will be an infringement of natural right.

MEMORIAL AND REMONSTRANCE AGAINST RELIGIOUS ASSESSMENTS

BY JAMES MADISON, 1785

Though Patrick Henry was a strong supporter of religious tolerance—the idea that people should not be punished because of their religion—he felt the state had a legitimate interest in promoting religion generally. In 1784, Henry proposed in the Virginia Assembly "A Bill Establishing a Provision for Teachers of the Christian Religion." Henry's bill did not favor any particular denomination. All Protestant sects were eligible for state support on an equal basis. Initially, most legislators favored the proposal, but James Madison, who supported an absolute separation between church and state, did not.

To marshal opposition to Henry's bill, Madison wrote his "Memorial and Remonstrance against Religious Assessment." In this brief tract—today it would probably be called a talking-points memo"—Madison lays out his opinion that the state should adopt a policy of absolute neutrality toward religious belief. Religious belief, he argues, falls outside the social contract; it's a matter to be addressed between an individual and his or her conscience, with no interference—be it help or hindrance—from any government agency.

Madison's arguments against Henry's religious-assessment bill were so successful that, after defeating it in 1785, he was able to reintroduce Jefferson's Statute for Religious Freedom, which passed by a large margin in 1786. Madison would later work the principles he espoused in the Virginia religious-freedom debate into the First Amendment to the Constitution, which stipulates that "Congress shall make no law respecting an establishment of religion, or prohibiting the free exercise thereof."

❧

To the Honorable the General Assembly of the Commonwealth of Virginia

A Memorial and Remonstrance Against Religious Assessments

We the subscribers, citizens of the said Commonwealth, having taken into serious consideration, a Bill printed by order of the last Session of General Assembly, entitled "A Bill establishing a provision for Teachers of the Christian Religion," and conceiving that the same if finally armed with the sanctions of a law, will be a dangerous abuse of power, are bound as faithful members of a free State to remonstrate against it, and to declare the reasons by which we are determined. We remonstrate against the said Bill,

1. **Because** we hold it for a fundamental and undeniable truth, "that religion or the duty which we owe to our Creator and the manner of discharging it, can be directed only by reason and conviction, not by force or violence." The Religion then of every man must be left to the conviction and conscience of every man; and it is the right of every man to exercise it as these may dictate. This right is in its nature an unalienable right. It is unalienable, because the opinions of men, depending only on the evidence contemplated by their own minds cannot follow the dictates of other men: It is unalienable also, because what is here a right towards men, is a duty towards the Creator. It is the duty of every man to render to the Creator such homage and such only as he believes to be acceptable to him. This duty is precedent, both in order of time and in degree of obligation, to the claims of Civil Society. Before any man can be considered as a member of Civil Society, he must be considered as a subject of the Governour of the Universe: And if a member of Civil Society, do it with a saving of his allegiance to the Universal Sovereign. We maintain therefore that in matters of Religion, no man's right is abridged by the institution of Civil Society and that Religion is wholly exempt from its cognizance. True it is, that no other rule exists, by which any question which may divide a Society, can be ultimately determined, but the

will of the majority; but it is also true that the majority may trespass on the rights of the minority.

2. **Because** Religion be exempt from the authority of the Society at large, still less can it be subject to that of the Legislative Body. The latter are but the creatures and vicegerents of the former. Their jurisdiction is both derivative and limited: it is limited with regard to the co-ordinate departments, more necessarily is it limited with regard to the constituents. The preservation of a free Government requires not merely, that the metes and bounds which separate each department of power be invariably maintained; but more especially that neither of them be suffered to overleap the great Barrier which defends the rights of the people. The Rulers who are guilty of such an encroachment, exceed the commission from which they derive their authority, and are Tyrants. The People who submit to it are governed by laws made neither by themselves nor by an authority derived from them, and are slaves.

3. **Because** it is proper to take alarm at the first experiment on our liberties. We hold this prudent jealousy to be the first duty of Citizens, and one of the noblest characteristics of the late Revolution. The free men of America did not wait till usurped power had strengthened itself by exercise, and entangled the question in precedents. They saw all the consequences in the principle, and they avoided the consequences by denying the principle. We revere this lesson too much soon to forget it. Who does not see that the same authority which can establish Christianity, in exclusion of all other Religions, may establish with the same ease any particular sect of Christians, in exclusion of all other Sects? that the same authority which can force a citizen to contribute three pence only of his property for the support of any one establishment, may force him to conform to any other establishment in all cases whatsoever?

4. **Because** the Bill violates the equality which ought to be the basis of every law, and which is more indispensible, in proportion as the validity or expediency of any law is more liable to be impeached. If "all men are by nature equally free and independent," all men are to be considered as entering into Society on equal conditions; as relinquishing no more, and therefore retaining no less, one than another, of their natural rights. Above all are they to be considered as

retaining an "equal title to the free exercise of Religion according to the dictates of Conscience." Whilst we assert for ourselves a freedom to embrace, to profess and to observe the Religion which we believe to be of divine origin, we cannot deny an equal freedom to those whose minds have not yet yielded to the evidence which has convinced us. If this freedom be abused, it is an offence against God, not against man: To God, therefore, not to man, must an account of it be rendered. As the Bill violates equality by subjecting some to peculiar burdens, so it violates the same principle, by granting to others peculiar exemptions. Are the Quakers and Menonists the only sects who think a compulsive support of their Religions unnecessary and unwarrantable? Can their piety alone be entrusted with the care of public worship? Ought their Religions to be endowed above all others with extraordinary privileges by which proselytes may be enticed from all others? We think too favorably of the justice and good sense of these denominations to believe that they either covet pre-eminences over their fellow citizens or that they will be seduced by them from the common opposition to the measure.

5. **Because** the Bill implies either that the Civil Magistrate is a competent Judge of Religious Truth; or that he may employ Religion as an engine of Civil policy. The first is an arrogant pretension falsified by the contradictory opinions of Rulers in all ages, and throughout the world: the second an unhallowed perversion of the means of salvation.

6. **Because** the establishment proposed by the Bill is not requisite for the support of the Christian Religion. To say that it is, is a contradiction to the Christian Religion itself, for every page of it disavows a dependence on the powers of this world: it is a contradiction to fact; for it is known that this Religion both existed and flourished, not only without the support of human laws, but in spite of every opposition from them, and not only during the period of miraculous aid, but long after it had been left to its own evidence and the ordinary care of Providence. Nay, it is a contradiction in terms; for a Religion not invented by human policy, must have pre-existed and been supported, before it was established by human policy. It is moreover to weaken in those who profess this Religion a pious confidence in its innate excellence and the patronage of its Author; and

to foster in those who still reject it, a suspicion that its friends are too conscious of its fallacies to trust it to its own merits.

7. **Because** experience witnesseth that ecclesiastical establishments, instead of maintaining the purity and efficacy of Religion, have had a contrary operation. During almost fifteen centuries has the legal establishment of Christianity been on trial. What have been its fruits? More or less in all places, pride and indolence in the Clergy, ignorance and servility in the laity, in both, superstition, bigotry and persecution. Enquire of the Teachers of Christianity for the ages in which it appeared in its greatest lustre; those of every sect, point to the ages prior to its incorporation with Civil policy. Propose a restoration of this primitive State in which its Teachers depended on the voluntary rewards of their flocks, many of them predict its downfall. On which Side ought their testimony to have greatest weight, when for or when against their interest?

8. **Because** the establishment in question is not necessary for the support of Civil Government. If it be urged as necessary for the support of Civil Government only as it is a means of supporting Religion, and it be not necessary for the latter purpose, it cannot be necessary for the former. If Religion be not within the cognizance of Civil Government how can its legal establishment be necessary to Civil Government? What influence in fact have ecclesiastical establishments had on Civil Society? In some instances they have been seen to erect a spiritual tyranny on the ruins of the Civil authority; in many instances they have been seen upholding the thrones of political tyranny: in no instance have they been seen the guardians of the liberties of the people. Rulers who wished to subvert the public liberty, may have found an established Clergy convenient auxiliaries. A just Government instituted to secure & perpetuate it needs them not. Such a Government will be best supported by protecting every Citizen in the enjoyment of his Religion with the same equal hand which protects his person and his property; by neither invading the equal rights of any Sect, nor suffering any Sect to invade those of another.

9. **Because** the proposed establishment is a departure from the generous policy, which, offering an Asylum to the persecuted and oppressed of every Nation and Religion, promised a lustre to our country, and an accession to the number of its citizens. What a

melancholy mark is the Bill of sudden degeneracy? Instead of holding forth an Asylum to the persecuted, it is itself a signal of persecution. It degrades from the equal rank of Citizens all those whose opinions in Religion do not bend to those of the Legislative authority. Distant as it may be in its present form from the Inquisition, it differs from it only in degree. The one is the first step, the other the last in the career of intolerance. The magnanimous sufferer under this cruel scourge in foreign Regions, must view the Bill as a Beacon on our Coast, warning him to seek some other haven, where liberty and philanthrophy in their due extent, may offer a more certain repose from his Troubles.

10. **Because** it will have a like tendency to banish our Citizens. The allurements presented by other situations are every day thinning their number. To superadd a fresh motive to emigration by revoking the liberty which they now enjoy, would be the same species of folly which has dishonoured and depopulated flourishing kingdoms.

11. **Because** it will destroy that moderation and harmony which the forbearance of our laws to intermeddle with Religion has produced among its several sects. Torrents of blood have been spilt in the old world, by vain attempts of the secular arm, to extinguish Religious discord, by proscribing all difference in Religious opinion. Time has at length revealed the true remedy. Every relaxation of narrow and rigorous policy, wherever it has been tried, has been found to assuage the disease. The American Theatre has exhibited proofs that equal and compleat liberty, if it does not wholly eradicate it, sufficiently destroys its malignant influence on the health and prosperity of the State. If with the salutary effects of this system under our own eyes, we begin to contract the bounds of Religious freedom, we know no name that will too severely reproach our folly. At least let warning be taken at the first fruits of the threatened innovation. The very appearance of the Bill has transformed "that Christian forbearance, love and charity," which of late mutually prevailed, into animosities and jealousies, which may not soon be appeased. What mischiefs may not be dreaded, should this enemy to the public quiet be armed with the force of a law?

12. **Because** the policy of the Bill is adverse to the diffusion of the light of Christianity. The first wish of those who enjoy this precious gift

ought to be that it may be imparted to the whole race of mankind. Compare the number of those who have as yet received it with the number still remaining under the dominion of false Religions; and how small is the former! Does the policy of the Bill tend to lessen the disproportion? No; it at once discourages those who are strangers to the light of revelation from coming into the Region of it; and countenances by example the nations who continue in darkness, in shutting out those who might convey it to them. Instead of Levelling as far as possible, every obstacle to the victorious progress of Truth, the Bill with an ignoble and unchristian timidity would circumscribe it with a wall of defence against the encroachments of error.

13. **Because** attempts to enforce by legal sanctions, acts obnoxious to so great a proportion of Citizens, tend to enervate the laws in general, and to slacken the bands of Society. If it be difficult to execute any law which is not generally deemed necessary or salutary, what must be the case, where it is deemed invalid and dangerous? And what may be the effect of so striking an example of impotency in the Government, on its general authority?

14. **Because** a measure of such singular magnitude and delicacy ought not to be imposed, without the clearest evidence that it is called for by a majority of citizens, and no satisfactory method is yet proposed by which the voice of the majority in this case may be determined, or its influence secured. "The people of the respective counties are indeed requested to signify their opinion respecting the adoption of the Bill to the next Session of Assembly." But the representation must be made equal, before the voice either of the Representatives or of the Counties will be that of the people. Our hope is that neither of the former will, after due consideration, espouse the dangerous principle of the Bill. Should the event disappoint us, it will still leave us in full confidence, that a fair appeal to the latter will reverse the sentence against our liberties.

Because finally, "the equal right of every citizen to the free exercise of his Religion according to the dictates of conscience" is held by the same tenure with all our other rights. If we recur to its origin, it is equally the gift of nature; if we weigh its importance, it cannot be less dear to us; if we consult the "Declaration of those rights which pertain to the good people of Virginia, as the basis and foundation of Government," it is enumerated with equal solemnity, or rather studied emphasis. Either then, we must say, that the Will of the Legislature is the only measure of their authority; and that in the plenitude of this authority, they may sweep away all our fundamental rights; or, that they are bound to leave this particular right untouched and sacred: Either we must say, that they may controul the freedom of the press, may abolish the Trial by Jury, may swallow up the Executive and Judiciary Powers of the State; nay that they may despoil us of our very right of suffrage, and erect themselves into an independent and hereditary Assembly or, we must say, that they have no authority to enact into the law the Bill under consideration.

We the Subscribers say, that the General Assembly of this Commonwealth have no such authority: And that no effort may be omitted on our part against so dangerous an usurpation, we oppose to it, this remonstrance; earnestly praying, as we are in duty bound, that the Supreme Lawgiver of the Universe, by illuminating those to whom it is addressed, may on the one hand, turn their Councils from every act which would affront his holy prerogative, or violate the trust committed to them: and on the other, guide them into every measure which may be worthy of his blessing, may redound to their own praise, and may establish more firmly the liberties, the prosperity and the happiness of the Commonwealth.

CORRESPONDENCE BETWEEN THE DANBURY BAPTIST ASSOCIATION AND THOMAS JEFFERSON, 1801–1802

The Jeffersonian Republican Party in the early 1800s was a fairly large tent, religiously speaking. It included freethinkers and intellectuals who were skeptical of Christianity and its claims. But it also included a fair number of devout New England Protestants who resented the Congregational Church's privileged position as the established religion of Massachusetts, New Hampshire, and Connecticut. While the Constitution prohibited the federal government from establishing any religion, the states were permitted to do so for most of the nineteenth century.

The Danbury Baptist Association in Danbury, Connecticut, was among the most powerful groups advocating religious disestablishment in New England. They wrote to Jefferson soon after he became president to express their support for him and to request his assistance in securing the same kind of religious-freedom bill in Connecticut that Jefferson had written in Virginia. Jefferson saw the letter as an opportunity to make a political statement. During the election of 1800, Jefferson had been roundly criticized as an atheist and a libertine, and his views on religious freedom had been presented as an affront to the faithful of all religions. More recently, Jefferson had been criticized in the press for refusing to follow his predecessors in proclaiming national days of prayer and fasting to commemorate important events.

But Jefferson knew his views on religious freedom had the support of minority religions everywhere. In January of 1802, Jefferson sent a reply to the Danbury Baptist Association, with copies sent to area newspapers, that he specifically crafted to emphasize the importance of state neutrality to religion itself. In this letter, Jefferson first uses the phrase "wall of separation between church and state," one of the most quoted and least understood phrases of the Founding era.

❧

LETTER TO THOMAS JEFFERSON

Danbury Baptist Association's letter to Thomas Jefferson, October 7, 1801.

Sir,—Among the many millions in America and Europe who rejoice in your Election to office; we embrace the first opportunity which we have enjoyed in our collective capacity, since your Inauguration, to express our great satisfaction, in your appointment to the chief Majestracy in the United States; And though our mode of expression may be less courtly and pompous than what many others clothe their addresses with, we beg you, Sir to believe, that none are more sincere.

Our Sentiments are uniformly on the side of Religious Liberty—That Religion is at all times and places a matter between God and individuals—That no man ought to suffer in name, person, or effects on account of his religious Opinions—That the legitimate Power of civil government extends no further than to punish the man who works *ill to his neighbor*: But Sir our constitution of government is not specific. Our ancient charter together with the Laws made coincident therewith, were adopted on the Basis of our government, at the time of our revolution; and such had been our Laws & usages, and such still are; that Religion is considered as the first object of Legislation; and therefore what religious privileges we enjoy (as a minor part of the State) we enjoy as favors granted, and not as inalienable rights: and these favors we receive at the expense of such degrading acknowledgements, as are inconsistent with the rights of freemen. It is not to be wondered at therefore; if those, who seek after power & gain under the pretense of *government & Religion* should reproach their fellow men—should reproach their chief Magistrate, as an enemy of religion Law & good order because he will not, dare not assume the prerogatives of Jehovah and make Laws to govern the Kingdom of Christ.

Sir, we are sensible that the President of the United States, is not the national legislator, and also sensible that the national government cannot destroy the Laws of each State; but our hopes are strong that the sentiments of our beloved President, which have had such genial affect already, like the radiant beams of the Sun, will shine and prevail through all these States and all the world till Hierarchy and Tyranny be destroyed from the Earth. Sir, when we reflect on your past services, and see a glow of philanthropy and good will shining forth in a course of more than thirty years we have reason to believe that America's God has raised you up to fill the chair of State out of that good will which he bears to the Millions which you preside over. May God strengthen you for the arduous task which providence & the voice of the people have called you to sustain and support you in your Administration against all the predetermined opposition of those who wish to rise to wealth & importance on the poverty and subjection of the people.

And may the Lord preserve you safe from every evil and bring you at last to his Heavenly Kingdom through Jesus Christ our Glorious Mediator.

Signed in behalf of the Association.
Nehh. Dodge, Ephm. Robbins
The Committee, Stephen S. Nelson

LETTER TO THE DANBURY BAPTIST ASSOCIATION

To Messrs. Nehemiah Dodge and Others, a Committee of the Danbury Baptist Association, in the State of Connecticut. January 1, 1802. by Thomas Jefferson

Gentlemen,—The affectionate sentiments of esteem and approbation which you are so good as to express towards me, on behalf of the Danbury Baptist Association, give me the highest satisfaction. My duties dictate a faithful and zealous pursuit of the interests of my constituents, and in proportion as they are persuaded of my fidelity to those duties, the discharge of them becomes more and more pleasing.

Believing with you that religion is a matter which lies solely between man and his God, that he owes account to none other for his faith or his worship, that the legislative powers of government reach actions only, and not opinions, I contemplate with sovereign reverence that act of the whole American people which declared that their legislature should "make no law respecting an establishment of religion, or prohibiting the free exercise thereof," thus building a wall of separation between church and State. Adhering to this expression of the supreme will of the nation in behalf of the rights of conscience, I shall see with sincere satisfaction the progress of those sentiments which tend to restore to man all his natural rights, convinced he has no natural right in opposition to his social duties.

I reciprocate your kind prayers for the protection and blessing of the common Father and Creator of man, and tender you for yourselves and your religious association, assurances of my high respect and esteem.

FEDERALIST NO. 10

BY JAMES MADISON, 1787

The new American Constitution faced stiff public opposition before it was ever finalized and signed by the delegates to the Federal Convention. Two of New York's delegates—John Lansing and Robert Yates—left the convention early in protest of the delegates' nationalistic inclinations and returned to New York to begin organizing the opposition. Within weeks of the Constitution's signing, Yates, under the pen name "Brutus," published the first of a series of all-out attacks on the Constitution.

The third delegate from New York, Alexander Hamilton, knew New York would be a crucial state in the ratification debate. He immediately recruited James Madison and John Jay to help him write a series of rebuttals to "Brutus" under the collective pseudonym "Publius." "Publius" would eventually write eighty-five essays that would become famous as the Federalist papers, which remain to this day the most important commentaries ever written on the American Constitution.

The first nine Federalist essays were written by either Hamilton (nos. 1, 6–9) or Jay (nos. 2–5). Madison's first essay, Federalist no. 10, was published on November 22, 1787. In this essay, Madison addresses the most devastating argument that "Brutus" and other Anti-Federalists had made: that the American colonies were too large to form a single united republic. No less an authority than the Baron de Montesquieu—the source of much of the Framers' understanding of the separation-of-powers doctrine—had written that "it is natural to a republic to have only a small territory, otherwise it cannot long subsist."

In Federalist no. 10, however, Madison argues that large republics are necessary to control the effects that different factions have on the body politic. Factions, Madison believed, could be controlled only through multiplication. In a small republic, it would be possible for a political faction to achieve a permanent majority status and use that status to invade the rights

of the minority. A large republic, on the other hand, has so many different fac-
tions that no single one can remain in the majority long enough to use the
instruments of democracy as tools of oppression.

⟋∿⟍

AMONG the numerous advantages promised by a well constructed Union, none deserves to be more accurately developed than its tendency to break and control the violence of faction. The friend of popular governments never finds himself so much alarmed for their character and fate, as when he contemplates their propensity to this dangerous vice. He will not fail, therefore, to set a due value on any plan which, without violating the principles to which he is attached, provides a proper cure for it. The instability, injustice, and confusion introduced into the public councils, have, in truth, been the mortal diseases under which popular governments have everywhere perished; as they continue to be the favorite and fruitful topics from which the adversaries to liberty derive their most specious declamations. The valuable improvements made by the American constitutions on the popular models, both ancient and modern, cannot certainly be too much admired; but it would be an unwarrantable partiality, to contend that they have as effectually obviated the danger on this side, as was wished and expected. Complaints are everywhere heard from our most considerate and virtuous citizens, equally the friends of public and private faith, and of public and personal liberty, that our governments are too unstable, that the public good is disregarded in the conflicts of rival parties, and that measures are too often decided, not according to the rules of justice and the rights of the minor party, but by the superior force of an interested and overbearing majority. However anxiously we may wish that these complaints had no foundation, the evidence, of known facts will not permit us to deny that they are in some degree true. It will be found, indeed, on a candid review of our situation, that some of the distresses under which we labor have been erroneously charged on the operation of our governments; but it will be found, at the same time, that other causes will not alone account for many of our heaviest misfortunes; and, particularly, for that prevailing and increasing distrust of public engagements, and alarm for private rights, which are echoed from one end of the continent to the other. These must be chiefly, if not wholly, effects of the unsteadiness and injustice with which a factious spirit has tainted our public administrations.

By a faction, I understand a number of citizens, whether amounting to a majority or a minority of the whole, who are united and actuated by some common impulse of passion, or of interest, adversed to the rights of other citizens, or to the permanent and aggregate interests of the community.

There are two methods of curing the mischiefs of faction: the one, by removing its causes; the other, by controlling its effects.

There are again two methods of removing the causes of faction: the one, by destroying the liberty which is essential to its existence; the other, by giving to every citizen the same opinions, the same passions, and the same interests.

It could never be more truly said than of the first remedy, that it was worse than the disease. Liberty is to faction what air is to fire, an aliment without which it instantly expires. But it could not be less folly to abolish liberty, which is essential to political life, because it nourishes faction, than it would be to wish the annihilation of air, which is essential to animal life, because it imparts to fire its destructive agency.

The second expedient is as impracticable as the first would be unwise. As long as the reason of man continues fallible, and he is at liberty to exercise it, different opinions will be formed. As long as the connection subsists between his reason and his self-love, his opinions and his passions will have a reciprocal influence on each other; and the former will be objects to which the latter will attach themselves. The diversity in the faculties of men, from which the rights of property originate, is not less an insuperable obstacle to a uniformity of interests. The protection of these faculties is the first object of government. From the protection of different and unequal faculties of acquiring property, the possession of different degrees and kinds of property immediately results; and from the influence of these on the sentiments and views of the respective proprietors, ensues a division of the society into different interests and parties.

The latent causes of faction are thus sown in the nature of man; and we see them everywhere brought into different degrees of activity, according to the different circumstances of civil society. A zeal for different opinions concerning religion, concerning government, and many other points, as well of speculation as of practice; an attachment to different leaders ambitiously contending for pre-eminence and power; or to persons of other descriptions whose fortunes have been interesting to the human passions, have, in turn, divided mankind into parties, inflamed them with mutual animosity, and rendered them much more disposed to vex and oppress each other than to co-operate for their common good. So strong is this propensity of mankind to fall into mutual animosities, that where no substantial occasion presents itself, the most frivolous and fanciful distinctions have been sufficient to kindle their unfriendly passions and excite their most violent conflicts. But the most common and durable source of factions has been the various and unequal distribution of property. Those who hold and those who are without property have ever formed distinct interests in society. Those who are creditors, and those who are debtors, fall under a like discrimination. A landed interest, a manufacturing interest, a mercantile interest, a moneyed interest, with many lesser interests, grow up of necessity in civilized nations, and divide them into different classes, actuated by different sentiments and views. The regulation of these various and interfering interests forms the principal task of modern legislation, and involves the spirit of party and faction in the necessary and ordinary operations of the government.

No man is allowed to be a judge in his own cause, because his interest would certainly bias his judgment, and, not improbably, corrupt his integrity. With equal, nay with greater reason, a body of men are unfit to be both judges and parties at the same time; yet what are many of the most important acts of legislation, but so many judicial determinations, not indeed concerning the rights of single persons, but concerning the rights of large bodies of citizens? And what are the different classes of legislators but advocates and parties to the causes which they determine? Is a law proposed concerning private debts? It is a question to which the creditors are parties on one side and the debtors on the other. Justice ought to hold the balance between them. Yet the parties are, and must be, themselves the judges; and the most numerous party, or, in other words, the most powerful faction must be expected to prevail. Shall domestic manufactures be encouraged, and in what degree, by restrictions on foreign manufactures? are questions which would be differently decided by the landed and the manufacturing classes, and probably by neither with a sole regard to justice and the public good. The apportionment of taxes on the various descriptions of property is an act which seems to require the most exact impartiality; yet there is, perhaps, no legislative act in which greater opportunity and temptation are given to a predominant party to trample on the rules of justice. Every shilling with which they overburden the inferior number, is a shilling saved to their own pockets.

It is in vain to say that enlightened statesmen will be able to adjust these clashing interests, and render them all subservient to the public good. Enlightened statesmen will not always be at the helm. Nor, in many cases, can such an adjustment be made at all without taking into view indirect and remote considerations, which will rarely prevail over the immediate interest which one party may find in disregarding the rights of another or the good of the whole.

The inference to which we are brought is, that the *causes* of faction cannot be removed, and that relief is only to be sought in the means of controlling its *effects*.

If a faction consists of less than a majority, relief is supplied by the republican principle, which enables the majority to defeat its sinister views by regular vote. It may clog the administration, it may convulse the society; but it will be unable to execute and mask its violence under the forms of the Constitution. When a majority is included in a faction, the form of popular government, on the other hand, enables it to sacrifice to its ruling passion or interest both the public good and the rights of other citizens. To secure the public good and private rights against the danger of such a faction, and at the same time to preserve the spirit and the form of popular government, is then the great object to which our inquiries are directed. Let me add that it is the great desideratum by which this form of government can be rescued from the opprobrium under which it has so long labored, and be recommended to the esteem and adoption of mankind.

By what means is this object attainable? Evidently by one of two only. Either the existence of the same passion or interest in a majority at the same time must be prevented, or the majority, having such coexistent passion or interest, must be rendered, by their number and local situation, unable to concert and carry into effect schemes of oppression. If the impulse and the opportunity be suffered to coincide, we well know that neither moral nor religious motives can be relied on as an adequate control. They are not found to be such on the injustice and violence of individuals, and lose their efficacy in proportion to the number combined together, that is, in proportion as their efficacy becomes needful.

From this view of the subject it may be concluded that a pure democracy, by which I mean a society consisting of a small number of citizens, who assemble and administer the government in person, can admit of no cure for the mischiefs of faction. A common passion or interest will, in almost every case, be felt by a majority of the whole; a communication and concert result from the form of government itself; and there is nothing to check the inducements to sacrifice the weaker party or an obnoxious individual. Hence it is that such democracies have ever been spectacles of turbulence and contention; have ever been found incompatible with personal security or the rights of property; and have in general been as short in their lives as they have been violent in their deaths. Theoretic politicians, who have patronized this species of government, have erroneously supposed that by reducing mankind to a perfect equality in their political rights, they would, at the same time, be perfectly equalized and assimilated in their possessions, their opinions, and their passions.

A republic, by which I mean a government in which the scheme of representation takes place, opens a different prospect, and promises the cure for which we are seeking. Let us examine the points in which it varies from pure democracy, and we shall comprehend both the nature of the cure and the efficacy which it must derive from the Union.

The two great points of difference between a democracy and a republic are: first, the delegation of the government, in the latter, to a small number of citizens elected by the rest; secondly, the greater number of citizens, and greater sphere of country, over which the latter may be extended.

The effect of the first difference is, on the one hand, to refine and enlarge the public views, by passing them through the medium of a chosen body of citizens, whose wisdom may best discern the true interest of their country, and whose patriotism and love of justice will be least likely to sacrifice it to temporary or partial considerations. Under such a regulation, it may well happen that the public voice, pronounced by the representatives of the people, will be more consonant to the public good than if pronounced by the people themselves, convened for the purpose. On the other hand, the effect may be inverted. Men of factious tempers, of local prejudices, or of sinister designs, may, by intrigue, by corruption, or by other means, first obtain the suffrages, and then betray the interests, of the people. The question resulting is, whether small or extensive republics are more favorable to the election of proper guardians of the public weal; and it is clearly decided in favor of the latter by two obvious considerations:

In the first place, it is to be remarked that, however small the republic may be, the representatives must be raised to a certain number, in order to guard against the cabals of a few; and that, however large it may be, they must be limited to a certain number, in order to guard against the confusion of a multitude. Hence, the number of representatives in the two cases not being in proportion to that of the two constituents, and being proportionally greater in the small republic, it follows that, if the proportion of fit characters be not less in the large than in the small republic, the former will present a greater option, and consequently a greater probability of a fit choice.

In the next place, as each representative will be chosen by a greater number of citizens in the large than in the small republic, it will be more difficult for unworthy candidates to practice with success the vicious arts by which elections are too often carried; and the suffrages of the people being more free, will be more likely to centre in men who possess the most attractive merit and the most diffusive and established characters.

It must be confessed that in this, as in most other cases, there is a mean, on both sides of which inconveniences will be found to lie. By enlarging too much the number of electors, you render the representatives too little acquainted with all their local circumstances and lesser interests; as by reducing it too much, you render him unduly attached to these, and too little fit to comprehend and pursue great and national objects. The federal Constitution forms a happy combination in this respect; the great and aggregate interests being referred to the national, the local and particular to the State legislatures.

The other point of difference is, the greater number of citizens and extent of territory which may be brought within the compass of republican than of democratic government; and it is this circumstance principally which renders factious combinations less to be dreaded in the former than in the latter. The smaller the society, the fewer probably will be the distinct parties and interests composing it; the fewer the distinct parties and interests, the more frequently will a majority be found of the same party; and the smaller the number of individuals composing a majority, and the smaller the compass within which they are placed, the more easily will they concert and execute their plans of oppression. Extend the sphere, and you take in a greater variety of parties and interests; you make it less probable that a majority of the whole will have a common motive to invade the rights of other citizens; or if such a common motive exists, it will be more difficult for all who feel it to discover their own strength, and to act in unison with each other. Besides other impediments, it may be remarked that, where there is a consciousness of unjust or dishonorable purposes, communication is always checked by distrust in proportion to the number whose concurrence is necessary.

Hence, it clearly appears, that the same advantage which a republic has over a democracy, in controlling the effects of faction, is enjoyed by a large over a small republic,—is enjoyed by the Union over the States composing it. Does the advantage consist in the substitution of representatives whose enlightened views and virtuous sentiments render them superior to local prejudices and schemes of injustice? It will not be denied that the representation of the Union will be most likely to possess these requisite endowments. Does it consist in the greater security afforded by a greater variety of parties, against the event of any one party being able to outnumber and oppress the rest? In an equal degree does the increased variety of parties comprised within the Union, increase this security. Does it, in fine, consist in the greater obstacles opposed to the concert and accomplishment of the secret wishes of an unjust and interested majority? Here, again, the extent of the Union gives it the most palpable advantage.

The influence of factious leaders may kindle a flame within their particular States, but will be unable to spread a general conflagration through the other States. A religious sect may degenerate into a political faction in a part of the Confederacy; but the variety of sects dispersed over the entire face of it must secure the national councils against any danger from that source. A rage for paper money, for an abolition of debts, for an equal division of property, or for any other improper or wicked project, will be less apt to pervade the whole body of the Union than a particular member of it; in the same proportion as such a malady is more likely to taint a particular county or district, than an entire State.

In the extent and proper structure of the Union, therefore, we behold a republican remedy for the diseases most incident to republican government. And according to the degree of pleasure and pride we feel in being republicans, ought to be our zeal in cherishing the spirit and supporting the character of Federalists.

—PUBLIUS

APPENDIX E

FEDERALIST NO. 78

BY ALEXANDER HAMILTON, 1788

Anti-Federalists opposed to the Constitution frequently presented the proposed judiciary as a potentially tyrannical institution because, through the power of judicial review, they would have the ultimate say over whether a law was constitutional. Writing as "Brutus," Robert Yates argues that unchecked power inevitably leads to dictatorship and that "there is no power provided in the constitution, that can correct their errors, or controul [the judiciary's] adjudications." To Yates, and to many others, the notion of unelected judges seemed too reminiscent of the British courts of colonial times.

Hamilton's Federalist no. 78 *was written in direct response to Yates's objections. The judiciary, Hamilton argues, is the weakest branch of government because it lacks any way to enforce its mandates. The legislature has the power of the purse; it can enforce its will by appropriating (or refusing to appropriate) money. The executive has the power of the sword; the president can use military or police force to enforce its will. Lacking either power, the judiciary must rely on the other two branches of government to enforce its directives. Its lack of power becomes a significant check on its authority.*

Hamilton also argues that the power to declare laws unconstitutional—and to be the final authority on such matters—constitutes a vital check on the legislature. Without a Supreme Court empowered by judicial review, Congress could disregard the Constitution any time a majority chose to do so. In time, he felt, this would lead to the complete erosion of the Constitution. Only a judiciary complexly independent from the other branches of government could preserve the delicate system of checks and balances the Framers created.

We proceed now to an examination of the judiciary department of the proposed government.

In unfolding the defects of the existing Confederation, the utility and necessity of a federal judicature have been clearly pointed out. It is the less necessary to recapitulate the considerations there urged, as the propriety of the institution in the abstract is not disputed; the only questions which have been raised being relative to the manner of constituting it, and to its extent. To these points, therefore, our observations shall be confined.

The manner of constituting it seems to embrace these several objects: 1st. The mode of appointing the judges. 2d. The tenure by which they are to hold their places. 3d. The partition of the judiciary authority between different courts, and their relations to each other.

First. As to the mode of appointing the judges; this is the same with that of appointing the officers of the Union in general, and has been so fully discussed in the two last numbers, that nothing can be said here which would not be useless repetition.

Second. As to the tenure by which the judges are to hold their places; this chiefly concerns their duration in office; the provisions for their support; the precautions for their responsibility.

According to the plan of the convention, all judges who may be appointed by the United States are to hold their offices during good behavior; which is conformable to the most approved of the State constitutions and among the rest, to that of this State. Its propriety having been drawn into question by the adversaries of that plan, is no light symptom of the rage for objection, which disorders their imaginations and judgments. The standard of good behavior for the continuance in office of the judicial magistracy, is certainly one of the most valuable of the modern improvements in the practice of government. In a monarchy it is an excellent barrier to the despotism of the prince; in a republic it is a no less excellent barrier to the encroachments and oppressions of the representative body. And it is the best expedient which can be devised in any government, to secure a steady, upright, and impartial administration of the laws.

Whoever attentively considers the different departments of power must perceive, that, in a government in which they are separated from each other, the judiciary, from the nature of its functions, will always be the least dangerous to the political rights of the Constitution; because it will be least in a capacity to annoy or injure them. The Executive not only dispenses the honors, but holds the sword of the community. The legislature not only commands the purse, but prescribes the rules by which the duties and rights of every citizen are to be regulated. The judiciary, on the contrary, has no influence over either the sword or the purse; no direction either of the strength or of the wealth of the society; and can take no active resolution whatever. It may truly be said to have neither FORCE nor WILL, but merely judgment; and must ultimately depend upon the aid of the executive arm even for the efficacy of its judgments.

This simple view of the matter suggests several important consequences. It proves incontestably, that the judiciary is beyond comparison the weakest of the three departments of power; that it can never attack with success either of the other two; and that all possible care is requisite to enable it to defend itself against their attacks. It equally proves, that though individual oppression may now and then proceed from the courts of justice, the general liberty of the people can never be endangered from that quarter; I mean so long as the judiciary remains truly distinct from both the legislature and the Executive. For I agree, that "there is no liberty, if the power of judging be not separated from the legislative and executive powers." And it proves, in the last place, that as liberty can have nothing to fear from the judiciary alone, but would have everything to fear from its union with either of the other departments; that as all the effects of such a union must ensue from a dependence of the former on the latter, notwithstanding a nominal and apparent separation; that as, from the natural feebleness of the judiciary, it is in continual jeopardy of being overpowered, awed, or influenced by its co-ordinate branches; and that as nothing can contribute so much to its firmness and independence as permanency in office, this quality may therefore be justly regarded as an indispensable ingredient in its constitution, and, in a great measure, as the citadel of the public justice and the public security.

The complete independence of the courts of justice is peculiarly essential in a limited Constitution. By a limited Constitution, I understand one which contains certain specified exceptions to the legislative authority; such, for instance, as that it shall pass no bills of attainder, no ex post facto laws, and the like. Limitations of this kind can be preserved in practice no other way than through the medium of courts of justice, whose duty it must be to declare all acts contrary to the manifest tenor of the Constitution void. Without this, all the reservations of particular rights or privileges would amount to nothing.

Some perplexity respecting the rights of the courts to pronounce legislative acts void, because contrary to the Constitution, has arisen from an imagination that the doctrine would imply a superiority of the judiciary to the legislative power. It is urged that the authority which can declare the acts of another void, must necessarily be superior to the one whose acts may be declared void. As this doctrine is of great importance in all the American constitutions, a brief discussion of the ground on which it rests cannot be unacceptable.

There is no position which depends on clearer principles, than that every act of a delegated authority, contrary to the tenor of the commission under which it is exercised, is void. No legislative act, therefore, contrary to the Constitution, can be valid. To deny this, would be to affirm, that the deputy is greater than his principal; that the servant is above his master; that the representatives of the people are superior to the people themselves; that men acting by virtue of powers, may do not only what their powers do not authorize, but what they forbid.

If it be said that the legislative body are themselves the constitutional judges of their own powers, and that the construction they put upon them is conclusive upon the other departments, it may be answered, that this cannot be the natural presumption, where it is not to be collected from any particular provisions in the Constitution. It is not otherwise to be supposed, that the Constitution could intend to enable the representatives of the people to substitute their will to that of their constituents. It is far more rational to suppose, that the courts were designed to be an intermediate body between the people and the legislature, in order, among other things, to keep the latter within the limits assigned to their authority. The interpretation of the laws is the proper and peculiar province of the courts. A constitution is, in fact, and must be regarded by the judges, as a fundamental law. It therefore belongs to them to ascertain its meaning, as well as the meaning of any particular act proceeding from the legislative body. If there should happen to be an irreconcilable variance between the two, that which has the superior obligation and validity ought, of course, to be preferred; or, in other words, the Constitution ought to be preferred to the statute, the intention of the people to the intention of their agents.

Nor does this conclusion by any means suppose a superiority of the judicial to the legislative power. It only supposes that the power of the people is superior to both; and that where the will of the legislature, declared in its statutes, stands in opposition to that of the people, declared in the Constitution, the judges ought to be governed by the latter rather than the former. They ought to regulate their decisions by the fundamental laws, rather than by those which are not fundamental.

This exercise of judicial discretion, in determining between two contradictory laws, is exemplified in a familiar instance. It not uncommonly happens, that there are two statutes existing at one time, clashing in whole or in part with each other, and neither of them containing any repealing clause or expression. In such a case, it is the province of the courts to liquidate and fix their meaning and operation. So far as they can, by any fair construction, be reconciled to each other, reason and law conspire to dictate that this should be done; where this is impracticable, it becomes a matter of necessity to give effect to one, in exclusion of the other. The rule which has obtained in the courts for determining their relative validity is, that the last in order of time shall be preferred to the first. But this is a mere rule of construction, not derived from any positive law, but from the nature and reason of the thing. It is a rule not enjoined upon the courts by legislative provision, but adopted by themselves, as consonant to truth and propriety, for the direction of their conduct as interpreters of the law. They thought it reasonable, that between the interfering acts of an EQUAL authority, that which was the last indication of its will should have the preference.

But in regard to the interfering acts of a superior and subordinate authority, of an original and derivative power, the nature and reason of the thing indicate the converse of that rule as proper to be followed. They teach us that the prior act of a superior ought to be preferred to the subsequent act of an inferior and subordinate authority; and that accordingly, whenever a particular statute contravenes the Constitution, it will be the duty of the judicial tribunals to adhere to the latter and disregard the former.

It can be of no weight to say that the courts, on the pretense of a repugnancy, may substitute their own pleasure to the constitutional intentions of the legislature. This might as well happen in the case of two contradictory statutes; or it might as well happen in every adjudication upon any single statute. The courts must declare the sense of the law; and if they should be disposed to exercise WILL instead of JUDGMENT, the consequence would equally be the substitution of their pleasure to that of the legislative body. The observation, if it proves anything, would prove that there ought to be no judges distinct from that body.

If, then, the courts of justice are to be considered as the bulwarks of a limited Constitution against legislative encroachments, this consideration will afford a strong argument for the permanent tenure of judicial offices, since nothing will contribute so much as this to that independent spirit in the judges which must be essential to the faithful performance of so arduous a duty.

This independence of the judges is equally requisite to guard the Constitution and the rights of individuals from the effects of those ill humors, which the arts of designing men, or the influence of particular conjunctures, sometimes disseminate among the people themselves, and which, though they speedily give place to better information, and more deliberate reflection, have a tendency, in the meantime, to occasion dangerous innovations in the government, and serious oppressions of the minor party in the community. Though I trust the friends of the proposed Constitution will never concur with its enemies, in questioning that fundamental principle of republican government, which admits the right of the people to alter or abolish the established Constitution, whenever they find it inconsistent with their happiness, yet it is not to be inferred from this principle, that the representatives of the people, whenever a momentary inclination happens to lay hold of a majority of their constituents, incompatible with the provisions in the existing Constitution, would, on that account, be justifiable in a violation of those provisions; or that the courts would be under a greater obligation to connive at infractions in this shape, than when they had proceeded wholly from the cabals of the representative body. Until the people have, by some solemn and authoritative act, annulled or changed the established form, it is binding upon themselves collectively, as well as individually; and no presumption, or even knowledge, of their sentiments, can warrant their representatives in a departure from it, prior to such an act. But it is easy to see, that it would require an uncommon portion of fortitude in the judges to do their duty as faithful guardians of the Constitution, where legislative invasions of it had been instigated by the major voice of the community.

But it is not with a view to infractions of the Constitution only, that the independence of the judges may be an essential safeguard against the effects of occasional ill humors in the society. These sometimes extend no farther than to the injury of the private rights of particular classes of citizens, by unjust and partial laws. Here also the firmness of the judicial magistracy is of vast importance in mitigating the severity and confining the operation of such laws. It not only serves to moderate the immediate mischiefs of those which may have been passed, but it operates as a check upon the legislative body in passing them; who, perceiving that obstacles to the success of iniquitous intention are to be expected from the scruples of the courts, are in a manner compelled, by the very motives of the injustice they meditate, to qualify their attempts. This is a circumstance calculated to have more influence upon the character of our governments, than but few may be aware of. The benefits of the integrity and moderation of the judiciary have already been felt in more States than one; and though they may have displeased those whose sinister expectations they may have disappointed, they must have commanded the esteem and applause of all the virtuous and disinterested. Considerate men, of every description, ought to prize whatever will tend to beget or fortify that temper in the courts: as no man can be sure that he may not be to-morrow the victim of a spirit of injustice, by which he may be a gainer to-day. And every man must now feel, that the inevitable tendency of such a spirit is to sap the foundations of public and private confidence, and to introduce in its stead universal distrust and distress.

That inflexible and uniform adherence to the rights of the Constitution, and of individuals, which we perceive to be indispensable in the courts of justice, can certainly not be expected from judges who hold their offices by a temporary commission. Periodical appointments, however regulated, or by whomsoever made, would, in some way or other, be fatal to their necessary independence. If the power of making them was committed either to the Executive or legislature, there would be danger of an improper complaisance to the branch which possessed it; if to both, there would be an unwillingness to hazard the displeasure of either; if to the people, or to persons chosen by them for the special purpose, there would be too great a disposition to consult popularity, to justify a reliance that nothing would be consulted but the Constitution and the laws.

There is yet a further and a weightier reason for the permanency of the judicial offices, which is deducible from the nature of the qualifications they require. It has been frequently remarked, with great propriety, that a voluminous code of laws is one of the inconveniences necessarily connected with the advantages of a free government. To avoid an arbitrary discretion in the courts, it is indispensable that they should be bound down by strict rules and precedents, which serve to define and point out their duty in every particular case that comes before them; and it will readily be conceived from the variety of controversies which grow out of the folly and wickedness of mankind, that the records of those precedents must unavoidably swell to a very considerable bulk, and must demand long and laborious study to acquire a competent knowledge of them. Hence it is, that there can be but few men in the society who will have sufficient skill in the laws to qualify them for the stations of judges. And making the proper deductions for the ordinary depravity of human nature, the number must be still smaller of those who unite the requisite integrity with the requisite knowledge. These considerations apprise us, that the government can have no great option between fit character; and that a temporary duration in office, which would naturally discourage such characters from quitting a lucrative line of practice to accept a seat on the bench, would have a tendency to throw the adminis-tration of justice into hands less able, and less well qualified, to conduct it with utility and dignity. In the present circumstances of this country, and in those in which it is likely to be for a long time to come, the disadvantages on this score would be greater than they may at first sight appear; but it must be confessed, that they are far inferior to those which present themselves under the other aspects of the subject.

Upon the whole, there can be no room to doubt that the convention acted wisely in copying from the models of those constitutions which have estab-lished good behavior as the tenure of their judicial offices, in point of dura-tion; and that so far from being blamable on this account, their plan would have been inexcusably defective, if it had wanted this important feature of good government. The experience of Great Britain affords an illustrious comment on the excellence of the institution.

—PUBLIUS

THE NATIONAL BANK DEBATE

BY THOMAS JEFFERSON AND ALEXANDER HAMILTON, 1791

When Treasury Secretary Alexander Hamilton proposed the creation of the Bank of the United States in 1791, he unknowingly set off a firestorm that would define American politics for a generation. In the North, merchants and industrialists were suffering from a severe shortage of credit and from a lack of any kind of national currency—two issues a national bank would address. Southern plantation owners, on the other hand, wanted nothing to do with banks, national or otherwise, which they saw as entities that created wealth out of air.

The congressional debate over the bank soon became a debate over the powers of the federal government. Madison, Jefferson, and their allies believed the Constitution did not give the national government the power to create banks; thus, Hamilton's plan was plainly unconstitutional. Hamilton, on the other hand, argued that the Constitution contained implied powers that allowed the government to undertake any reasonable means necessary to accomplish its delegated powers. Since the Constitution empowers Congress to borrow money, regulate commerce, and collect taxes, he insisted, it empowers it to create a bank to facilitate these objectives.

After both the House and the Senate passed legislation to create the Bank of the United States, Madison urged President Washington to exercise his veto on constitutional grounds. Washington was genuinely perplexed about the issue, and he asked both Hamilton and his secretary of state, Thomas Jefferson, to give him a written assessment of the constitutionality of the national bank. Jefferson responded with a brief paper advocating a limited reading of the powers granted to Congress by the Constitution. Hamilton responded with a massive document outlining his view of the powers implied by—but not stated directly in—the Constitution.

Jefferson's "Opinion on the Constitutionality of a National Bank" has been reprinted here in its entirety. Hamilton's "Opinion on the Constitutionality of a National Bank"—which is six times longer than Jefferson's paper— has been excerpted.

Please note the numbering in the following document remains true to the original.

೧౪౯

JEFFERSON'S "OPINION ON THE CONSTITUTIONALITY OF A NATIONAL BANK," 1791

The bill for establishing a National Bank undertakes among other things:

1. To form the subscribers into a corporation.

2. To enable them in their corporate capacities to receive grants of land; and so far is against the laws of *Mortmain*.

3. To make alien subscribers capable of holding lands, and so far is against the laws of *Alienage*.

4. To transmit these lands, on the death of a proprietor, to a certain line of successors; and so far changes the course of *Descents*.

5. To put the lands out of the reach of forfeiture or escheat, and so far is against the laws of *Forfeiture and Escheat*.

6. To transmit personal chattels to successors in a certain line and so far is against the laws of *Distribution*.

7. To give them the sole and exclusive right of banking under the national authority; and so far is against the laws of *Monopoly*.

8. To communicate to them a power to make laws paramount to the laws of the States; for so they must be construed, to protect the institution from the control of the State legislatures, and so, probably, they will be construed.

I consider the foundation of the Constitution as laid on this ground: That "all powers not delegated to the United States, by the Constitution, nor prohibited by it to the States, are reserved to the States or to the people." [XIIth amendment.] To take a single step beyond the boundaries thus specially drawn around the powers of Congress, is to take possession of a boundless field of power, no longer susceptible of any definition.

The incorporation of a bank, and the powers assumed by this bill, have not, in my opinion, been delegated to the United States, by the Constitution.

I. They are not among the powers specially enumerated: for these are: 1st A power to lay taxes for the purpose of paying the debts of the United States; but no debt is paid by this bill, nor any tax laid. Were it a bill to raise money, its origination in the Senate would condemn it by the Constitution.

2. "To borrow money." But this bill neither borrows money nor ensures the borrowing it. The proprietors of the bank will be just as free as any other money holders, to lend or not to lend their money to the public. The operation proposed in the bill first, to lend them two millions, and then to borrow them back again, cannot change the nature of the latter act, which will still be a payment, and not a loan, call it by what name you please.

3. To "regulate commerce with foreign nations, and among the States, and with the Indian tribes." To erect a bank, and to regulate commerce, are very different acts. He who erects a bank, creates a subject of commerce in its bills, so does he who makes a bushel of wheat, or digs a dollar out of the mines; yet neither of these persons regulates commerce thereby. To make a thing which may be bought and sold, is not to prescribe regulations for buying and selling. Besides, if this was an exercise of the power of regulating commerce, it would be void, as extending as much to the internal commerce of every State, as to its external. For the power given to Congress by the Constitution does not extend to the internal regulation of the commerce of a State, (that is to say of the commerce between citizen and citizen,) which remain exclusively with its own legislature; but to its external commerce only, that is to say, its commerce with another State, or with foreign nations, or with the Indian tribes. Accordingly the bill does not propose the measure as a regulation of trace, but as "productive of considerable advantages to trade." Still less are these powers covered by any other of the special enumerations.

II. Nor are they within either of the general phrases, which are the two following:

1. To lay taxes to provide for the general welfare of the United States, that is to say, "to lay taxes for *the purpose of* providing for the general welfare." For the laying of taxes is the *power*, and the general welfare

the *purpose* for which the power is to be exercised. They are not to lay taxes *ad libitum for any purpose they please*; but only *to pay the debts or provide for the welfare of the Union*. In like manner, they are not *to do anything they please* to provide for the general welfare, but only to *lay taxes* for that purpose. To consider the latter phrase, not as describing the purpose of the first, but as giving a distinct and independent power to do any act they please, which might be for the good of the Union, would render all the preceding and subsequent enumerations of power completely useless.

It would reduce the whole instrument to a single phrase, that of instituting a Congress with power to do whatever would be for the good of the United States; and, as they would be the sole judges of the good or evil, it would be also a power to do whatever evil they please.

It is an established rule of construction where a phrase will bear either of two meanings, to give it that which will allow some meaning to the other parts of the instrument, and not that which would render all the others useless. Certainly no such universal power was meant to be given them. It was intended to lace them up straitly within the enumerated powers, and those without which, as means, these powers could not be carried into effect. It is known that the very power now proposed *as a means* was rejected *as an end* by the Convention which formed the Constitution. A proposition was made to them to authorize Congress to open canals, and an amendatory one to empower them to incorporate. But the whole was rejected, and one of the reasons for rejection urged in debate was, that then they would have a power to erect a bank, which would render the great cities, where there were prejudices and jealousies on the subject, adverse to the reception of the Constitution.

2. The second general phrase is, "to make all laws Necessary and Proper for carrying into execution the enumerated powers." But they can all be carried into execution without a bank. A bank therefore is not necessary, and consequently not authorized by this phrase.

It has been urged that a bank will give great facility or convenience in the collection of taxes, Suppose this were true: yet the Constitution allows only the means which are "necessary," not those which are merely "convenient" for effecting the enumerated powers. If such a latitude of construction be allowed to this phrase as to give any non-enumerated power, it will go to everyone, for there is not one which ingenuity may not torture into a convenience in some instance or other, to some one of so long a list of enumerated powers. It would swallow up all the delegated powers, and reduce the whole to one power, as before observed. Therefore it was that the Constitution restrained them to the necessary means, that is to say, to those means without which the grant of power would be nugatory.

But let us examine this convenience and see what it is. The report on this subject, page 3, states the only general convenience to be, the preventing the transportation and re-transportation of money between the States and the treasury, (for I pass over the increase of circulating medium, ascribed to it as a want, and which, according to my ideas of paper money, is clearly a demerit.) Every State will have to pay a sum of tax money into the treasury; and the treasury will have to pay, in every State, a part of the interest on the public debt, and salaries to the officers of government resident in that State. In most of the States there will still be a surplus of tax money to come up to the seat of government for the officers residing there. The payments of interest and salary in each State may be made by treasury orders on the State collector. This will take up the greater part of the money he has collected in his State, and consequently prevent the great mass of it from being drawn out of the State. If there be a balance of commerce in favor of that State against the one in which the government resides, the surplus of taxes will be remitted by the bills of exchange drawn for that commercial balance. And so it must be if there was a bank. But if there be no balance of commerce, either direct or circuitous, all the banks in the world could not bring up the surplus of taxes, but in the form of money. Treasury orders then, and bills of exchange may prevent the displacement of the main mass of the money collected, without the aid of any bank; and where these fail, it cannot be prevented even with that aid.

Perhaps, indeed, bank bills may be a more convenient vehicle than treasury orders. But a little difference in the degree of convenience cannot constitute the necessity which the Constitution makes the ground for assuming any non-enumerated power.

Besides, the existing banks will, without a doubt, enter into arrangements for lending their agency, and the more favorable, as there will be a competition among them for it; whereas the bill delivers us up bound to the national bank, who are free to refuse all arrangement, but on their own terms, and the public not free, on such refusal, to employ any other bank. That of Philadelphia I believe, now does this business, by their post-notes, which, by an arrangement with the treasury, are paid by any State collector to whom they are presented. This expedient alone suffices to prevent the existence of that necessity which may justify the assumption of a non-enumerated power as a means for carrying into effect an enumerated one. The thing may be done, and has been done, and well done, without this assumption, therefore it does not stand on that degree of necessity which can honestly justify it.

It may be said that a bank whose bills would have a currency all over the States, would be more convenient than one whose currency is limited to a single State. So it would be still more convenient that there should be a bank, whose bills should have a currency all over the world. But it does not follow from this superior conveniency, that there exists anywhere a power to establish such a bank; or that the world may not go on very well without it.

Can it be thought that the Constitution intended that for a shade or two of convenience, more or less, Congress should be authorized to break down the most ancient and fundamental laws of the several States; such as those against Mortmain, the laws of Alienage, the rules of descent, the acts of distribution, the laws of escheat and forfeiture, the laws of monopoly? Nothing but a necessity invincible by any other means, can justify such a prostitution of laws, which constitute the pillars of our whole system of jurisprudence. Will Congress be too strait-laced to carry the Constitution into honest effect, unless they may pass over the foundation-laws of the State government for the slightest convenience of theirs?

The negative of the President is the shield provided by the Constitution to protect against the invasions of the legislature: 1. The right of the Executive. 2. Of the Judiciary. 3. Of the States and State legislatures. The present is the case of a right remaining exclusively with the States, and consequently one of those intended by the Constitution to be placed under its protection.

It must be added, however, that unless the President's mind on a view of everything which is urged for and against this bill, is tolerably clear that it is unauthorized by the Constitution; if the pro and the con hang so even as to balance his judgment, a just respect for the wisdom of the legislature would naturally decide the balance in favor of their opinion. It is chiefly for cases where they are clearly misled by error, ambition, or interest, that the Constitution has placed a check in the negative of the President.

SELECTION FROM HAMILTON'S "OPINION AS TO THE CONSTITUTIONALITY OF THE BANK OF THE UNITED STATES," 1791

The Secretary of the Treasury having perused with attention the papers containing the opinions of the Secretary of State and Attorney General, concerning the constitutionality of the bill for establishing a National Bank, proceeds, according to the order of the President, to submit the reasons which have induced him to entertain a different opinion.

It will naturally have been anticipated, that in performing this task, he would feel uncommon solicitude. Personal considerations alone, arising from the reflection that the measure originated with him, would be sufficient to produce it. The sense which he has manifested of the great importance of such an institution to the successful administration of the department under his particular care, and an expectation of serious ill consequences to result from a failure of the measure, do not permit him to be without anxiety on public accounts. But the chief solicitude arises from a firm persuasion, that principles of construction like those espoused by the Secretary of State and Attorney General, would be fatal to the just and indispensable authority of the United States.

In entering upon the argument, it ought to be premised that the objections of the Secretary of State and Attorney General are founded on a general denial of the authority of the United States to erect corporations. The latter, indeed, expressly admits, that if there be anything in the bill which is not warranted by the Constitution, it is the clause of incorporation.

Now it appears to the Secretary of the Treasury that this general principle is inherent in the very definition of government, and essential to every step of progress to be made by that of the United States, namely: That every power vested in a government is in its nature sovereign, and includes, by force of the term, a right to employ all the means requisite and fairly applicable to the attainment of the ends of such power, and which are not precluded by restrictions and exceptions specified in the Constitution, or not immoral, or not contrary to the essential ends of political society.

This principle, in its application to government in general, would be admitted as an axiom; and it will be incumbent upon those who may incline to deny it, to prove a distinction, and to show that a rule which, in the general system of things, is essential to the preservation of the social order, is inapplicable to the United States.

The circumstance that the powers of sovereignty are in this country divided between the National and State governments, does not afford the distinction required. It does not follow from this, that each of the portion of powers delegated to the one or to the other, is not sovereign with regard to its proper objects. It will only follow from it, that each has sovereign power as to certain things, and not as to other things. To deny that the government of the United States has sovereign power, as to its declared purposes and trusts, because its power does not extend to all cases would be equally to deny that the State governments have sovereign power in any case, because their power does not extend to every case. The tenth section of the first article of the Constitution exhibits a long list of very important things which they may not do. And thus the United States would furnish the singular spectacle of a political society without sovereignty, or of a people governed, without government.

If it would be necessary to bring proof to a proposition so clear, as that which affirms that the powers of the federal government, as to its objects, were sovereign, there is a clause of its Constitution which would be decisive. It is that which declares that the Constitution, and the laws of the United States made in pursuance of it, and all treaties made, or which shall be made, under their authority, shall be the serene law of the land. The power which can create the supreme law of the land in any case, is doubtless sovereign as to such case.

This general and indisputable principle puts at once an end to the abstract question, whether the United States have power to erect a corporation; that is to say, to give a legal or artificial capacity to one or more persons, distinct from the natural. For it is unquestionably incident to sovereign power to erect corporations, and consequently to that of the United States, in relation to the objects intrusted to the management of the government. The difference is this: where the authority of the government is general, it can create corporations in ad cases, where it is confined to certain branches of legislation, it can create corporations only in those cases."

Here then, as far as concerns the reasonings of the Secretary of State and the Attorney General, the affirmative of the constitutionality of the bill might be permitted to rest. It will occur to the President, that the principle here advanced has been untouched by either of them.

For a more complete elucidation of the point, nevertheless, the arguments which they had used against the power of the government to erect corporations, however foreign they are to the great and fundamental rule which has been stated, shall be particularly examined. And after showing that they do not tend to impair its force, it shall also be shown that the power of incorporation, incident to the government in certain cases, does fairly extend to the particular case which is the object of the bill.

The first of these arguments is, that the foundation of the Constitution is laid on this ground: "That all powers not delegated to the United States by the Constitution, nor prohibited to it by the States, are reserved for the States, or to the people." Whence it is meant to be inferred, that Congress can in no case exercise any power not Included in those not enumerated in the Constitution. And it is affirmed, that the power of erecting a corporation is not included in any of the enumerated powers.

The main proposition here laid down, in its true signification is not to be questioned. It is nothing more than a consequence of this republican maxim, that all government is a delegation of power. But how much is delegated in each case, is a question of fact, to be made out by fair reasoning and construction, upon the particular provisions of the Constitution, taking as guides the general principles and general ends of governments.

It is not denied that there are implied as well as express powers, and that the former are as effectually delegated as the latter. And for the sake of accuracy it shall be mentioned, that there is another class of powers, which may be properly denominated resting powers. It will not be doubted, that if the United States should make a conquest of any of the territories of its neighbors, they would possess sovereign jurisdiction over the conquered territory. This would be rather a result, from the whole mass of the powers of the government, and from the nature of political society, than a consequence of either of the powers specially enumerated.

But be this as it may, it furnishes a striking illustration of the general doctrine contended for; it shows an extensive case in which a power of erecting corporations is either implied in or would result from, some or all of the powers vested in the national government. The jurisdiction acquired over such conquered country would certainly be competent to any species of legislation.

To return: It is conceded that implied powers are to be considered as delegated equally with express ones. Then it follows, that as a power of erecting a corporation may as well be implied as any other thing, it may as well be employed as an instrument or mean of carrying into execution any of the specified powers, as any other instrument or mean whatever. The only question must be in this, as in every other case, whether the mean to be employed or in this instance, the corporation to be erected, has a natural relation to any of the acknowledged objects or lawful ends of the government. Thus a corporation may not be erected by Congress for superintending the police of the city of Philadelphia, because they are not authorized to regulate the police of that city. But one may be erected in relation to the collection of taxes, or to the trade with foreign countries, or to the trade between the States, or with the Indian tribes; because it is the province of the federal government to regulate those objects, and because it is incident to a general sovereign or legislative power to regulate a thing, to employ all the means which relate to its regulation to the best and greatest advantage.

A strange fallacy seems to have crept into the manner of thinking and reasoning upon the subject. Imagination appears to have been unusually busy concerning it. An incorporation seems to have been regarded as some great independent substantive thing; as a political end of peculiar magnitude and moment; whereas it is truly to be considered as a quality, capacity, or mean to an end. Thus a mercantile company is formed, with a certain capital, for the purpose of carrying on a particular branch of business. Here the business to be prosecuted is the end. The association, in order to form the requisite capital, is the primary mean. Suppose that an incorporation were added to this, it would only be to add a new quality to that association, to give it an artificial capacity, by which it would be enabled to prosecute the business with more safety and convenience.

That the importance of the power of incorporation has been exaggerated, leading to erroneous conclusions, will further appear from tracing it to its origin. The Roman law is the source of it, according to which a voluntary association of individuals, at any time, or for any purpose, was capable of producing it. In England, whence our notions of it are immediately borrowed, it forms part of the executive authority, and the exercise of it has been often delegated by that authority. Whence, therefore, the ground of the supposition that it lies beyond the reach of all those very important portions of sovereign power, legislative as well as executive, which belongs to the government of the United States.

To this mode of reasoning respecting the right of employing all the means requisite to the execution of the specified powers of the government, it is objected, that none but Necessary and Proper means are to be employed; and the Secretary of State maintains, that no means are to be considered as necessary but those without which the grant of the power would be nugatory. Nay, so far does he go in his restrictive interpretation of the word, as even to make the case of necessity which shall warrant the constitutional exercise of the power to depend on casual and temporary circumstances; an idea which alone refutes the construction. The expediency of exercising a particular power, at a particular time, must, indeed depend on circumstances, but the constitutional right of exercising it must be uniform and invariable, the same to-day as to-morrow.

All the arguments, therefore, against the constitutionality of the bill derived from the accidental existence of certain State banks, institutions which happen to exist to-day, and, for aught that concerns the government of the United States, may disappear tomorrow, must not only be rejected as fallacious, but must be viewed as demonstrative that there is a radical source of error in the reasoning.

It is essential to the being of the national government, that so erroneous a conception of the meaning of the word necessary should be exploded.

It is certain that neither the grammatical nor popular sense of the term requires that construction. According to both, necessary often means no more than needful, requisite, incidental, useful, or conducive to. It is a common mode of expression to say, that it is necessary for a government or a person to do this or that thing, when nothing more is intended or understood, than that the interests of the government or person require, or will be promoted by, the doing of this or that thing. The imagination can be at no loss for exemplifications of the use of the word in this sense. And it is the true one in which it is to be understood as used in the Constitution. The whole turn of the clause containing it indicates, that it was the intent of the Convention, by that clause, to give a liberal latitude to the exercise of the specified powers. The expressions have peculiar comprehensiveness. They are thought "to make all laws Necessary and Proper for carrying into execution the foregoing powers, and all other powers vested by the Constitution in the government of the United States, or in any department or officer thereof."

To understand the word as the Secretary of State does, would be to depart from its obvious and popular sense, and to give it a restrictive operation, an idea never before entertained. It would be to give it the same force as if the word absolutely or indispensably had been prefixed to it.

Such a construction would beget endless uncertainty and embarrassment. The cases must be palpable and extreme, in which it could be pronounced, with certainty, that a measure was absolutely necessary, or one, without which, the exercise of a given power would be nugatory. There are few measures of any government which would stand so severe a test. To insist upon it, would be to make the criterion of the exercise of any implied power, a case of extreme necessity; which is rather a rule to justify the over-leaping of the bounds of constitutional authority, than to govern the ordinary exercise of it.

It may be truly said of every government, as well as of that of the United States, that it has only a right to pass such laws as are Necessary and Proper to accomplish the objects intrusted to it. For no government has a right to do merely what it pleases. Hence, by a process of reasoning similar to that of the Secretary of State, it might be proved that neither of the State governments has a right to incorporate a bank. It might be shown that all the public business of the state could be performed without a bank, and inferring thence that it was unnecessary, it might be argued that it could not be done, because it is against the rule which has been just mentioned. A like mode of reasoning would prove that there was no power to incorporate the inhabitants of a town, with a view to a more perfect police. For it is certain that an incorporation may be dispensed with, though it is better to have one. It is to be remembered that there is no express power in any State constitution to erect corporations.

The degree in which a measure is necessary, can never be a test of the legal right to adopt it; that must be a matter of opinion, and can only be a test of expediency. The relation between the measure and the end; between the nature of the mean employed toward the execution of a power, and the object of that power must be the criterion of constitutionality, not the more or less of necessity or utility.

The practice of the government is against the rule of construction advocated by the Secretary of State. Of this, the Act concerning lighthouses, beacons, buoys, and public piers, is a decisive example. This, doubtless, must be referred to the powers of regulating trade, and is fairly relative to it. But it cannot be affirmed that the exercise of that power in this instance was strictly necessity or that the power itself would be nugatory, without that of regulating establishments of this nature.

This restrictive interpretation of the word necessary is also contrary to this sound maxim of construction, namely, that the powers contained in a constitution of government, especially those which concern the general administration of the affairs of a country, its finances, trade, defense, etc., ought to be construed liberally in advancement of the public good. This rule does not depend on the particular form of a government, or on the particular demarcation of the boundaries of its powers, but on the nature and object of government itself. The means by which national exigencies are to be provided for, national inconveniences obviated, national prosperity promoted, are of such infinite variety, extent, and complexity, that there must of necessity be great latitude of discretion in the selection and application of those means. Hence, consequently, the necessity and propriety of exercising the authorities intrusted to a government on principles of liberal construction.

NOTES

1. HOW I LEARNED TO STOP WORRYING ABOUT GLENN BECK AND WRITE THIS BOOK

1. Juvenal, *The Satires*, trans. Niall Rudd (New York: Oxford University Press, 1991), pp. 15–24.

2. George L. Hart, *Official Report of the Proceedings of the Sixteenth Republican National Convention* (New York: Tenny, 1916), pp. 14–15.

3. *Inaugural Addresses of the Presidents of the United States Volume 2: Grover Cleveland (1885) to George W. Bush (2001)* (Bedford, MA: Applewood Books, 2001), p. 65.

4. Richard B. Bernstein, *The Founding Fathers Reconsidered* (New York: Oxford University Press, 2009), p. 5.

5. Glenn Beck and Joe Kerry, *Glenn Beck's Common Sense* (New York: Mercury Radio Arts/Threshold Editions, 2009), p. 9; Glenn Beck, Being George (New York: Threshold Editions, 2011).

6. Glenn Beck and Joshua Charles, *The Original Argument* (New York: Threshold Editions, 2011), p. xii.

7. Ibid., p. 12.

8. Ibid., p. 154.

9. Ibid., p. 282.

10. Ibid., p. 242.

11. Ibid., p. 320.

12. Two of the more recent of these are Richard Brookhiser, *What Would the Founders Do? Our Questions, Their Answers* (New York: Basic Books, 2007), written from a center-left perspective; and Larry Schweikart, *What Would the Founders Say? A Patriot's Answers to America's Most Pressing Problems* (New York: Sentinel, 2011), written from an ultraconservative point of view.

13. In 1856, Representative Preston Brooks of South Carolina nearly killed Massachusetts senator Charles Sumner by beating him with a cane in the Senate chamber. In 1798, Representative Matthew Lyon of Vermont spit tobacco juice at Representative Roger Griswold of Connecticut, who promptly attacked him with a cane. Alexander Hamilton was killed by Aaron Burr (the sitting vice president of the United States) in a famous 1804 duel. Button Gwinnett, a signer of the Declaration

of Independence, was killed in a duel with his political rival, Lachlan McIntosh, who insulted him on the floor of the Georgia General Assembly. Richard Dobbs Spaight, a signer of the Constitution, was killed in a duel with John Stanley, who had earlier defeated him in a race for a congressional seat.

14. See Eric Burns, *Infamous Scribblers: The Founding Fathers and the Rowdy Beginnings of American Journalism* (New York: Public Affairs, 2006), pp. 262–92.

15. Philadelphia *Aurora*, Decem

ber 23, 1796, quoted in James Tagg, *Benjamin Franklin Bache and the Philadelphia* Aurora (Philadelphia: University of Pennsylvania Press, 1991), p. 282.

16. Burns, *Infamous Scribblers*, pp. 355–56.

2. FOUNDERSTEIN

1. "America's God and Country: Encyclopedia of Quotations," Patriot Depot, http://www.patriotdepot.com/products/America's-God-and-Country -Encyclopedia-of-Quotations.html (accessed January 15, 2012).

2. Alexander Hamilton, *The Revolutionary Writings of Alexander Hamilton*, ed. Richard B. Vernier (Indianapolis: Liberty Fund, 2008), p. 89.

3. Glenn Beck and Joshua Charles, *The Original Argument* (New York: Threshold Editions, 2011), p. 12.

4. Clinton Rossiter, ed., *The Federalist Papers* (New York: Mentor, 1961), p. 33.

5. Hamilton, *Revolutionary Writings*, p. 53.

6. Larry Schweikart, *What Would the Founders Say? A Patriot's Answers to America's Most Pressing Problems* (New York: Sentinel, 2011), pp. 69, 75, 101.

7. Ibid., p. 153–54.

8. John C. Hamilton, ed., *The Works of Alexander Hamilton*, 7 vols. (New York: J. F. Trow, 1850), 1:125.

9. Alexander Hamilton, *Writings*, ed. Joanne B. Freeman (New York: Library of America, 2001), p. 115.

10. Glenn Beck, *Being George Washington* (New York: Threshold Editions, 2011), pp. 240–44.

11. "Quotes about Religion and Government," Christian Apologetics and Research Ministry, http://carm.org/quotes-religion-government (accessed June 30, 2012); "Positive Atheism's Big List of John Adams Quotations," *Positive Atheism*, http://www.positiveatheism.org/hist/quotes/adams.htm (accessed June 30, 2012).

12. Charles Francis Adams, ed., *The Works of John Adams, Second President of the United States*, 10 vols. (Boston: Little, 1850), 9:635.

13. George A. Peek, ed., *The Political Writings of John Adams* (New York: Liberal Arts Press, 1954), p. 118.

14. George Washington, *Writings*, ed. John H. Rhodehamel (New York: Library of America, 1997), p. 351.

15. David Barton, *Original Intent: The Courts, the Constitution, and Religion*, 5th ed. (Aledo, TX: WallBuilder Press, 2008), p. 91.

16. Forrest Church, *So Help Me God: The Founding Fathers and the First Great Battle over Church and State* (Orlando, FL: Harcourt, 2007), p. 46.

3. THE FALLACY OF "ORIGINAL INTENT"

1. Glenn Beck, *Arguing with Idiots* (New York: Threshold Editions, 2009), p. 267.

2. Sean Hannity, *Conservative Victory: Defeating Obama's Radical Agenda* (New York: Harper, 2010), p. 230.

3. Mark R. Levin, *Men in Black: How the Supreme Court Is Destroying America* (Lanham, MD: Regnery, 2005), p. 13.

4. Mark R. Levin, *Liberty and Tyranny: A Conservative Manifesto* (New York: Threshold Editions, 2009), p. 52.

5. "Overview," WallBuilders, http://www.wallbuilders.com/ABT Overview.asp (accessed June 30, 2012).

6. David Barton, *Original Intent: The Courts, the Constitution, and Religion*, 5th ed. (Aledo, TX: WallBuilder Press, 2008), pp. 6, 8.

7. Ibid., p. 153.

8. Antonin Scalia, *A Matter of Interpretation: Federal Courts and the Law* (Princeton, NJ: Princeton University Press, 1997), p. 17.

9. Ibid., pp. 31–32.

10. Barton, *Original Intent*, pp. 29–30.

11. Thomas Jefferson, *Writings*, ed. Merrill D. Peterson (New York: Library of America, 1984), p. 959.

12. Ibid., p. 963.

13. H. Jefferson Powell, "The Original Understanding of Original Intent," *Harvard Law Review* 98, no. 5 (1985): 903.

14. Ibid., p. 915.

15. Alexander Hamilton, *Writings*, ed. Joanne B. Freeman (New York: Library of America, 2001), p. 625.

16. Cong. Globe, 4th Cong., 1st Sess. 4 (1795).

17. Scalia, *Matter of Interpretation*, p. 17.

18. James Madison, *Writings*, ed. Jack N. Rakove (New York: Library of America, 1999), p. 99.

19. Ibid., p. 149.

20. James Madison, *Notes of Debates in the Federal Convention of 1787 Reported by James Madison*, ed. Adrienne Koch (New York: Norton, 1987), pp. 305–306.

21. Christopher Collier and James Lincoln Collier, *Decision in Philadelphia: TheConstitutional Convention of 1787* (New York: Ballantine Books, 1987), p. 268.

22. George Will, "An Argument to Be Made about Immigrant Babies and Citizenship," *Washington Post*, March 28, 2010, p. A15.

23. P. A. Madison, "The UnConstitutionality of Citizenship by Birth to Non-Americans," The Fourteenth Amendment, February 1, 2005, http://www.14thamendment.us.articles/anchor_babies_unconstitutionality.html (accessed July 15, 2012).

24. Levin, *Liberty and Tyranny*, p. 168.

25. Garrett Epps, "Phony 'Originalism' and the Assault on Birthright Citizenship,"*Atlantic*, August 10, 2010, http://www.theatlantic.com/national/archive/2010/08/phony-originalism-and-the-assault-on-birthright-citizenship/61224/ (accessed February 11, 2012).

26. Levin, *Liberty and Tyranny*, p. 168.

27. Antonin Scalia, "On Interpreting the Constitution" (speech, Manhattan Institute, New York, November 17, 1997), transcript available at http://www.manhattan-institute.org/html/wl1997.htm (accessed June 30, 2012).

4. THE FOUNDERS ON RELIGION AND LIBERTY

1. William J. Federer, *America's God and Country: Encyclopedia of Quotations* (Coppell, TX: Fame, 1994), p. 13.

2. Ibid., p. 410.

3. Ibid., p. 331.

4. Ibid., p. 246.

5. Ibid., p. 289.

6. Thomas Paine, *Collected Writings*, ed. Eric Foner (New York: Library of America, 1995), p. 677.

7. Thomas Jefferson, *Writings*, ed. Merrill D. Peterson (New York: Library of America, 1984), p. 1112.

8. John Adams, *The Political Writings of John Adams*, ed. George A. Peek (New York: Liberal Arts Press, 1954), p. 118.

9. Benjamin Franklin, *Writings*, ed. J. A. Leo Lemay (New York: Library of America, 1987), p. 1359.

10. For the full treaty, see "The Barbary Treaties 1786–1816," Avalon Project, http://avalon.law.yale.edu/18th_century/bar1796t.asp (accessed June 30, 2012).

11. David Barton, *Separation of Church and State: What the Founders Meant* (Aledo, TX: WallBuilder Press, 2007), p. 7.

12. Ibid., p. 13.

13. Tim LaHaye, *Faith of Our Founding Fathers* (Brentwood, TN: Wolgemunth & Hyatt, 1987), p. 196.

14. Jefferson, *Writings*, pp. 346–48.

15. Merrill D. Peterson, *Thomas Jefferson and the New Nation* (New York: Oxford University Press, 1970), p. 134.

16. Ibid., p. 137.

17. Patrick Henry, "Appendix B: A Bill 'Establishing a Provision for Teachers of the Christian Religion,'" in *God and the Founders*, by Vincent Phillip Muñoz (New York: Cambridge University Press, 2009).

18. Ibid.

19. Muñoz, *God and the Founders*, pp. 229–30.

20. Mark R. Levin, *Liberty and Tyranny: A Conservative Manifesto* (New York: Threshold Editions, 2009), pp. 46–47.

21. Ibid.

22. Ibid., pp. 46, 48.

23. James Madison, *Writings*, ed. Jack N. Rakove (New York: Library of America, 1999), p. 30.

24. Ibid., p. 31.

25. Ibid.

26. Ibid.

27. Ibid.

28. Ibid., p. 30.

29. Muñoz, *God and the Founders*, p. 12.

30. Madison, *Writings*, p. 30.

31. Robert S. Alley, ed., *James Madison on Religious Liberty* (Buffalo, NY: Prometheus Books, 1985), p. 62.

32. Garry Wills, *Under God: Religion and American Politics* (New York: Simon & Schuster, 1990), p. 374.

33. Richard Labunski, *James Madison and the Struggle for the Bill of Rights* (New York: Oxford University Press, 2006), pp. 227–28.

34. Alley, *Madison on Religious Liberty*, pp. 79, 239.

35. Gaillard Hunt, ed., *The Writings of James Madison*, 9 vols. (New York: G. P. Putnam's Sons, 1819), 8:133.

36. Wills, *Under God*, p. 354.

37. LaHaye, *Faith of Our Founding Fathers*, p. 13.

38. Quoted in Derek Davis, "Thomas Jefferson and the 'Wall of Separation' Metaphor," *Journal of Church and State* 45, no. 1 (2003): 6–7.

39. Barton, *Separation of Church and State*, pp. 12–13.

40. David Barton, *The Myth of Separation* (Aledo, TX: WallBuilder Press, 1989), p. 41.

41. Davis, "Jefferson and the Wall of Separation," p. 9.

42. Andrew Lipscomb and Albert Bergh, *The Writings of Thomas Jefferson* (Washington, DC: Thomas Jefferson Memorial Association, 1904), 10:305.

43. Ibid.

44. The full text of the letter to Jefferson and Jefferson's letters to Lincoln and preliminary draft response can be found in Daniel L. Dreisbach, *Thomas Jefferson and the Wall of Separation between Church and State* (New York: New York University Press, 2002), pp. 142–47.

45. Jefferson, *Writings*, p. 510.

46. Ibid., p. 286.

47. Quoted in Peterson, *Jefferson and the New Nation*, p. 138.

48. Jefferson, *Writings*, p. 285.

5. STATES' RIGHTS/STATES' WRONGS

1. Rand Paul, *The Tea Party Goes to Washington* (Nashville, TN: Center Street, 2011), p. 172.

2. Catherine Drinker Bowen, *Miracle at Philadelphia* (Boston: Little, Brown, 1966), p. 4.

3. Bernard Bailyn, *The Debate on the Constitution*, 2 vols. (New York: Library of America, 1993), 1:164–75.

4. Richard Labunski, *James Madison and the Struggle for the Bill of Rights* (New York: Oxford University Press, 2006), pp. 229–32.

5. Jackson Turner Main, *The Antifederalists: Critics of the Constitution, 1781–1788* (New York: Norton, 1974), p. viii.

6. U.S. Const. article I, § 8, paragraph 18.

7. Mark R. Levin, *Liberty and Tyranny: A Conservative Manifesto* (New York: Threshold Editions, 2009), p. 74.

8. Clinton Rossiter, ed., *The Federalist Papers* (New York: Mentor, 1961), p. 246.

9. Rick Perry, *Fed Up! Our Fight to Save America from Washington* (New York: Little, Brown, 2010), pp. 26–27.

10. Mike Lee, *The Freedom Agenda* (Washington, DC: Regnery, 2011), p. 25.

11. Charles de Secondat Montesquieu, *The Spirit of Laws*, vol. 35, *Great Books of the Western World* (Chicago: Encyclopedia Britannica, 1990), p. 56.

12. Bailyn, *Debate on the Constitution*, 1:172.

13. Rossiter, *Federalist Papers*, p. 78.

14. Ibid., p. 83.

15. Perry, *Fed Up!*, p. 27.

16. "Controversies over Mosques and Islamic Centers across the U.S.," Pew Research Center, September 29, 2011, http://features.pewforum.org/muslim/contro versies-over-mosque-and-islamic-centers-across-the-us.html (accessed June 30, 2012).

17. Perry, *Fed Up!*, p. 27.

18. Bailyn, *Debate on the Constitution*, 1:1053–54.

19. Labunski, *Madison and the Struggle for the Bill of Rights*, pp. 227–28.

20. James Madison, *Writings*, ed. Jack N. Rakove (New York: Library of America, 1999), p. 470.

21. Paul Finkelman, *Slavery and the Founders*, 2nd ed. (Armonk, NY: M. E. Sharpe, 2001), p. 27.

22. Ibid., p. 83.

23. Ibid., p. 7.

24. Ibid., p. 9.

25. Glenn Beck, *Arguing with Idiots* (New York: Threshold Editions, 2009), p. 271.

26. Ibid., p. 278.

27. Perry, *Fed Up!*, pp. 33–34.

28. Bailyn, *Debate on the Constitution*, 1:15.

29. Ibid., 1:57.

30. Ibid., 1:165.

31. Mark Levin, *The Mark Levin Show*, Cumulus Media Networks, August 2, 2010.

6. THE JEFFERSONIAN MYTH AND THE HAMILTONIAN BOGEYMAN

1. Joseph Ellis, *American Sphinx* (New York: Vintage, 1998), p. 8.

2. Thomas J. DiLorenzo, *Hamilton's Curse: How Jefferson's Arch Enemy Betrayed the American Revolution—and What It Means for Americans Today* (New York: Three Rivers Press, 2008), pp. 208–209.

3. The fascinating story of the compromise Jefferson engineered between Hamilton and Madison is the subject of "The Dinner," chapter 2 of Joseph Ellis's Pulitzer Prize–winning *Founding Brothers* (New York: Vintage, 2000), pp. 48–80.

4. Quoted in Dumas Malone, *Jefferson and His Time*, vol 2, *Jefferson and the Rights of Man* (Boston: Little, Brown, 1951), p. 90.

5. Ralph Louis Ketcham, *James Madison: A Biography* (Charlottesville, VA: University Press of Virginia, 1990), p. 308.

6. Alexander Hamilton, *Writings*, ed. Joanne B. Freeman (New York: Library of America, 2001), p. 538.

7. Thomas Jefferson, *Writings*, ed. Merrill D. Peterson (New York: Library of America, 1984), pp. 666–67.

8. Ron Chernow, *Alexander Hamilton* (New York: Penguin, 2004), p. 306.

9. Roger Pilon, *The Purpose and Limits of Government*, Cato's Letters 13 (Washington, DC: Cato Institute, 1999), p. 25.

10. Edward J. Larson, ed., *The Constitutional Convention: A Narrative History* (New York: Modern Library, 2005), p. 123.

11. Clinton Rossiter, ed., *The Federalist Papers* (New York: Mentor, 1961), p. 285.

12. Jefferson, *Writings*, p. 416–17.

13. Ibid., p. 419.

14. Hamilton, *Writings*, pp. 615–16.

15. Ibid., p. 618.

16. DiLorenzo, *Hamilton's Curse*, p. 26.

17. The actual vote was 60:23, which represents a 38:20 vote in the House and a 22:3 in the Senate. See the Library of Congress's *Annals of Congress* site at http://memory.loc.gov/ammem/amlaw/lwaclink.html. The House vote was taken on February 8, 1791, and the Senate vote on February 24, 1791.

18. Paul Leicester Ford, ed., *The Writings of Thomas Jefferson*, 10 vols. (New York: Putnam's Sons, 1892), 8:245.

19. Charles Francis Adams, ed., *Memoirs of John Quincy Adams*, 12 vols. (Philadelphia: J. B. Lippincott, 1848), 5:364–65.

20. Ibid.

21. Jefferson, *Writings*, p. 672.

22. George Washington, *Writings*, ed. John H. Rhodehamel (New York: Library of America, 1997), p. 840.

23. Dumas Malone, *Jefferson and His Time*, vol. 3, *Jefferson and the Ordeal of Liberty* (Boston: Little, Brown, 1962), p. 48.

24. David G. McCullough, *John Adams* (New York: Simon & Schuster, 2001), pp. 417–18.

25. Thomas Jefferson to John Adams, January 11, 1816, in Lester J. Cappon, ed., *The Adams-Jefferson Letters: The Complete Correspondence between Thomas Jefferson and Abigail and John Adams* (Chapel Hill, NC: University of North Carolina Press, 1988) p. 459.

26. Jefferson, *Writings*, p. 1009.

27. Ibid., 1006.

28. Malone, *Jefferson and His Time*, p. 69.

29. Hamilton, *Writings*, p. 806.

30. Ibid., p. 805.

31. Ibid., p. 801.

32. Ibid., pp. 805–806.

33. Alexander Hamilton and James Madison, *Letters of Pacificus and Helvidius on the Proclamation of Neutrality of 1793* (Washington, DC: J. & G. S. Gideon, 1845), p. 34.

34. Ketcham, *James Madison*, p. 345.

35. James Madison, *Writings*, ed. Jack N. Rakove (New York: Library of America, 1999), pp. 537.

36. Ibid., p. 541.

37. Ibid., p. 545.

7. GROVER NORQUIST AND THE TAX PLEDGE VERSUS ALEXANDER HAMILTON AND GOOD GOVERNMENT

1. Bernard Bailyn, *The Debate on the Constitution*, 2 vols. (New York: Library of America, 1993), 1:691.

2. David Wootton, *The Essential Federalist and Anti-Federalist Papers* (Indianapolis: Hackett, 2003), pp. 34–35.

3. Bailyn, *Debate on the Constitution*, 2:649–50.

4. Glenn Beck, *Arguing with Idiots* (New York: Threshold Editions, 2009), pp. 277–78.

5. James Taranto, "Big Lies and Little Ones," *Wall Street Journal*, January 12, 2011, http://online.wsj.com/article/SB1000142405274870480360457607789200668 3586.html?mod=WSJ_Opinion_MIDDLETopOpinion (accessed January 16, 2012).

6. Thomas Jefferson, *Writings*, ed. Merrill D. Peterson (New York, Library of America, 1984), p. 911.

7. Ruth Marcus, "Unhinged on the Right," *Washington Post*, June 30, 2010, A17; Bernie Becker, "Talking about a Revolution: A Call to Arms? It's an Option," *New York Times*, October 23, 2010, A11.

8. George Washington, *Writings*, ed. John H. Rhodehamel (New York: Library of America, 1997), p. 882.

9. Copies of the Taxpayer Protection Pledge for different state and federal officials can be found on the website of the Americans for Tax Reform (http://www.atr.org/tax payer-protection-pledge).

10. Steve Benen, "Ten-to-One Isn't Good Enough for the GOP," *Washington Monthly*, August 12, 2011, http://www.washingtonmonthly.com/political-animal/2011_08/tentoone_isnt_good_enough_for031484.php (accessed January 16, 2012).

11. House Joint Economic Committee Republicans, *Spend Less, Owe Less, Grow the Economy: Executive Summary*, March 15, 2011, http://www.speaker.gov/UploadedFiles/JEC_Jobs_Study.pdf (accessed January 16, 2012).

12. Frank Wolf, *Congressional Record–House*, October 4, 2011, H6509–10. Also available online at http://www.gpo.gov/fdsys/pkg/CREC-2011-10-04/pdf/CREC-2011-10-04-pt1-PgH6509.pdf (accessed August 1, 2012).

13. Clinton Rossiter, ed., *The Federalist Papers* (New York: Mentor, 1961), p. 207.

14. Ibid., p. 233.

15. Bruce Bartlett, "Tax Cuts and 'Starving the Beast,'" *Forbes*, May 7, 2010, http://www.forbes.com/2010/05/06/tax-cuts-republicans-starve-the-beast-columnists-bruce-bartlett.html (accessed January 16, 2012).

16. Ibid.

17. William Niskanen, "Limiting Government: The Failure of 'Starve the Beast,'" *Cato Journal* 2, no. 3 (2006): 554.

18. Bruce Bartlett, "Norquist Holds the Deficit Hostage to 'Starve the Beast' Theory," *Tax Notes*, March 21, 2011, p. 1492.

19. Jackie Calms, "Criticism of GOP Is Growing," *New York Times*, August 12, 2011, B1.

20. Bruce Bartlett correlated the results of twenty-seven polls taken between September 16 and November 26, 2011, on the blog *Capital Gains and Games* at http://capitalgainsandgames.com/blog/bruce-bartlett/2368/updated-tax-polls. On the average, polls reported that 64.5 percent of Americans would rather balance the budget with a combination of tax increases and spending cuts than with spending cuts alone.

21. Bartlett, "Norquist Holds the Deficit Hostage," p. 1491.

22. Harold Coffin Syrett and Jacob Ernest Cooke, ed., *The Papers of Alexander Hamilton*, 27 vols. (New York: Columbia University Press, 1961), 11:365.

23. Alexander Hamilton, *Writings*, ed. Joanne B. Freeman (New York: Library of America, 2001), p. 531.

24. Ibid., p. 532.

25. Ibid., p. 569.

26. See chapter 6, note 3.

27. Hamilton, *Writings*, p. 562.

28. Ron Chernow, *Alexander Hamilton* (New York: Penguin, 2004), p. 342.

29. Nikola G. Swann, "United States of America Long-Term Rating Lowered to 'AA+' on Political Risks and Rising Debt Burden; Outlook Negative," Standard and Poor's, August 5, 2011, p. 3, http://msnbcmedia.msn.com/i/MSNBC/Sections/NEWS/SPdowngrade.pdf (accessed August 1, 2012).

30. Ibid., p. 4.

31. Ibid., p. 3.

32. Peter Nicholas, "Seeking Political Leverage from Economic Turmoil," *Los Angeles Times*, August 9, 2011, A6.

8. COURTING DISASTER

1. Amy Gardner and Matt DeLong, "Newt Gingrich's Assault on 'Activist Judges' Draws Criticism, Even from Right," *Washington Post*, December 17, 2011, http://www.washingtonpost.com/politics/newt-gingrichs-assault-on-activist-judges-draws-criticism-even-from-right/2011/12/17/gIQAoYa80O_story.html (accessed June 14, 2012).

2. Ibid.

3. Josh Feldman, "Ann Coulter: Gingrich's 'Outrageous' Threat to Subpoena Justices Threatens Checks and Balances," *Mediaite*, December 16, 2011, http://www.mediaite.com/tv/ann-coulter-to-bill-oreilly-gingrichs-outrageous-threat-to-subpoena-justices-threatens-checks-balances/ (accessed June 14, 2012).

4. The official version of the 2010 State of the Union Address can be found on the White House website at http://www.whitehouse.gov/the-press-office/remarks-president-state-union-address.

5. Clinton Rossiter, ed., *The Federalist Papers* (New York: Mentor, 1961), pp. 465–66.

6. Newt Gingrich, *Winning the Future* (Washington, DC: Regnery, 2005; rev. ed., 2006), p. 62.

7. Rossiter, *Federalist Papers*, p. 465.

8. Ibid., p. 384.

9. Ibid.

10. Mark Levin, *Men in Black: How the Supreme Court Is Destroying America* (Washington, DC: Regnery, 2005), p. 199.

11. Gingrich, *Winning the Future*, p. 84.

12. Jonathan Elliot, ed., *The Debates in the Several State Conventions on the Adoption of the Federal Constitution* (Washington, DC: Printed for the editor, 1836), p. 444.

13. James F. Simon, *What Kind of Nation* (New York: Simon & Schuster, 2002), pp. 192–97.

14. Ibid., p. 209.

15. William H. Rehnquist, *Grand Inquests* (New York: William Morrow, 1992), p. 114.

16. Levin, *Men in Black*, p. 26.

17. Ibid., pp. 30–32.

18. See Jefferson's letter to Abigail Adams on September 11, 1804, in which he says, "Nothing in the constitution has given [judges] a right to decide for the executive, more than to the Executive to decide for them. The magistracies are equally independent in the sphere of action assigned to them. The judges, believing the law constitutional, had a right to pass a sentence of fine and imprisonment, because that power was placed in their hands by the constitution. But the Executive, believing the law to be unconstitutional, was bound to remit the execution. . . . The opinion which gives to the judges the right to decide what laws are constitutional, and what not, not only for themselves in their own sphere of action, but for the legislature and executive also in their spheres, would make the Judiciary a despotic branch." Lester J. Cappon, ed., *The Adams-Jefferson Letters* (Chapel Hill, NC: University of North Carolina Press, 1987), p. 279.

19. James Madison, *Notes of Debates in the Federal Convention of 1787 Reported by James Madison*, ed. Adrienne Koch (New York: Norton, 1987), p. 32.

20. Levin, *Men in Black*, p. 26.

21. Madison, *Notes of Debates*, p. 61.

22. Ibid., p. 336–37.

23. Ibid., p. 340.

24. Ibid., p. 341.

25. Saikrishna Prakash and John C. Yoo, "The Origins of Judicial Review," *University of Chicago Law Review* 70 (2003): 64.

26. Ibid., p. 67.

27. Bernard Bailyn, *The Debate on the Constitution*, 2 vols. (New York: Library of America, 1993), 2:132.

28. Rossiter, *Federalist Papers*, p. 477.

29. Cliff Sloan and David McKean, *The Great Decision* (New York: Public Affairs, 2009), p. 166.

30. James Madison, *Writings*, ed. Jack N. Rakove (New York: Library of America, 1999), p. 777.

9. WHY AMERICA, THE CONSTITUTION, AND GOD WILL (PROBABLY) SURVIVE

1. "Michelle Obama in Madison," YouTube video, 9:45, speaking at the Oscar Meyer Theater the day before the Wisconsin Primary, February 18, 2008, posted by "annalthouse," February 18, 2008, http://www.youtube.com/watch?v=Nh1Tdd L9YvQ (accessed August 3, 2012).

2. Mark Levin, *The Mark Levin Show*, Cumulus Media Networks, February 23, 2008.

3. Glenn Beck, *The Glenn Beck Program*, Premiere Radio Networks, November 4, 2008.

4. Rush Limbaugh, *The Rush Limbaugh Show*, Premiere Radio Networks, July 27, 2009.

5. Mark Levin, *Ameritopia* (New York: Threshold Editions, 2012).

6. Ibid., pp. 187–88.

7. Ibid., p. 198.

8. Ibid., p. 201.

9. Glenn Beck, *Arguing with Idiots* (New York: Threshold Editions, 2009), p. 222.

10. John R. Vile, *The Constitutional Convention of 1787: A Comprehensive Encyclopedia of America's Founding*, 2 vols. (Santa Barbara, CA: ABC-CLIO, 2005), 2:14.

11. Laurence H. Tribe, "America's Constitutional Narrative," *Daedalus* 141, no. 1 (2012): 18–19.

12. Stephen Breyer, *Active Liberty* (New York: Vintage, 2005), pp. 131–32.

13. Mark Levin, *Men in Black: How the Supreme Court Is Destroying America* (Washington, DC: Regnery, 2005), pp. 12–13.

14. Antonin Scalia, "Originalism: The Lesser Evil," quoted in David Andrew Schultz and Christopher E. Smith, *The Jurisprudential Vision of Justice Antonin Scalia* (Lanham, MD: Rowman and Littlefield, 1996), p. 190.

15. Tribe, "America's Constitutional Narrative," p. 21.

16. Clinton Rossiter, ed., *The Federalist Papers* (New York: Mentor, 1961), p. 322.

17. Ibid., p. 324.

18. Ibid., p. 322.

19. Ibid., p. 227.

20. Stephen Breyer, *Making Our Democracy Work* (New York: Knopf, 2010), p. 10.

21. Alexis de Tocqueville, *Democracy in America*, trans. Arthur Goldhammer (New York: Library of America, 2004), p. 352.

22. Breyer, *Active Liberty*, p. 6.

INDEX